The New York Times

CROSSWORDS FOR A RELAXING WEEKEND
Easy, Breezy 200-Puzzle Omnibus

Edited by Will Shortz

ST. MARTIN'S GRIFFIN ⚓ NEW YORK

All of the puzzles that appear in this work were originally published
in *The New York Times* from April 29, 2002, to August 6, 2003.
Copyright © 2002, 2003 by The New York Times Company.
All rights reserved. Reprinted by permission.

ISBN-13: 978-0-312-37829-5
ISBN-10: 0-312-37829-7

10   9   8   7

The New York Times

CROSSWORDS FOR A RELAXING WEEKEND

ACROSS

1 Steals from
5 Inferior, as writing
11 1936 candidate Landon
14 Norway's capital
15 Certain apartment
16 Hair styling stuff
17 Robert Mitchum drama, 1958
19 "___ Got You Under My Skin"
20 "Beetle Bailey" character
21 Big I.R.S. mo.
22 Out of the wind
23 Home of Bert and Ernie
27 Educ. group
30 Mal de ___
31 Feather's partner
32 Seniors' org.
34 Golf targets
37 Michelangelo masterpiece
41 Billy Wilder film starring Gloria Swanson
44 Fulton's power
45 ___ mater
46 Buffalo's lake
47 Kind of service
49 Charlottesville sch.
51 Chaney of horror films
52 A trusting person may be led down it
58 Millions of years
59 Calif. airport
60 Lhasa's land
64 In the past
65 Source of many old pop songs
68 Baseball score
69 Eight-armed creatures
70 Frolic
71 Rocker Tommy
72 Pop maker
73 Brake part

DOWN

1 Goes bad
2 Dept. of Labor watchdog
3 Make less clear
4 The 40 in a "top 40"
5 Mao ___-tung
6 Karel Capek play
7 The "A" in James A. Garfield
8 Slippery ___
9 Citizen Kane's real-life model
10 Balance sheet abbr.
11 Spry
12 Embankment
13 Naval force
18 Consider
22 Get there
24 Small group of believers
25 Popular vacation isle
26 Cash register output
27 Quarterback's option
28 Drawn tight
29 "Rule Britannia" composer
33 Writings by David
35 D.C. type
36 Recapitulate
38 "Duke of ___" (1962 hit)
39 Wynken, Blynken and Nod, e.g.
40 Mideast's Gulf of ___
42 40-Down V.I.P.
43 Popular hand soap
48 Constabulary
50 Lead-in to girl
52 Oyster's prize
53 Scalawag
54 Hole ___ (golfer's dream)
55 "Ho ho ho" crier
56 Montreal team til 2004
57 "Rolling" things
61 Dull
62 Architect Saarinen
63 Toddler
65 Pull along
66 Gibbon, for one
67 Zippo

by Holden Baker

ACROSS

1 Lash of oaters
6 Buccaneers' home
11 Iranian city: Var.
14 Bowl
15 "Are you calling me ___?"
16 Actress Merkel
17 Very best
19 "___ bin ein Berliner"
20 Gas of the past
21 Gore's "___ My Party"
22 Lullaby rocker
24 Amigo of Fidel
26 More acute
27 Scores for Shaq
31 Pianist Nero
32 Renée's pal
33 Police offer
35 Scattered
38 Wash cycle
40 Detergent brand
41 Close-fitting hat
42 Journey for Kirk
43 Where 17- and 61-Across and 11- and 29-Down might be used
45 Olympics chant
46 "Shush!"
48 Consumer's bottom line
50 Academic AWOL's
52 Gloppy stuff
53 Friars' fetes
54 Wilder's "___ Town"
56 Location
60 Swabber's org.
61 Ceaselessly
64 A.F.L.'s former partner
65 ___ Kid of early TV
66 Like helium, chemically
67 Barbie's sometime beau
68 Heads overseas?
69 Job extras

DOWN

1 Lois of the Daily Planet
2 God of war
3 Sales force, for short
4 Use a key on
5 ___ Claire, Wis.
6 Ex-lax?
7 Word before fair or well
8 Cambridge univ.
9 More than thirsty
10 Noah's landfall
11 Fair exchange
12 Cry of surrender
13 Mr. Politically Incorrect
18 Pedro's lucky number?
23 Playground retort
25 "Take one!"
26 Wrist injury, maybe
27 Homer's boy
28 Mideast chief: Var.
29 Prerequisite
30 Gym garb
34 Tate collection
36 Hardly a he-man
37 Without ice
39 Gull-like predators
41 Josip Broz ___
43 Makes no attempt to save
44 Actress Pola
47 Not damaged
49 Trig function
50 Teamster's transport
51 "Sweet" O'Grady of song
54 Long ago
55 Roswell sightings
57 Roman's way
58 Istanbul native
59 CPR pros
62 Believer's suffix
63 Quick drink

by John F. Hughes

ACROSS

1 Garlicky sauce
6 Mother ___
10 Soft, white cheese
14 Like a depth finder
15 Financial page heading
16 Commentator Keyes
17 Pay, in a modern way
20 Adderley of bop
21 French painter Charles Le ___
22 Wee
23 Fire
24 Show interrupter
25 Make a disclosure
29 Mrs., in Barcelona
32 Letter before beth
33 Trauma ctrs.
34 "It's So Nice to Have ___ Around the House"
35 Sweater letter
36 Word with mass or mixed
38 Arabian plateau region
39 Work without ___
40 Former press secretary Fleischer
41 Sign for an audience
42 Part of Roy G. Biv
43 Cause pain or numbness, maybe
46 Traffic marker
47 "Family Ties" role
48 Colt .45's, now
51 Film rating org.
52 Proof's end
55 Upstage everyone, maybe
58 ___ bath
59 Big model
60 Unoriginal
61 Long basket, in hoops lingo
62 Put the end first?
63 Evaluated, with "up"

DOWN

1 Org.
2 "The Music Man" setting
3 "Step ___!"
4 Collagen injection site
5 Cool dip?
6 Nader's 2000 running mate
7 Dark clouds, say
8 One coming out
9 Emigrant's document
10 Met squarely
11 Verve
12 Pine products
13 "Handy" one
18 Enemy leader?
19 Shade of blue
23 Mar. honoree
24 Actress Polo of "Meet the Parents"
25 Agent Swifty
26 "Prince Valiant" princess
27 Threw a party for
28 Of Hindu scriptures
29 Makeup problem
30 A Gandhi
31 Wrestling's ___ the Giant
34 New wing
36 Trunk
37 Fish-eating flier
41 Theatrical shorts
43 Betting group
44 Come to pass
45 Jai ___
46 Cuckoo
48 ___ prof.
49 The big house
50 French bean?
51 Boss's writing
52 Interrogate
53 Art Deco artist
54 Scout's doing
56 Med. plan
57 TNT part

by Steve Jones

ACROSS

1 Maker of Space Invaders
6 Cut with scissors
10 Verdant
14 Batman's sidekick
15 "Voilà!"
16 Gazetteer datum
17 Punch in the mouth
20 Locale
21 Clean air org.
22 Lovers' secret meetings
23 "___ está usted?"
25 Roller coaster cry
26 Token punishment
32 Not tacit
33 Billy Joel's "Tell ___ About It"
34 Sgt., e.g.
35 Pooped out
36 Boeing 747, e.g.
37 The Jetsons' dog
39 Royal flush card
40 Cheerios grain
41 Bordeaux wine
42 Having drinks
46 They're exchanged at the altar
47 "So what ___ is new?"
48 Sitting room
51 Iceland's ocean: Abbr.
52 It's $24 on Marvin Gardens
56 Item for an armed detective, maybe
59 Chimney grime
60 Lake touching four states
61 French city, in song
62 Moppet
63 Caboose's spot
64 Dag Hammarskjöld, for one

DOWN

1 Clumsy boats
2 Singer Braxton
3 Border on
4 Low-calorie snack
5 Calligrapher's purchase
6 Walk over
7 Shuttle org.
8 Neighbor of Wyo.
9 Black cat
10 Perry Mason or Ally McBeal
11 "QB VII" author
12 Splinter group
13 Triumphant cries
18 Iced tea garnish
19 Didn't stand pat
24 Newspaper's ___ page
25 Sharpen
26 It might be put on the rack
27 "Two Women" star Sophia
28 Letter before iota
29 Preface
30 It has a groovy head
31 Choo-choo's sound
32 Pierce
36 Fancy sports cars, for short
37 "___ fair in love . . ."
38 Portable cutter
40 Not in stock yet
41 String quartet instrument
43 Weaken with water
44 Screen favorite
45 Infernal
48 "Hey, you!"
49 Sailor's greeting
50 Piece next to a knight
51 Opera highlight
53 French 101 verb
54 Require
55 Orchard unit
57 Poetic preposition
58 Turntable turners, briefly

by Peter Gordon

ACROSS
1 Plays the ponies
5 Dads
10 Suitcase
14 Part of Hawaii
15 Make amends
16 Philosopher Descartes
17 Unleashes
19 Penny ___
20 What the neophyte jester didn't feel like?
22 Building addition
24 Bagel topper
25 Officeholders
26 Curtain holder
27 Fashion
30 Relative of a rabbit
32 Common term for strabismus
35 Bill
36 What the part-time abacus user didn't feel like?
40 Likely
41 And so forth
43 Relative of a rabbit
45 God of war
46 Tire filler
47 Hold up
48 German cathedral city
50 Castaway's place
52 What the queasy rodeo rider didn't feel like?
57 Savior, to Bach
58 "Family Affair" star of 1960's–70's TV
61 "Jeopardy!" host Trebek
62 Reached in a hurry
63 Rock band Better Than ___
64 Gardener's need
65 Thrown for ___
66 Pond duck

DOWN
1 Big Apple subway inits.
2 ___ de cologne
3 Puccini's last opera
4 Because
5 Magician's hiding spot
6 At the peak of
7 Gene group
8 Founder of Scholasticism
9 Take care of
10 Tennis's Steffi
11 "Le Moulin de la Galette" artist
12 Chant
13 Strips
18 White ___
21 Sigh with relief, say
22 Bow
23 Writer Ephron
27 Accomplishment
28 Popeye's Olive ___
29 Direct (to)
31 Touch
33 Get really wet
34 A twin city
35 Twitches
37 Dined
38 Not shrunk or enlarged
39 Tribe with palisaded villages
42 "Jeopardy!" host Fleming
43 Big citrus fruit
44 Sacred birds, to some
45 Unprincipled
47 Indian prince
49 The Balance
50 Opposite of "Yum!"
51 ___ shooting
53 Elegance
54 Boy, in Barcelona
55 Flying mammals
56 Spanish articles
59 ___-la-la
60 Shakespearean prince

by Steven Dorfman

ACROSS

1 They may be jerked
6 Leisurely time to arrive at work
11 Sounds at a masseur's
14 Ten sawbucks
15 Deposed leader, perhaps
16 Web search result
17 Cereal for squirrels?
19 Ethyl ender
20 Distribute anew
21 Where to find Sonora: Abbr.
22 Miami-___ County
23 See 34-Down
25 Evaluated
27 Like the lunar surface
31 Enrapture
32 Down for the count
33 Become established
35 Jocks' antitheses
38 Tuck away
40 Hunk of fairway
42 Shade of red
43 Sunni's belief
45 Expressed orally
47 The Mustangs' sch.
48 Wasn't straight
50 Prepares for a rough ride
52 Olympics vehicle
55 Clinton's birthplace
56 Oodles
57 "A jealous mistress": Emerson
59 Tens, perhaps
63 Natural leader, in astrology
64 Perfumed actress?
66 One who can't pass the bar?
67 Penalized
68 Advance in age
69 Silver-gray
70 Most mall rats
71 Site of two famous banks

DOWN

1 Lasting impression
2 "___ bitten . . ."
3 "I ___ it!": Red Skelton
4 Motionless
5 Legislative houses
6 Business card abbr.
7 Physical, e.g.
8 Some sneaks
9 Joan's "Dynasty" role
10 ___ amis
11 Futuristic woman's chapeau?
12 Yoga practitioner
13 Hardly cheap
18 Erupted suddenly
22 Star in Cygnus
24 Fix, as a pool cue
26 Buddhist sect
27 "___ fan tutte"
28 Where wheels roll
29 Island's source of revenue?
30 Temperamental types
34 With 23-Across, a guiding light
36 Prefix with god
37 Leave speechless
39 Place for a spare tire?
41 Doughnut-shaped
44 Sportscaster Allen
46 Mini-pooches
49 Snookums
51 Kind of league
52 Corkwood
53 Dinner substitutes
54 Hive member
58 Some feds
60 Opposed to
61 Boxer Spinks
62 New Year's word
64 Time in 65-Down
65 Want ___

by Fred Piscop

ACROSS

1 Pilfer
6 Mars' counterpart
10 Waiflike
14 French wine valley
15 Expert
16 Texas city on the Brazos
17 Bearer of the heavens, in myth
18 Memo abbr.
19 Bullfight cheers
20 Craziness
23 Pigs' digs
24 French friend
25 Lowly abode
28 Stomach muscles, for short
29 Talk like th-th-this
33 Most-wanted invitees
35 "___ bin ein Berliner"
36 Rubik of Rubik's cube fame
37 No-goodnik
41 ___ a one
42 Observe
43 Any Time
44 Happy-go-lucky syllables
46 ___ Francisco
48 Men
49 Money for old age: Abbr.
50 South-of-the-border friend
52 Slight hoarseness
59 "I do" or "Drat!"
60 One way to settle a dispute
61 It's just over a foot
62 Sandpaper coating
63 And others: Abbr.
64 Alfred E. Neuman, for one
65 Back talk
66 Former mayor Giuliani
67 Sports figures

DOWN

1 Extra fat
2 Tiny bit
3 Cheerful tune
4 Vulgar
5 Say "um . . ."
6 Some marbles
7 Baseball's Babe and others
8 Old Harper's Bazaar designer
9 Lie on the beach, perhaps
10 Common soda bottle capacity
11 Football game division
12 Cake decorator
13 Prying
21 Penpoint
22 Earthbound bird
25 Lacks, briefly
26 Of an armbone
27 Princess's headwear
29 Coll. or univ.
30 Reduce to ruins
31 Result
32 Tournament of ___
34 Features of some bright rooms
35 Suffix with Israel
38 New York hockey player
39 Teachers' org.
40 Cotton fabrics
45 Jackie's second
46 Odoriferous
47 Spot in a river
50 Leading
51 "Ready ___ . . ."
52 Reasons for lighthouses
53 ___ avis
54 Singer Redding
55 Ballerina's dress
56 Gumbo ingredient
57 Tons
58 Column next to the ones

by Patrick Merrell

8

ACROSS

1 Purple bloomer
6 Hardly tanned
10 Vegan's no-no
14 Staffordshire stench
15 Factual
16 First name in scat
17 Dire early
   morning warning?
20 Sort
21 Ga. neighbor
22 Takes potshots
23 Used up
25 Cools down
26 Doll's cry
28 Big cheeses
32 Author Jong
34 Do damage to
35 To and ___
38 Joey's place?
42 "Lah-di-___!"
43 Kauai keepsakes
44 Pan-fry
45 Most fearless
48 Golfer's
   selection
49 Hood's blade
51 Snitches (on)
53 Orbital high
   point
55 Blood fluids
56 Jefferson Davis's org.
59 Buzz over
   New York City
   animals?
62 Powerful shark
63 Enlarge,
   as a hole
64 Spooky
65 Gaelic tongue
66 ___ a soul
67 Lively dances

DOWN

1 Centers of activity
2 Teen fave
3 Yale person?
4 Diving bird
5 Rugged box
6 "Right away!"
7 Long, long
   time
8 Little shaver
9 New wings
10 Army docs
11 Skip the big
   wedding
12 Balm additives
13 Highland hats
18 Fender blemish
19 Riddles
24 Nafta, for one
26 Pinochle combo
27 Diva's delivery
29 Part of a
   lunar cycle
30 Newsman Rather
31 Nonprofit's
   U.R.L. ending
33 Here, there and
   everywhere
35 Gettysburg
   Address opener
36 Old newspaper
   section
37 Foreboding
39 Fish caught in a pot
40 Tease
41 Alternative to air
   or highway
45 Often-stubbed digit
46 Hot and humid
47 Status before
   statehood: Abbr.
49 Asparagus unit
50 Sounds of
   frustration
52 Los Angeles hoopster
53 Pinnacle
54 Make, as money
55 Debate (with)
57 Make dirty
58 Home of Iowa State
60 Pasture
61 Tappan ___ Bridge

by Barry Callahan

ACROSS

1 Stick on a spit
7 "M" director Fritz
11 Sun. speech
14 Shop worker
15 Takeoff artist
16 ___ polloi
17 Lawgivers
18 900-line psychic
   Miss ___
19 It may be worn
   under a tunicle
20 "It's getting late!"
   abroad?
23 Kofi ___ Annan
25 CD-___
26 Kind of star
27 Token of welcome
28 It may be taken
   with a raised hand
30 Nothing, at
   a poker table
32 Upper-left key
33 "Tristia" poet
35 Long distance
   letters, once
36 "What'll you have?"
   abroad?
41 Morsel for Dobbin
42 Taunt
43 It's twice-eaten
45 Rushed violently
49 Old saying
50 Old NOW cause
51 Early computer
52 O'Hare
   monitor abbr.
54 Go to and fro
55 "Baloney!"
   abroad?
59 Crackpot
60 Horse of
   different colors
61 Ringmaster's
   place
64 ___ de France
65 Two tablets, say
66 "Psst!" follower,
   perhaps
67 Days of yore
68 Agenda, informally
69 Excessive

DOWN

1 T.G.I.F. part
2 Lea call
3 Many a
   conventiongoer
4 Hilo hello
5 Yakutsk's river
6 Once, once
7 Milk: Prefix
8 Poise
9 Not e'en once
10 Airline gang
11 Cascades peak
12 Windblown
13 Like Playboy
   cartoons
21 Stu of early TV
22 Mumbai master
23 Schooner filler
24 New Ager John
28 Coloratura's
   asset
29 Humpty
   Dumpty-shaped
31 Pseudopod
   former
34 Understand,
   slangily
37 Odin, to the Germans
38 Hemp source
39 Diner freebie
40 Pervasive quality
44 Dennis or Doris
45 Tush
46 Exciting
47 Smashed
   windows, maybe
48 Adulterate
53 Got into shape
54 Aid in aiming
56 Captured
57 Term paper abbr.
58 Tarzan's transport
62 Montana
   motto starter
63 Zip

by Kumar Balani

ACROSS

1 Garage sale tag
5 The whole spectrum
9 Sea creatures with claws
14 Worker's ___ (insurance)
15 Catch rodeo-style
16 "Scheherazade" locale
17 Knight's protection
19 Quite sharp
20 Marisa of "What Women Want"
21 Bad firecracker
22 James Dean persona
23 Econ. yardstick
25 Letter distribution on base
27 "Close, but no cigar"
31 Mermaid's home
32 Phone the folks
34 Despot
38 ___ Khan
39 Sheetful of cookies
41 Twinings product
42 Italian cheese
45 Money for the house
48 Fellows
49 Certain spiders in "Spider-Man"
50 Linguistic borrowing
55 Moo ___ pork
56 Fouled up
57 "___ you sure?"
59 Ice house
63 Treat badly
64 Theme of this puzzle
66 "Hasta la ___, baby!"
67 NBC's peacock, e.g.
68 Sitting on one's hands
69 Gas additive
70 Smudge
71 Loch ___

DOWN

1 It's got your number: Abbr.
2 London shopping district
3 Muslim holy man
4 Big name in catalogs
5 Pitcher's pride
6 Warty hopper
7 Poppy product
8 Mrs. F. Scott Fitzgerald
9 Pride of country music
10 Indy entry
11 Island near Curaçao
12 Tropical nut
13 Whiff
18 Final inning, usually
24 Gratis, to a lawyer
26 Land bridge
27 Raleigh's state: Abbr.
28 Othello's undoer
29 Chowder morsel
30 Vocalist Sumac
33 Biblical verb ending
35 Plenty, and then some
36 In apple-pie order
37 Shades from the sun
40 See 65-Down
43 General pardon
44 F.D.R.'s plan
46 Code of conduct
47 Rowan & Martin's show
50 Sailor's shore time
51 Planet's path
52 In ___ (hurriedly)
53 R & B singer Lou
54 Start to wilt
58 It follows that
60 Put on board, as cargo
61 Lubricates
62 Small bills
65 With 40-Down, a modern company

by Nancy Salomon and Harvey Estes

ACROSS

1 High school outbreak?
5 Afternoon affairs
9 Witty Wilde
14 Person of action
15 Sitar master Shankar
16 Fern-to-be
17 Rapscallions
18 McCain's state: Abbr.
19 Spills the beans
20 Thomas Mann classic
23 Home of the Braves: Abbr.
24 Photo ___ (camera sessions)
25 See 48-Across
28 Bakes, as eggs
30 Place for pennies
32 Inc., abroad
33 Angry
35 Classic toothpaste
37 Halving
40 Partner of dined
41 Golfer's concern
42 Jiffy
43 "Gotcha!"
44 "ER" extras
48 With 25-Across, speaker of the quote hidden in 20-, 37- and 53-Across
51 Watch chain
52 ABBA's "Mamma ___"
53 Nearby
57 Dunkable treat
59 Hamlet, e.g.
60 Old English letters
61 Grenoble's river
62 Astronaut Shepard
63 Newshawk's query
64 Passover supper
65 Tuna ___
66 Newbie

DOWN

1 Nike competitor
2 O'Neill title ender
3 Himalayan denizen
4 Start with while
5 Walked about
6 Brings in
7 Tel ___
8 XXL, e.g.
9 Old port on the Tiber
10 #, to a proofreader
11 Deli dish
12 Object of Indiana Jones's quest
13 In medias ___
21 Abominable
22 A.T.M. maker
26 ___ time (never)
27 Nutritional fig.
29 Tear apart
30 Coup d'état group
31 Seaweed, for one
34 Drop a line?
35 Spirits that victimize the sleeping
36 Wing: Prefix
37 Prie-___ (prayer bench)
38 Not level
39 Like a lamb
40 Financial daily, initially
43 Bat wood
45 Shop with an anvil
46 Choice word
47 Refuses
49 Habituate
50 Out-and-out
51 Big test
54 Dutch cheese
55 Greece's ___ of Tempe
56 Adult eft
57 Speak ill of, in slang
58 Sugar suffix

by Paula Gamache

ACROSS

1 Treaty subject
5 Broadway's Bob
10 Org. of which Nancy Lopez was once champion
14 Hang over one's head
15 For the birds?
16 Neighbor of Azerbaijan
17 Prediction basis #1
19 Author __ Neale Hurston
20 Biblical landfall
21 Diving bird
23 Chess champ before and after Botvinnik
24 Hem again
25 Prediction basis #2
28 60's campus org.
29 Card balance
31 Draws out
32 Old yellers?
34 Was second-best
35 Prediction basis #3
38 English painter John
40 Buttinskies
41 Prod
44 Robt. E. Lee, e.g.
45 Côte __, France
48 Prediction basis #4
50 "The Three Faces __"
52 Car ad abbr.
53 Hoop grp.
54 Wept wildly, maybe
55 Ties up the line
57 Prediction basis #5
60 Suffix with stink
61 Cause to swell
62 Adriatic resort
63 Like a pinup
64 Check mates?
65 Toil wearily

DOWN

1 Sacred places
2 Laughed loudly
3 Swampy area
4 Chocolaty campfire treat
5 Almanac bit
6 Egg cells
7 Lady's man
8 1978 Peace co-Nobelist
9 Guarantee
10 Gossipy Smith
11 The right stuff?
12 Some sale sites
13 Assayer, e.g.
18 Cheaply showy
22 Sent to the mat
25 Cases the joint for, say
26 Way out
27 Slow times
30 Frozen Wasser
32 Angler's basket
33 Tart fruits
35 Container with a lid that flips
36 Voyage beginning?
37 Self-confidence
38 Power problems
39 Whip up
42 Vintner's prefix
43 Moguls
45 Micromanager's concern
46 Carry too far
47 Football blitz
49 Safe place
51 Nincompoops
54 Takes in
56 Sauce source
58 Promise to pay
59 The "one" of a one-two

by Sherry O. Blackard

ACROSS

1 Listened to
6 Nickname for a good ol' boy
11 Entrepreneur's deg.
14 "The Goat" playwright Edward
15 Zones
16 Seek office
17 Etiquette expert
19 Wager
20 They're not yet adults
21 Conductors' sticks
23 Head of a fleet
26 Colorful crested bird
27 Photocopier attachment
28 Rice dish
29 Part of a printing press
30 Least good
31 Actress Peeples
34 Solicits for payment
35 Organ features
36 10-percenters: Abbr.
37 W.W. II region: Abbr.
38 Eiffel Tower's home
39 Falling sound
40 Rabbit's home
42 Mississippi city where Elvis was born
43 Alcohol
45 Reveals secrets about
46 "I'm in a rush!"
47 Lessen
48 Suffix with schnozz
49 Language mangler
54 ___ and vinegar
55 Boner
56 Weeper of myth
57 Office seeker, for short
58 Raises, as children
59 Not on the perimeter

DOWN

1 Popular Easter dish
2 Inventor Whitney
3 Stomach muscles, briefly
4 Breathers
5 More reserved
6 Trite
7 Coffee vessels
8 "Busy" one
9 Free of pointed parts
10 Military offensive
11 Famous tap-dancer
12 ___ Vista Lake, Calif.
13 Anxious
18 On ___ with (equal to)
22 ___ Aviv
23 Parenthetical comment
24 Food with a hole in the middle
25 One with encyclopedic knowledge
26 Exposes
28 Stop by
30 Electrical lines
32 From Rome: Prefix
33 ___ Martin (auto)
35 Back section of seats
36 Dessert often served à la mode
38 More fastidious
39 Islamic chiefs
41 Former Bush spokesman Fleischer
42 Dabbling duck
43 Busybody
44 Old disease
45 Skiers' transports
47 Love god
50 Mex. lady
51 Rubbish
52 ___-Wan Kenobi
53 Paper Mate product

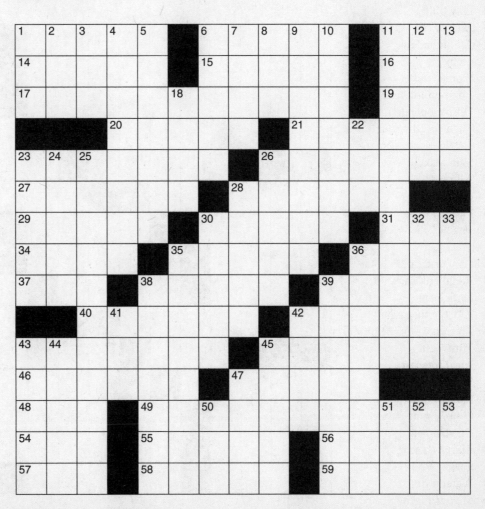

by Norman Wizer

ACROSS

1 Not that
5 Plods along
10 Take it easy
14 Open to inspection
16 Showy flower
17 Citrus fruit waste
18 Coal deposits?
19 Thieves' hangout
20 Employee's reward
21 Hippie's catchword
22 Intrinsically
23 Place for a cold one
24 Play time
27 N.L. or A.L. division
31 A criminal may go by it
32 Stomach filler
34 Log-burning time
35 D.E.A. operative
36 Theme of this puzzle
37 Ship lockup
38 Allergy consequence
39 Field of expertise
40 The "L" in 51-Down
41 Erne or tern
43 Radio talk show participant
44 L.B.J.'s successor
45 Tree knot
47 Throw out
50 April forecast
51 Santa __, Calif.
54 Lena of "Havana"
55 Q-tip, e.g.
57 Come down
58 Ruin a shot, in a way
59 Water swirl
60 Mexican bread
61 "Ah, me!"

DOWN

1 Walked (on)
2 Call to Fido
3 "Terrible" czar
4 Lust, for one
5 Takes an oath
6 __ lazuli
7 More than heavy
8 Jubilation
9 French seasoning
10 Philadelphia tourist attraction
11 Pavarotti specialty
12 Brass component
13 North Carolina motto starter
15 Exit
21 Give a scathing review
22 Sweet drink
23 Hospital capacity
24 Indian royalty
25 Make jubilant
26 Around
27 Drink with fast food
28 Like Mayberry
29 Well's partner
30 Cubist Fernand
32 Explorer maker
33 Be beholden to
36 Country dance spot
40 Adam's apple's place
42 Dennis the Menace, e.g.
43 Rapids transit?
45 Microsoft honcho
46 Explosion maker
47 Shoe bottom
48 Decked out
49 Cheese coating
50 Wander
51 Mil. truant
52 Canaveral letters
53 Beame and Saperstein
55 __ a plea
56 Baden-Baden or Évian

by Ed Early

ACROSS

1 "Belling the Cat" author
6 Kind of code
11 New Year overseas
14 Ignorance, they say
15 Love of Livorno
16 Word of farewell
17 Start of a quote by John Kenneth Galbraith
19 Reunion group
20 Cousin of a foil
21 Unearthly
22 Sander part
23 Not the first transaction
25 Register
27 Quote, part 2
32 Tried to stop from scoring
36 Surgically bind
37 Jewish month
38 Actor Stephen
40 Times to call, in ads
41 Society stalwart
44 Goal-oriented sorts
47 Quote, part 3
49 Item for a fairy?
50 Brings to a boil?
55 Switch's partner
57 Early computer language
60 Math computation
61 Resistance unit
62 End of the quote
64 Draw upon
65 Choir's platform
66 Africa's largest country
67 Rocky hill
68 Take care of
69 Gregg expert

DOWN

1 A Yokum
2 Split to unite
3 Many end in .com
4 Actor Milo
5 Trident-shaped letter
6 Summon
7 Mideast bigwig
8 More meddlesome
9 Magazine store?
10 Charlemagne's crowner
11 Depart
12 Satan's doings
13 Carnival sight
18 Has to have
22 Lahr co-star of 1939
24 PC linkup
26 Stat for Sosa
28 Mal de ___
29 "Gibraltar may be strong, but ___ are impregnable": Emerson
30 Cato's way
31 Capone's nemesis
32 Johnny of "Ed Wood"
33 Director Petri
34 40-hour-a-weeker
35 Mama Cass ___
39 King of Judah
42 From ___ Z
43 Valens who sang "Donna"
45 Sacred song
46 Writer Fleming
48 Pick out
51 Full range
52 Chip away
53 Showed over
54 Refuse
55 Event on a card
56 Facetious "I see"
58 A Maverick
59 Other, in Acapulco
62 Ones of the highest grade: Abbr.
63 Highway curve

by Alan Olschwang

ACROSS

1 Eye amorously
5 No ifs, ___ or buts
9 Partners
14 Place for seagulls to sit
15 Not shallow
16 Oven emanation
17 "What ___ is new?"
18 Dance in a grass skirt
19 Neglected neighborhoods
20 Classic Salinger novel, with "The"
23 Poi root
24 Yang's complement
25 Favorite project
28 Make, as a guess
31 Land for a house
34 Without help
36 Tijuana gold
37 Celebration
38 Behave promiscuously
42 Erupt
43 Bemoan
44 Put back to zero, say
45 Electric fish
46 Goulash seasoning
49 Make an effort
50 1040 initials
51 Old-fashioned containers
53 Repeated lyric in a children's song
61 Clay brick
62 "Incredible" one
63 Follow orders
64 Neighbor of Earth
65 Comedic actress McClurg
66 Took a train, say
67 Beauty, brawn or brains
68 "I haven't a thing to ___!"
69 Egg holder

DOWN

1 Letters from the Persian Gulf?
2 Southwestern river
3 For fear that
4 Put up
5 Cling (to)
6 Brain cell
7 Supermarket part
8 C-___
9 #5 iron
10 "Over the Rainbow" composer Harold
11 Studio visit
12 TV honor
13 Enclosure with a MS.
21 Any port in a storm
22 Mountainous area of Austria
25 No longer in fashion
26 Secretly tie the knot
27 Dry (off)
29 ___ of London
30 Mentalist Geller
31 Opposite of most
32 Playful animal
33 Cantankerous
35 This instant
37 Goliath, to David, e.g.
39 Use the backspace key
40 Break bread
41 Toped
46 Mass figure
47 Firenze's land
48 Field goal specialist
50 Fill (with)
52 Heap ___ upon
53 Coffee, slangily
54 Middle of March
55 Starts of workweeks: Abbr.
56 Not just swallow whole
57 Ill-mannered
58 Clarinet's kin
59 Cincinnati nine
60 Russian rejection

by Gregory E. Paul

ACROSS

1 Underwater predator
5 Letters on a Soyuz rocket
9 October stones
14 Fermented honey drink
15 Bona fide
16 Running wild
17 Indigo dye source
18 School for a future ens.
19 NBC staple since 1/14/52
20 Either 38- or 53-Across
23 Privy to
24 Pizarro's prize
25 Clod buster
28 Priests' subordinates
31 Automobile sticker fig.
34 Boredom
36 Trucker's truck
37 Fly high
38 "The Last Supper" artist
42 Battering wind
43 Out ___ limb
44 Largish combo
45 In the style of
46 Tableland
49 Hosp. units
50 Iron man Ripken
51 Ten: Prefix
53 "The Divine Comedy" author
60 Canon competitor
61 Grease monkey's job
62 The "S" in CBS: Abbr.
63 Muse of poetry
64 Bruins' sch.
65 First name in jeans
66 Surrenders
67 Deportment
68 "Baseball Tonight" channel

DOWN

1 Barbra's "Funny Girl" co-star
2 Philosopher Descartes
3 Genesis son
4 He finished second to Ike
5 Friend of Friday
6 Big name in small planes
7 Scene of Jesus's first miracle
8 Blueprint
9 Many John Wayne films
10 TV teaser
11 Verdi heroine
12 It can generate a lot of interest
13 Porker's pad
21 Land of a billion
22 Line dance
25 Hägar's wife, in the comics
26 N.B.A.'s Shaquille
27 ___ Gay (plane)
29 Zagreb resident
30 Suffix with fact
31 Three-card hustle
32 Indiana hoopster
33 Dixie dish
35 Arles article
37 [not a typo]
39 Esther of "Good Times"
40 Heredity helix
41 ___ for (substantiate)
46 Feeling of pity
47 Unlike toadstools
48 Cyclades' sea
50 Big bill
52 Airplane seat option
53 Calamitous
54 Part of 18-Across: Abbr.
55 Reunion attendee
56 ___ Baines Johnson
57 Ogles
58 Invitation letters
59 "Put ___ writing"
60 Boom box button

by Matthew J. Koceich

ACROSS

1 Kindergarten lesson
5 1957 Literature Nobelist
10 Lay an egg
14 Source of caffeine
15 Valuable violin
16 First-sight phenomenon
17 Top 10 hit for the Impressions, 1964
18 Leaves for lunch?
19 Out of port
20 Russia's cold war beer?
23 She played Ginger on "Gilligan's Island"
24 Corona's end
25 Weather changer
28 Site of El Misti volcano
30 Self starter?
33 Nifty
34 Destiny
35 Diminutive suffix
36 Deep-sea brew?
40 Cable network
41 Leave the sack
42 Unit charge
43 ___ roll (sushi selection)
44 Basketball Hall-of-Famer Archibald
45 Plower's creation
47 Shade of black
48 Wide-eyed
49 Presidential pint?
55 Go cold turkey
56 Laughing
57 Overcast
59 Suffix with kitchen
60 Opening words
61 Shade of green
62 Action figure?
63 None of the above
64 Where county offices are

DOWN

1 Blotter letters
2 Long pass
3 Laine of jazz
4 Holiness
5 James Bond locale
6 Whirlpool competitor
7 Many a beer
8 Its motto is "Industry"
9 Pistols and swords
10 Instant
11 Red ink amount
12 Through
13 Shade of green
21 They're all in the family
22 Customary
25 Provide
26 Flat agreement
27 Fleet-related
28 Bel ___ cheese
29 Gaelic tongue
30 "King Olaf" composer
31 Look after
32 Sprinkle around
34 Make stockings, say
37 One of the Jacksons
38 Haydn's "The Seasons," e.g.
39 Calls before a court
45 Divisor
46 "Yech!"
47 2000 World Series M.V.P.
48 Art style
49 Mercury or Saturn
50 Lo-cal
51 Salon request
52 Biblical verb
53 War of 1812 battle site
54 F.D.R.'s Scottie
55 Mathematician's sign-off
58 To this day

by Richard Silvestri

ACROSS

1 Male voice
5 Destroy
9 Ralph ___ Emerson
14 Gem with a play of colors
15 Scores to shoot for
16 Love affair
17 Lawman of the Old West
19 Hindu queen
20 Home on the range
21 Old West cemetery
23 Off-road transport: Abbr.
25 Family girl, for short
26 Burn
30 Construction piece
33 Winter clock setting in S.F.
36 Grand lineup
37 Location of 21-Across
39 Weaver's apparatus
40 Durable fabric
41 Upon
42 Location of 51-Across
44 Explorer Sir Francis
45 Music with jazzlike riffs
46 Electric dart shooter
47 Twisty turns
48 ___ tai
49 Boo-hoo
51 Site of a famous gunfight
56 Squiggly marks
61 Not suitable
62 Legendary lawman of the Old West
64 Mow down
65 Art Deco artist
66 Poet Pound
67 Neighbor of a Finn
68 Nostradamus, reputedly
69 Take five

DOWN

1 Boxing match
2 Church alcove
3 Ditto
4 Smack
5 Discombobulate
6 "Count me out"
7 Lackluster
8 Capital once known as Christiania
9 1941–45, for the United States
10 Nanking nannies
11 Actress Anderson
12 Event done at 20 paces, maybe
13 Pitcher Hershiser
18 Word before "set, go!"
22 Missouri river
24 MTV features
26 Seasons, as steak
27 Petty thief
28 Wonderful smell
29 Suckling sheep
31 Shouldered
32 Trimming tools
33 Sandwich breads
34 Stir up, as a fire
35 Uses a Smith Corona
38 Mustang and Impala
40 Connector of floors
43 Scare suddenly
44 Amount to subtract
48 Bike that zips
50 Glossy brown fur
51 Fixes a squeak
52 Had a gut feeling
53 Bat's hangout
54 Amazes
55 Instrument for a Muse
57 Wanton look
58 Muddleheadedness
59 Flubs
60 Tiff
63 Gobbled up

by Sherry O. Blackard

20

ACROSS

1 Lady's shoe
5 Diamond measure
10 Prefix with legal
14 Phone button below the 7
15 Egg-shaped
16 Lighted sign
17 Delhi wrap
18 Information-gathering mission
19 Gin flavoring
20 Wall Street Journal beat
23 Many a legal holiday: Abbr.
24 Bill-blocking vote
25 Sapporo sash
28 Spoon-___
30 Part of a play
31 Call to Bo-peep
34 Macintosh and others
38 Deep sleep
39 Luau dish
40 Fly traps
41 Those not on the guest list
46 King: Lat.
47 Fire remnant
48 Stud site
49 Things that go together
50 To's reverse
51 Chest protector?
53 What 20-, 34- and 41-Across have in common
61 Photographed
62 Newsman Newman
63 One for the road
64 Keokuk's home
65 Chaucer pilgrim
66 Diver Louganis
67 Legally invalid
68 Not so crazy
69 What fellers need

DOWN

1 "Hey, you!"
2 D-Day beachhead
3 Filly's mother
4 Spectrum creator
5 Princess topper
6 ___ plaisir
7 Billiard hall item
8 Proton's place
9 Period of occupancy
10 Annoying, as a gnat
11 Wheel connector
12 Side-splitter
13 Polished off
21 Soy product
22 "Darn it!"
25 Come about
26 Wilderness Road blazer
27 Blend
29 Pool measure
30 In reserve
31 Sounds from R2-D2
32 Stroll along
33 Good thing
35 Zero-star review
36 Fish eggs
37 It's "company"
42 Diversify
43 Certain similar chemical compounds
44 Burns, to Allen
45 ___ the Red
50 Of the unborn
52 Acts the blowhard
53 Biblical pronoun
54 Vigorous protest
55 Creative spark
56 Verdon of "Damn Yankees"
57 Honeycombed home
58 Atmosphere
59 Ragout or burgoo
60 Takes most of
61 Pride or lust

by Nancy Kavanaugh

ACROSS

1 Cuts blades
5 Slack-jawed
10 Fit together
14 Sound return
15 Cut up
16 Photographer's setting
17 Photograph bands?
19 1963 role for Liz
20 In concert
21 Dallas sch.
22 Out in front
23 Writer
24 Make a video about lowlifes?
26 More just
29 Sparkler
30 Old inits. in telecommunications
31 Tire filler
35 Sorry to say
39 Censor's target
41 Problem-solving advice appropriate for this puzzle?
42 "Liquor is quicker" poet
43 Pueblo Indian
44 Pilot, slangily
46 Cultural funding org.
47 Close one
49 N.Y.S.E. alternative
51 Take pictures of heads?
57 IV units
58 OPEC land
59 Catwoman, to Batman
60 Meteorological effects
63 Where to get off
64 Make an X-rated movie, perhaps?
66 Dumb cluck
67 Jazzman Shapiro
68 Score after deuce
69 Old-fashioned knife
70 Certain cup maker
71 Epitomes of busyness

DOWN

1 Arizona city
2 Publisher Adolph
3 Celebrate noisily
4 Cornhusker archrival
5 Shade of blonde
6 Hamlet's father, e.g.
7 Bouquet
8 Give some zing
9 Newspaper staffers, for short
10 Guy's guy
11 Noted blind mathematician
12 It may be let off
13 Gangsters
18 Basic belief
22 Leave 5-Across
25 Spurs
26 School group?
27 Prefix with sphere
28 Mess up
32 La Paz's land: Abbr.
33 Ultra-aloof
34 Gist
36 One-sided victory
37 Cruising
38 ___ attack
40 What a child may stand on
45 Millionaire's transport
48 Attorney's org.
50 Egyptian beetle
51 Mushers' vehicles
52 Resigned president
53 Put up with
54 In flames
55 Nick of "Affliction"
56 Some playoffs
61 Aunt Bee's boy
62 ID's for the I.R.S.
64 Where achievers go
65 "What'd I tell you?!"

by Nancy Salomon and Bill Zais

22

ACROSS

1 Instrument with a bow
6 Trucker with a handle
10 Like stallions and bulls
14 Heavenly hunter
15 Sharpen
16 Touched down
17 Two for breakfast?
20 Play ___ (do some tennis)
21 Deuce, in tennis
22 Baltimore player
23 Mink or sable
24 Not as dusty
25 Taiwan's capital
29 Stout drinks
30 Money in the bank, say
31 A ___ apple
32 Mailed
36 Two for dinner?
39 Ponies up
40 Summer coolers
41 Redhead's dye
42 "You said it!"
43 Diviner, of a sort
44 All-night studier
48 "Psst!"
49 What cable TV renders unnecessary
50 Bambi's mother, for one
51 Without cost
55 Two for dessert?
58 Isle of exile
59 Pro or con, in a debate
60 Dumbwaiter, essentially
61 Radiator sound
62 "Don't move!"
63 Actress Moorehead

DOWN

1 ___-Cola
2 Libido, in psychiatry
3 Vitality
4 Place for hay
5 Loved ___
6 Head of a meeting
7 Radius or rib
8 Finale
9 Aromatic
10 Craze
11 "March comes in like ___ . . ."
12 Fine thread
13 It'll knock you out
18 Needle case
19 War god
23 Crumbly white cheese
24 Ad biz awards
25 Push (down)
26 Away from port
27 Brit's exclamation
28 Beloved animals
29 Colorado town on the Roaring Fork River
31 Venomous snake
32 Fret
33 Almost forever
34 State bird of Hawaii
35 Peter I, II or III
37 How some shall remain
38 Chips ___! (cookies)
42 Asian nurse
43 Owner's proof
44 Sleeveless wraps
45 Spools
46 Riyadh residents
47 Flaky minerals
48 Sweetie pie
50 Bit of baby talk
51 Symbol of the WB network
52 Bit attachment
53 Relieve
54 Ambulance grp.
56 "Take a load off!"
57 When repeated, a Latin dance

by Janice M. Putney

ACROSS

1 Shoe blemish
6 Sean Connery, for one
10 Plod along
14 Trivial objection
15 Grandma
16 Like some tales or orders
17 Mountain ridge
18 Uzis and AK-47's
19 Columnist Bombeck
20 Barely wound Lee's men?
22 Affirm
23 Math course, briefly
24 Intertwine
26 ___ room (place for tots)
30 Van Gogh home
32 Skater's jump
33 Ricky player
35 Skylit lobbies
39 Elude capture
41 Primal therapy sounds
43 Beachhead of 1/22/44
44 Dance at a barn dance
46 Braun and Gabor
47 "Julius" in Gaius Julius Caesar
49 Join the navy, say
51 Major publicity
54 Weight not charged for
56 Airline to Ben-Gurion
57 Examine an Eastern European language?
63 Moreno of "West Side Story"
64 To laugh, to Lafayette
65 One-tenth payment
66 Oast
67 More than
68 Per ___ (yearly)
69 Bohr or Borge
70 Many a Bosnian
71 Lots and lots

DOWN

1 Heroin, slangily
2 Mystery writer John Dickson ___
3 Iris's place
4 Irish surname starter
5 Lamb's cover
6 Traffic problem
7 Venezuela's capital
8 "Gentle ___ Mind" (country classic)
9 Mortarboard attachment
10 Pilfer I-beams?
11 Caterpillar, e.g.
12 Ancient Mexican
13 Menacing look
21 Italy's largest lake
25 In the area
26 Sitar selection
27 Yoked pair
28 City on the Moselle
29 No-frills Cessna?
31 Greet the day
34 Brontë heroine
36 26-Down player Shankar
37 "___ corny . . ."
38 Kind of prof.
40 Moth's temptation
42 Office worker
45 One on the way in
48 Computer shortcuts
50 Sweet stuff
51 Judean king
52 Three-time batting champ Tony
53 Like Cheerios
55 Sour-tasting
58 Busy place
59 Fan's publication, for short
60 Sicilian spouter
61 Ground-up bait
62 Clothes lines

by Eugene W. Sard

ACROSS

1 North African capital
6 Fit one inside another
10 Bit of change
14 Farsi speaker
15 Linchpin site
16 Bibliography abbr.
17 Religious artwork
18 Sidesplitter
19 Actress ___ Flynn Boyle
20 More out of control?
23 Boot reinforcement
25 When it's broken, that's good
26 Cyclotron bit
27 Cousin of a caribou
28 Database operations
31 Goosy
33 Long in the tooth
35 Bill's partner
36 M.B.A. holder, maybe
37 Not as tall?
43 Shindigs
44 It may be brewing
45 Not aweather
46 Blouse ruffle
49 Conductor Sir Georg
51 Jet ___
52 Latin 101 word
53 Notable period
55 Punches in
57 More secure?
61 Mirth
62 Baal, e.g.
63 Cut into
66 Turkish money
67 1986 #1 hit by Starship
68 Outpost group
69 Magi's origin
70 North Carolina college
71 Nasal dividers

DOWN

1 Letters sometimes inscribed above a name
2 Former press secretary Fleischer
3 Traveler's guidebook
4 Prank
5 Royal toppers
6 D.E.A. agent
7 Way out
8 Some fore-and-afters
9 Prefix with hydrozoline
10 Bologna home
11 Bologna home
12 Actor Brando
13 Comedienne Boosler
21 Noteworthy periods
22 Bring up-to-date
23 Kind of spirit
24 "Three Sisters" sister
29 Milne youngster
30 Old TV sidekick
32 Nick's wife
34 Pedestal part
36 Lunar locale
38 Tribal symbol
39 Sinuous swimmer
40 Basketball maneuver
41 Close
42 They're tapped
46 Sound of keys
47 Bloomer who popularized bloomers
48 Shaded recesses
49 Flip-flop, e.g.
50 Coastal features
54 Union demand
56 ___ Haute, Ind.
58 Place in the House
59 Former P.M. of 11-Down
60 Pearl Buck heroine
64 URL part
65 Raters of m.p.g.

by Janet R. Bender

ACROSS

1 West Point institution, for short
5 Made a gaffe
10 Bathroom powder
14 Enter
15 Exit
16 Is in arrears
17 Quick race
20 Sisters' daughters
21 It's connected to the left ventricle
22 Sportscaster Garagiola
24 Sault ___ Marie
25 Basketball hoop
27 Patriotic women's org.
28 Insurance company with a duck in its TV ads
30 Lament
32 Engine additive letters
33 Munchie in a brownie, perhaps
35 Doesn't wander
37 Rock band with the platinum album "The Downward Spiral"
41 Sleeping disorder
42 Kind of valve in a car
44 "Leaving ___ Vegas"
47 Commit to memory
49 Spacey of "American Beauty"
50 Granola morsel
51 Egyptian reptile
52 Praiseful poem
54 Big galoot
55 Eventual oak
57 Imaginary
59 1979 nuclear accident site
64 Pay attention to
65 Gift recipient
66 Onetime Atlanta arena
67 At loose ___
68 Oodles
69 Light blade

DOWN

1 "How revolting!"
2 Old French coin
3 Liza . . . with a Z
4 "Me, myself ___"
5 Put into power
6 Cash in
7 Suntanners catch them
8 Sister of Zsa Zsa
9 Architect Mies van ___ Rohe
10 Kind of list
11 Medals and trophies, e.g.
12 Vampire in Anne Rice novels
13 D flat's equivalent
18 Salvation for someone stranded in the Arctic, say
19 "Whatever Lola Wants" musical
22 Long feature of a crocodile
23 In the blink ___ eye
25 Book after Judges
26 Citizen of Tehran
29 Ballerina Pavlova
31 Recognition from "the Academy"
34 Food spearers
36 Location
38 ___ tide
39 Groovy light source
40 Gambol
43 Chemical suffix
44 Despise
45 German city near the Belgian border
46 In an attic
48 "Really, you don't have to"
53 Towels off
56 Dark wines
57 Bone by the humerus
58 Balm ingredient
60 Physicians, for short
61 Quadrennial games org.
62 SSW's reverse
63 Casino cube

by Trip Payne

ACROSS

1 Lines on a musical staff
6 Froth
10 Man trapper
14 Maui veranda
15 First name in scat
16 Needle holder
17 Muscle
18 Tibetan monk
19 Launch agcy.
20 Columnist for the lovelorn
23 Part of U.C.L.A.
24 Square-dancing call
25 Maximally
29 Strike callers
31 Shot onto a green
32 Columnist for the lovelorn
38 Citadel student
40 Texas tea
41 Pago Pago's place
42 20-Across, to 32-Across
45 Rumor generator?
46 "Trick" joint, maybe
47 Brunch dish
49 Beverage that soothes a sore throat
53 "Be Prepared" org.
54 Entreaty to 20- or 32-Across
61 Popeye's tooter
62 High time?
63 Autumn drink
64 Ode or haiku
65 Shirt brand
66 Go ___ with
67 Addition column
68 Addition column
69 Trappers' wares

DOWN

1 Napoleon was banished to it
2 Dress
3 ___ B'rith
4 Deputy ___ (cartoon canine)
5 Important exams
6 Chops down
7 Norwegian saint
8 ___ mater
9 The Kettles
10 Morning Star
11 Video game pioneer
12 Pondered
13 Softly, on scores
21 Teeny bit
22 Petty officers
25 Depositor's holding: Abbr.
26 Spring occurrence
27 Longish skirt
28 Dentist's direction
29 Bring together
30 Fr. miss
33 Beak
34 Title for Agatha Christie
35 Actor Jannings
36 Something to play
37 Put (away)
39 Expressed disapproval
43 Irritated
44 Parks on a bus
48 Like the Marx Brothers
49 Hulking herbivore
50 Burger topper
51 Portable dwelling
52 Abounds
53 Gives a bit
55 Seep
56 It may be new or blue
57 Awful-tasting
58 Hilary Duff, to teen girls
59 Euro part
60 Work units

by Kelly Clark

ACROSS
1 Father's offering
5 What will be
9 Not try very hard
14 Gator's kin
15 Tennis score after deuce
16 Completely anesthetized
17 Fashionable explosive?
19 Team track event
20 Tuba sound
21 Airline to Israel
23 From ___ Z
24 Fashionable view?
28 Took in with astonishment
29 Chanel of fashion
30 Clinches
31 Insolence
33 Marriage guide
37 Neighbor of Aus.
38 Fashionable dessert?
41 Justice Fortas
42 Sun Valley state
44 Splashy resort
45 Plodded
46 Friendly femme
49 New York tribe
51 Fashionable substitute?
55 Gardner on screen
56 Shaving stuff
57 "O Sole ___"
58 Relatively red
60 Fashionable conveyance?
65 Like some remarks
66 Vincent Lopez's theme song
67 Garr of "Tootsie"
68 Undue speed
69 Make one's permanent mark?
70 Lyrical tributes

DOWN
1 Roast hosts, briefly
2 Recliner part
3 Ongoing saga
4 Set-tos
5 Terrif
6 Brouhaha
7 Kitchen counter?
8 As a whole
9 Fancy twist
10 United
11 Statesman Stevenson
12 Defense grp. of 1954–77
13 Check for fit
18 Impact sound
22 Mil. mail drop
24 Walked nervously
25 Film composer Schifrin
26 Quarreling
27 Discouraging words
28 Leslie Caron role
32 Gateway sales
34 Tough
35 W.W. II torpedo craft
36 Cold war foe
38 Out of jeopardy
39 Grp. of books in the Bible
40 Welles's "Citizen"
43 Kramden laugh syllable
45 Connect with
47 Wall St. debut
48 Pal of Jerry Seinfeld
50 Madame Bovary
51 Strident
52 The Donald's first ex
53 Rue de Rivoli city
54 Comeback to "Are too!"
59 Buffalo's summer hrs.
61 R.N.'s forte
62 "Go team!"
63 High dudgeon
64 Carol contraction

by Nancy Salomon

28

ACROSS

1 North Pole assistant?
4 Military bases
9 Lowly workers
14 Misstatement
15 In the upper berth
16 Brightest star in a constellation
17 Holiday ___
18 Postal device
19 Scent
20 Star of 36-Across
23 Insurance company worker
24 What an actor waits for
25 Terrier or retriever
28 Deli sandwich
29 Trails
32 Titled lady
33 Use an 18-Across
35 Kind of position
36 Series set at 328 Chauncey Street in Brooklyn
41 Wise one
42 Computer shortcut
43 All over
44 Put up, as a building
46 Sharp flavor
50 Sun. speaker
51 Wrath
52 "I agree!"
53 Co-star of 36-Across
58 About 39 inches, in England
60 Multiflavor ice cream
61 Touch of frost
62 Letter opposite 16-Across
63 Conspicuous success
64 WNW's opposite
65 Mass transit vehicles

66 Spicy sauce
67 Wilmington's state: Abbr.

DOWN

1 Hebrew prophet
2 Amount of space in a newspaper
3 Foil user
4 Suggest
5 First word in a fairy tale
6 Male deer
7 Turnpike charge
8 Oration
9 Not in anymore
10 Tickle Me ___
11 When no games are scheduled
12 Flyers' and Rangers' org.
13 Mule of old song
21 Ability
22 Vienna's home: Abbr.
26 Sharif of "Doctor Zhivago"
27 Hair goops
29 Wrestling win
30 Six, say, for a first-grader
31 Herb in soups
32 Signified
34 Long, long time
35 In favor of
36 Leader opposed by the Bolsheviks
37 Sharpen

38 Boosts
39 Bub
40 World Series mo.
44 "To ___ is human . . ."
45 ___ Pieces
47 Made good
48 In any way, in dialect
49 God's honest truth
51 Think tank output
52 Mediterranean land
54 Goad
55 Blue Triangle org.
56 Steelmaking site
57 Gay 90's and Roaring 20's
58 Mafia
59 Big bird

by Allan E. Parrish

ACROSS

1 Lay to rest
6 Up to, informally
9 Zest
14 Riyadh resident
15 Prefix with cycle
16 According to
17 Black Panthers, e.g.
19 Like Valhalla's heroes
20 "A-Tisket, A-Tasket" singer
22 "___ a deal!"
23 Victor's booty
24 "We want ___!" (baseball fans' cry)
26 ___ Speedwagon
27 Piece of field artillery
31 Was ill with
34 Faint with beating heart
36 Place for a béret
37 Like the Tower of Pisa
39 Hardship
40 Stuck in Pamplona?
41 Pro ___
42 Old Ford flop
44 Draft dodgers' bane: Abbr.
45 This puzzle's theme
48 Fallen space station
50 Concerning, in memos
51 Nail-___ (tense situations)
54 Catch some rays
56 Rite of passage, for some
59 ___ Fountain
61 Pertaining to tautness
63 Black ink item
64 Bard's before
65 Barely managing, with "out"
66 They're sometimes stolen
67 Match part
68 Actress Zellweger

DOWN

1 Doctrine
2 Artless ones
3 Dutch bloomer
4 Perry White, e.g.
5 Most elegant
6 Counterparts to lyrics
7 Verb type: Abbr.
8 Actress Kudrow
9 Father of independent India
10 Hope's road show org.
11 Wine drinks
12 Dry run
13 Miners' finds
18 Luminous
21 Some postgraduate study
25 "Tell ___ the judge!"
27 Young toughs
28 Teller's stack
29 Vacation times in Verdun
30 Some M&M's
31 Mata ___
32 Rat-___
33 Blonde's quality, in jokes
35 Ran a tab
38 Croquet area
40 More showy
43 Broadcasts
46 Asteroids' paths
47 New Deal org.
49 Annul
51 Stanford-___ (I.Q. rater)
52 Arrested
53 Classic Ladd western
54 Attempt
55 Celestial bear
57 Numbered hwys.
58 Insignificant
60 Neckline shape
62 T-shirt size: Abbr.

by John R. Conrad

30

ACROSS

1 Currency substitute
6 Big party
10 The Beatles'
"__ Madonna"
14 Japanese verse
15 Part of A.M.
16 Yellow spread
17 When many people
have cookouts
20 Formerly
21 They average 100
22 Free
23 Bug
24 Enter
25 Spanish snack
28 Monopoly game
token
30 Novelist Rona
35 Flamenco cries
36 It's nothing, really
37 Big name in beauty
products
38 Frédéric Auguste
Bartholdi creation
41 People in People
42 Energy
43 Uno y dos
44 Pittsburgh's
Mellon __
45 Speaker in the
Baseball Hall
of Fame
46 Elusive Stevenson
character
47 Emperor who
poisoned Britannicus
49 Singer Sumac
51 Feeling pins
and needles
55 Santa __
56 Unagi, at a sushi bar
59 Tablet inscription
on 38-Across that
commemorates
17-Across
62 Up to snuff
63 Actress Skye
64 Home on the range
65 Take a breather

66 Mmes., in Madrid
67 Embellish

DOWN

1 Painful place to
be kicked
2 Sugar source
3 Fairgrounds
attraction
4 War-hero president
5 Iris's center
6 Makes verboten
7 What's more
8 Walk over
9 Artist
Toulouse-Lautrec
10 "Stay" singer Lisa
11 Designer Gucci
12 Person with a list

13 Go up and down
rapidly
18 Zebras, e.g.
19 Grifter's ploy
23 Buckle
24 One who works
on a swing
25 Puccini opera
26 Adjust
27 "The Power of Positive
Thinking" writer
29 Carnival city
31 1986 self-titled
soul album
32 Boat to Staten Island
33 In the cards
34 "Family Ties" mom
37 Not really sing
39 Congo border river

40 Aloha shirt accessory
45 Aftershock
48 Graceland name
50 Island south of Sicily
51 Open slightly
52 Part of an IV
53 Troubles
54 Da's opposite
55 Pair in a dead
man's hand
56 Big fair
57 Penultimate fairy
tale word
58 Bank holding
60 Modern courtroom
evidence
61 Marked, as a ballot

by Peter Gordon

ACROSS

1 Fraud
5 Yemeni or Qatari
9 Coffee lightener
14 Show bravery
15 Over hill and ___
16 Oscar-winning Berry
17 Coal waste
18 Stir up
19 French clerics
20 Symbol marking a composer's music?
23 Early form of bridge
24 Waikiki wreath
25 Leave
28 Crossword solving, for one
32 Make happy
33 Land of O'Kelly and O'Keeffe
35 Woman's hairstyle
36 Composer's popular works?
40 Choose
41 Emulated Pinocchio
42 Close, in poetry
43 Gets hot under the collar
46 Spirited
47 Publicize
48 Powell of the Bush White House
50 Like the dog days of summer, for a composer?
56 Brilliance
57 One of five Norwegian kings
58 Thoroughly
60 Portion
61 Cry of greed
62 Writing of Chaucer
63 Marine detector
64 Ages
65 Verve

DOWN

1 60's protest grp.
2 Baby elephant
3 Asia's ___ Sea
4 It can provide a big jolt
5 Skillful
6 What the monsoon season brings
7 Parcel out
8 "It's ___ real!"
9 Pursues
10 Cottontail
11 Exile isle for Napoleon
12 One of the Baldwins
13 Fit well together
21 Flung
22 African antelope
25 Show cars
26 Leave via ladder, maybe
27 Stickum
28 ___ Piper
29 "Peer Gynt" dramatist
30 Background sound in a store
31 Door
33 Oklahoma city
34 1 or 95: Abbr.
37 Heads-up
38 10-Down fur
39 Deluge
44 Noted Las Vegas casino
45 Disorderly one
46 Toils (away)
48 Hue
49 John who wrote "Butterfield 8"
50 Hardy heroine
51 Cuatro + cuatro
52 Pearl Buck heroine
53 Volume
54 And others, for short
55 "Damn Yankees" seductress
59 Kind of Buddhism

by Sheldon Benardo

ACROSS

1 "Whatcha ___?"
5 Madonna musical
10 "Yikes!"
14 Big name in oil
15 Assaults with
a spray
16 "Adam ___"
(Eliot novel)
17 Elvis Presley hit
of 1956
20 Hippie
21 Without support
22 Like Coolidge's
utterances
23 Letter adornment
25 Volcanic spew
27 Gist
29 Portly plus
32 Record player
34 Losing tic-tac-toe
row
35 Pre-stereo
36 Stared at
37 Busy airport
38 Gluck's "___ ed
Euridice"
39 Hanging on
every word
40 Standard
41 Ralph Kramden,
for one
42 Sturdy tree
43 Bluesman McClinton
45 Mos. and mos.
46 Workout venues
48 Purple ___, New
Hampshire's
state flower
50 Very, to Verdi
52 Reject,
as a motion
55 Beatles hit of
1967
58 "The Little Mermaid"
baddies
59 Pitchfork wielder
60 Diversion
61 Box that crackers
go into?

62 Hair-raising
63 British P.M. before
Macmillan

DOWN

1 Children's author
Roald
2 Nabisco cookie
3 Four Tops hit of 1965
4 Scandinavian
land, to natives
5 Mission
6 Fluctuates
7 Cake finisher
8 Kind of party
9 One way to get
directions
10 Carlo Levi's "Christ
Stopped at ___"

11 Rolling Stones hit
of 1965
12 Yemeni port
13 Expunge, as text
18 Sewer line?
19 Fast runner
23 Stuck-up sort
24 Prefix with system
25 Really love
26 "Love Story"
author
28 Outlying community
30 Words after
bend or lend
31 Cel mates?
33 Widebody, e.g.
35 ___ Smith's pies
37 Haarlem painter
Frans

38 Start-up costs
40 Shooter pellet
41 Easily provoked
43 A fifth of MMMX
44 Medicine show
purchase
47 Parson's estate
49 Actress Woodard
50 Impresses
51 Long Island
Railroad stop
52 Opera persona
53 England's Great
___ River
54 Plump songbird
56 E.R. workers
57 "Hold on a ___"

by Robert Malinow

ACROSS

1 Monopoly square
5 Palladium, for one
10 Dumbfound
14 Biblical preposition
15 Not only like
16 Oscar Wilde poem "The Garden of ___"
17 Hubbub
18 About
19 Heist haul
20 Twelve inches of supply boat?
22 Break, in a way
23 "The Great Ziegfeld" co-star
24 Raspy
26 Quiver holder
30 Target of some collars
32 Out of this world?
33 Three feet of basketball floor?
38 Refrain syllables
39 Tasteless
40 Apple spray
41 Three miles of climbing vine?
43 Stopper
44 Pizzas
45 Bamboozled
46 Stoolies do it
50 Thai's neighbor
51 Bee or Em
52 39.37 inches of stream?
59 A dirty person may draw one
60 Foaming at the mouth
61 It's long in fashion
62 "___ From Muskogee"
63 Place for an urn
64 Flower of one's eye?
65 Show partner
66 Library device
67 "Valley of the Dolls" actress

DOWN

1 Like some deserts
2 Stud stake
3 Take ___ stride
4 Lady's man
5 Long-vowel mark
6 Enlighten
7 El Cordobés adversary
8 Sacramento's ___ Arena
9 Coriaceous
10 River feature
11 Sounding like lions
12 Skyrockets
13 First name in cosmetics
21 Pizazz
25 Bit in a horse's mouth
26 Lesser Sunda island
27 Patron saint of Norway
28 Guileful
29 Square ___
30 Try hard to visualize
31 New Testament book
33 It may be rattled
34 Fish story
35 Lyricist Lerner
36 Haymaking aid
37 Historic Scott
39 It speeds up flights
42 Org. that may be involved in a cleanup
43 Bust alternative
45 Calling
46 Cousin of a clog
47 Temblor
48 Up to
49 Waters of Hollywood
50 Oblivion
53 Horne solo
54 Boor's lack
55 Radiate
56 Butler's quarters?
57 Way out
58 Piece of high ground

by Richard Silvestri

34

ACROSS

1 Slice (off)
4 Indoor camera attachment
9 Rand McNally book
14 Gay 90's, e.g.
15 Spooky
16 One of the Allman Brothers
17 Prefix with puncture
18 Alfalfa's love in "The Little Rascals"
19 A-list group
20 "Freeze!"
22 Leader of reformers' 31-Down
24 Wet, weatherwise
26 Charged particle
27 Processes, as ore
29 Daily Hollywood publication
33 Signals goodbye
34 Sent a letter by phone
35 Playboy Mansion guy
37 The best three in a three-of-a-kind
38 Goofed
39 Concrete
40 One over a birdie
41 Use
42 Succinct
43 Using a blowtorch
45 Give
46 Fill one's stomach
47 Oscar winner Marisa
48 Leader of football's 31-Down
53 Dutch cheese
56 Stadium
57 Farsi speaker
59 Dolly the clone, e.g.
60 Nobleman
61 Snooped (around)
62 Operated
63 Skew
64 Wagner work
65 Pink Floyd co-founder Barrett

DOWN

1 Mrs. Rabin of Israel
2 Killer whale
3 Leader of pop music's 31-Down
4 G-man, e.g.
5 Gets smart
6 Ordered set
7 Pie-cooling spot
8 Mound
9 Throat tissue
10 The Green Wave, in college sports
11 With 54-Down, in reserve
12 Poker stake
13 Crystal ball user
21 Grimm works
23 Employed
25 "___ in his kiss" (1964 pop lyric)
27 Exchange
28 Parrot's cousin
29 Airline to Rio
30 Skater's jump
31 1960's group (in three different ways)
32 Brewer's need
34 Drescher of "The Nanny"
36 Turn tail
38 Musical with the song "Buenos Aires"
39 Girl's name meaning "born again"
41 Not budging
42 Mr. Turkey
44 "Instant Karma" singer
45 One of Santa's reindeer
47 Needle
48 Needles
49 Like some medicines
50 Zeus' wife
51 The Flintstones' pet
52 Plummet
54 See 11-Down
55 Darn
58 It borders Wash.

by John Leavy

ACROSS

1 Argentine plains
7 "Some of this, some of that" dish
11 School advisory grp.
14 Everlasting, old-style
15 The "C" in U.P.C.
16 Serving of corn
17 1925 musical featuring "Tea for Two"
19 Opposite of post-
20 Blue books?
21 Stereo forerunner
22 Number 2's
24 Make jubilant
26 Fish organ
27 Of one's surroundings
30 Hard to miss
33 1950's–60's guitar twanger Eddy
34 Get ___ (start work)
36 Ed of "Daniel Boone"
37 Like Shostakovich's Symphony No. 2
38 "I've Got the Music in Me" singer, 1974
41 Eggs
42 March Madness grp.
44 Stet's opposite
45 Quiz show host, often
47 Make a point, in a way
49 White knights
51 Les États-___
52 UFO occupant
53 Barber chair attachment
55 Sashes in "The Mikado"
56 Opera set along the Nile
60 Reaction to a back rub, maybe
61 Polynesian treat
64 Brooklyn campus, for short
65 Furies
66 Off course
67 Shade tree
68 Cloud ___
69 Insufficient

DOWN

1 They used to be lowered into wells
2 Nuclear energy source
3 Restaurant handout
4 Amino acid chain
5 Lee who founded the Shakers
6 Mariner
7 Part of an act
8 Oz visitor
9 Summer D.C. setting
10 Crop-destroying beetle
11 1937 Jean Gabin title role
12 Infield cover
13 Mars' counterpart
18 Like a road in a Frost poem
23 Charles Lamb's pen name
25 Soup ingredient
26 Golden ___
27 Tennis scores after deuce
28 Chew (on)
29 Liquor-flavored cake
30 Go askew
31 Emphatic refusal
32 Winter Palace residents
35 ". . . ___ the cows come home"
39 Bad time for Caesar
40 House overhang
43 The New Yorker cartoonist Peter
46 Original "Ocean's Eleven" star
48 1972 Ben Vereen musical
50 Bridal paths
52 Invective
53 Store sign
54 Follow
55 Store sign
57 "I'd consider ___ honor"
58 Collision memento
59 Like would-be bohemians
62 Mentalist Geller
63 Semicircle

by Ed Early

ACROSS

1 Construction co. projects
6 Chicago-to-Memphis dir.
9 Fighting
14 Lecherous looks
15 X
16 River past Liechtenstein
17 Father of the Pleiades
18 Some California baseball stars?
20 Ostracize
21 Propelled a lifeboat
22 Classic pop
23 California baseball players in trouble with the I.R.S.?
25 Hollywood, with "the"
26 Ace place?
27 Locker room item
29 Cause of a stomachache
33 Some noblemen
34 Gang of California baseball players?
37 Garlic piece
39 Company that made Pong
40 Brings on board, in a way
41 Like some inspections
46 Pack animal
47 What brainy California baseball players get?
51 Takes advantage of
53 Front wheel alignment
54 O.K. Corral figure
55 California baseball teammates?
57 Mother of Pebbles
58 PC letters
59 Start of Julius III's papacy
60 First name in 2000 news
61 Lets
62 What a contact contacts
63 Bangladesh's capital, old-style

DOWN

1 Good times
2 "___ Weapon"
3 Like the presidential suite
4 Starbucks size
5 Draft org.
6 Lean person
7 ___ Khan (tiger in "The Jungle Book")
8 Dentist's request
9 The Diamondbacks, on scoreboards
10 Comparison word
11 Sipping sites
12 Where soldiers may be busy
13 Adjusts, as a cap
19 Mdse.
21 Newbery Medal winner Scott
24 Small eggs
27 Involved with
28 "Silent" prez
30 Civil War letters
31 "Mangia!"
32 Messenger ___
34 Equestrian
35 Adam's apple picker
36 Common injury location
37 Writer buried at Westminster Abbey
38 Supple
42 Down Under girl
43 It leans
44 Runway
45 Madrileño's land
47 Regular: Abbr.
48 The Velvet Fog
49 Like marshes
50 Plane seating request
52 Fast-moving card game
56 Hirt and Hirschfeld
57 Get a wife

by Peter Gordon

ACROSS

1 Comical Laurel
5 All excited
9 Knights' ladies
14 Sexologist Shere
15 Sandy slope
16 "Remember the ___!"
17 Service status
18 Damon of "The Bourne Identity"
19 Disinfectant brand
20 Wind pointer
23 D.D.E.'s command in W.W. II
24 Some household heads
25 Not Rep. or Dem.
26 Myrna of "The Thin Man"
27 The hoop in hoops
28 Having good posture
30 Hissy fit
32 Meal in a shell
33 Quoits target
35 One ___ kind
36 Lay ___ the line
37 "Changing the subject . . ."
41 Raid rival
42 Pi follower
43 China's Sun ___-sen
44 Take a load off
45 Part of CNN
47 Flies alone
51 Leave dumbstruck
52 Confederate soldier
53 Lobbying grp.
55 Before, of yore
56 Ford or Lincoln
57 1972 Carly Simon hit
60 City near Syracuse
62 Stink to high heaven
63 Brain wave
64 Russian Revolution leader
65 Patiently wait

66 Dryer outlet
67 Rival of ancient Sparta
68 Winter blanket
69 Pay to play

DOWN

1 Missourian's demand
2 Musical ineptitude
3 "Relax, soldier!"
4 Shipshape
5 Product pitchers
6 Some football linemen
7 Airing
8 "Stop worrying about picayune stuff!"
9 Big name in Chicago politics
10 Prince ___ Khan
11 Grand Prix racer
12 :-) or :-(
13 Wise king of Israel
21 Woo in an unwelcome way
22 ___ public
29 Rooters' refrain
31 At all, in dialect
32 Connect with
34 Island on the Java Sea
37 Free serving at a restaurant
38 A bull may wear one
39 Many a commuter's base
40 Explorer ___ da Gama
41 Storied vampire
46 Popular swimwear
48 Hard to lift
49 Show the ropes to
50 100-member group
52 "___ Hope" (former soap)
54 Cockeyed
58 Horse halter?
59 Cheer starter
61 A.F.L.'s partner, once

by Harvey Estes and Nancy Salomon

ACROSS

1 Couch
5 Fail to act
10 Host before Carson
14 Grad
15 Think the world of
16 Light brown
17 Sask. neighbor
18 ___ palm
19 Whiz kids
20 Hoot at confined hooters?
23 Bank statement amt.
24 Have a bite
25 Eventually
27 Explorer Johnson
30 Captain's hook
33 Send via Western Union
34 Hamlet, in "Hamlet"
36 Bill Gates, to some
38 Supplies, as assistance
41 Claim Confederate leader has varied taste?
44 Winetaster's criterion
45 1970 Kinks hit
46 Triumphant cry
47 Room at San Quentin
49 Part of a basilica
51 Auction buy
52 Villain in Exodus
55 Response to a preacher
57 Tennis judge's cry
58 Entice W.W. II agents?
64 Racer Luyendyk
66 It's a fact
67 Site of the Taj Mahal
68 ___ suit (baggy outfit)
69 First name in cosmetics
70 "___ Over Beethoven"
71 Oscar winner Paquin
72 Takes five
73 Not just a five-minute jaunt

DOWN

1 German industrial region
2 ___ podrida
3 Play around (with)
4 Dumbfound
5 "Mission: Impossible" assignment, maybe
6 Thought: Prefix
7 Screen pooch of 1939
8 Makes suds
9 Shortest light
10 Unimpressive brain size
11 Unplanned
12 Rock concert venue
13 Out of practice
21 End of a two-part move
22 Request before a click
26 Build
27 Shamu, for one
28 Rise quickly
29 Divvying-up process
31 Natural gas, for one
32 Common refrigerant
35 "___ Gantry"
37 Pac-10 team, for short
39 "Thank You" singer, 2001
40 Leave in a hurry
42 Steven Bochco series
43 Doesn't skimp with
48 Window smasher, maybe
50 Actors Begley and Begley Jr.
52 Public square
53 "Great white" bird
54 Preakness entrant
56 It's eye-grabbing
59 On the ___ (bickering)
60 Let stand, in editorial parlance
61 Aviation pioneer Sikorsky
62 ___ Stanley Gardner
63 Polio vaccine developer
65 LAX info

by Randall J. Hartman

ACROSS

1 Puccini opera
6 Grasslands
10 Hole-making tool
13 "___ to Be You"
14 Laceless shoes
15 La-la lead-in
16 13
18 Obedience school command
19 Defensive tackle Warren ___
20 Suit to ___
21 Smallest postage hike
22 13
26 Abbreviate
28 Letter after epsilon
29 When repeated, a 1963 Kingsmen hit
30 Aim for many models
34 Abby's late sister
35 Bygone
37 Beyond tipsy
38 Hindmost brain parts
41 Rubbish
43 Rich soil
44 Side by side
46 13
50 "What's the ___?!"
51 Muzzleloader's load
52 Lacking thrills
55 "Scram!"
56 13
59 Bon ___
60 Like bustards and buzzards
61 One of the Muses
62 "Chasing ___" (1997 film)
63 Gravitate (toward)
64 Natural mimics

DOWN

1 Diner jarful
2 Other, to Ortega
3 Stuck on board
4 Italian aperitif
5 Sidewalk stand drink
6 "Deathtrap" director
7 Misappropriate
8 How fans may go
9 Former Asian map abbr.
10 Perplexed
11 Dry with a twist
12 Morning eye-opener
14 Apply (for)
17 Dogtag info
21 Sleuth created by Biggers
23 Road sign abbr.
24 Thin blue line, say
25 It requires a PIN
26 Dis
27 Give an edge to
30 New Left org.
31 Controversial Oscar recipient of 1999
32 Tastes
33 "Never mind" to an editor
35 One of five Norwegian kings
36 Glove material
39 It connects to the elbow
40 Place to go in London?
41 Capote nickname
42 Parish residence
44 Gild
45 Some diner orders
46 Science society ___ Xi
47 Colorful phrase
48 Los Angeles attraction, with "the"
49 Leading
53 Prefix with tarsal
54 Grandson of Adam
56 Hanger-on?
57 Many a Monopoly property: Abbr.
58 Like L.B.J.

by Eric Berlin

ACROSS

1 Old-time oath
5 Threaded fastener
10 Went out, as a fire
14 Auntie of Broadway
15 Fight site
16 Memo starter
17 Elvis's middle name
18 First line of a nursery rhyme
20 Creative guy
22 Make a goof
23 Matt of "Friends"
24 Delivery room doctors, for short
25 Hwy.
27 Symbol of slowness
28 Submarine sandwich
30 Colorado ski resort
31 Brother of Cain
33 Sign after Taurus
35 1961 Sinatra album
39 Divulge
40 He played Ricky on 50's TV
41 Took too much of a drug, briefly
42 Copycat
44 Japanese restaurant fare
49 "No ___" (Chinese menu phrase)
50 601, in old Rome
51 Place to play jai alai
53 Pamper
55 J. P. Morgan and others
56 Knocking sound
58 Cube inventor Rubik
59 Phoenix's state: Abbr.
60 Lab containers
61 Slippery part of a banana
62 Tennis great Sampras
63 White, to Latinos
64 Canvas bag

DOWN

1 Sends a message by computer
2 Madison Square ___
3 One-celled protozoan
4 National park in Alaska
5 Brand of wrap
6 Chewed noisily
7 Soldier in Dixie
8 Fill with love
9 All-Star third baseman, 1985–96
10 Have ___ on (claim)
11 Five-time Tour de France winner Miguel
12 Ejecting lava
13 Cotillion girl
19 Battleship letters
21 Spanish province or its wine
26 Yale player
29 Omit in pronunciation
30 Rival school of The Citadel: Abbr.
32 Skier's headgear
34 The Wizard of Menlo Park
35 Old anti-Communist reaction
36 "Eureka!"
37 Actor Beatty
38 Spongelike toy
39 CD-___
43 Frisbee's inspiration, supposedly
45 Given away
46 Not mono
47 Big stinger
48 Shoe part
50 Banned insecticide
52 "Midnight Cowboy" character
54 Stupefy
56 Run-D.M.C.'s music
57 "You're it!" game

by Peter Gordon

ACROSS

1 Nile slitherers
5 Masked critter
9 Expecting, as a raise
14 Opportunity, so to speak
15 Dagger handle
16 Monica of the courts
17 1999 Meryl Streep movie
20 "___ not fair!"
21 Gardener's need
22 Craving
23 Master's requirement, often
25 Met or Card, for short
27 Gateway Arch city: Abbr.
30 Midleg
32 Viands
34 Negative vote
36 Foolhardy
38 Interminably
39 Ayn Rand book
42 Out-and-out
43 Accordingly
44 Gives the nod
45 Ethel Waters classic
47 Fall shade
49 Twitch
50 Shows one's human side
52 Things with ___ (theme of this puzzle)
56 Yiddish plaints
57 Bread spread
59 Matterhorn, e.g.
60 1988 John Cleese movie, with "A"
65 Action spot
66 Easily molded
67 Bumped off
68 Fortuneteller's card
69 Golden rule word
70 Nothing more than

DOWN

1 Own up to
2 Pole position?
3 Group that's rounded up
4 ___ Lanka
5 Picky people?
6 Meatheads
7 "Come here ___?"
8 Extreme
9 Leading down the aisle
10 Hammer part
11 It has many keys: Abbr.
12 Anthem preposition
13 Queue after Q
18 Goatee site
19 Gave the once-over
24 First U.S. space station
26 MacNeil's longtime news partner
27 Built for speed
28 Looks after
29 60's turn-on
31 Egg roll time
33 Colombia's capital
34 One of the Judds
35 Storage spot
37 "Quiet, please!"
40 Back street prowler
41 Not familiar with
42 Make lace
46 ___ Minor
48 Flat-bottomed boat
51 Wise lawgiver
53 Cyclist Armstrong
54 Respected one
55 Gardener's need
56 "It can't be!"
58 Took off
60 "___ chance!"
61 Lyrical Gershwin
62 Sun. talk
63 Baton Rouge sch.
64 Prepare to shoot

by Sherry O. Blackard

ACROSS

1 ___ Lilly & Co.
4 Had creditors
8 Copier
14 Meld of the queen of spades and jack of diamonds
16 Some sorority women
17 Peruse?
18 Gets even with
19 Timeline segments
20 Chemin de ___
21 Lotion ingredient
22 Lith., formerly
23 Foreign exchange?
27 Takes a siesta
30 Touched down
31 Swimming (in)
33 "Believe it ___ . . ."
35 A founder of Dadaism
38 Beaten?
41 Oxford-to-London dir.
42 Simpleton
43 Job-specific vocabulary
44 Nut used to flavor Coke
45 Chip in
46 Atrophy?
51 Mathematician's degree?
54 In myth she was turned into a spring
55 Suffix with real
56 Ancient colonnade
57 Mere 1%, say
60 Shortstop?
62 Protective cover
63 Fix firmly in place
64 Plays the toady, perhaps
65 "The lady ___ protest . . ."
66 Sounds during doctor's exams

DOWN

1 They might touch one's heart
2 Yarn makers
3 Personified
4 Columbus Day mo.
5 Quick smells
6 Bull in advertising
7 "Nothing runs like a ___"
8 Narrow sailing rte.
9 Compadre of Fidel
10 Buffet, e.g.
11 Author Calvino
12 Marshy inlet
13 Winding paths
15 Circus cries
24 Capital of ancient Lorraine
25 Flow stopper
26 His job is murder
28 Agent of Cleopatra's demise
29 Carbolic acid
31 Ripen
32 Horror maven Craven
33 At the break ___
34 Blushing
35 "Evita" setting
36 "Citizen Kane" studio
37 Winter hrs. in L.A.
39 Lady Macbeth, e.g.
40 Busts inside a museum
44 Rascally sorts
45 Best suited
46 Impertinent
47 Veil fabric
48 Natural athlete, supposedly
49 Named
50 "___ hooks" (box caution)
52 Spelunker's aid
53 Detests
56 HBO rival
58 Forbidden fruit partaker
59 In medias ___
61 Educ. institution

by Jerry E. Rosman

ACROSS

1 Panorama
6 "I dare you!"
10 Meal-in-bed supporter
14 ___ and aahed
15 Upper hand
16 Hearty's companion
17 With 61-Across, a fictional pair who are hard to tell apart
19 Jane Austen heroine
20 Toward sunrise
21 Res ___ loquitur (legal phrase)
22 Face-valued, as stocks
23 Scurries
25 El ___ (Pacific phenomenon)
27 Family pair who are hard to tell apart
33 56-Across + 56-Across
34 For takeout
35 Enamored of
36 Writer Wharton
38 "___ about that?!"
40 Hertz competitor
41 Satellite TV receivers
43 ___ is to say
45 Court subject
46 Routine that's hard to tell apart from past routines
49 "It's c-c-c-cold!"
50 Minipie
51 Laugh-filled
54 Prefix with potent
56 Fair share, maybe
60 Song for a diva
61 See 17-Across
63 Dovetail
64 Powerful auto engine
65 Remove from the blackboard
66 Feathery scarves
67 Shipped
68 So far

DOWN

1 November catchword
2 Dubuque's state
3 The Rolling Stones' "___ a Rainbow"
4 Prepare to bite?
5 Say further
6 Sound that's heaved
7 Bookie's quote
8 Big lizard
9 Chairman pro ___
10 What a loser may throw in
11 Interstate entrance/exit
12 ___ mater
13 1776 or 1945
18 Deceive
22 Aardvark
24 On paper
26 Sort
27 Place for a sacred cow
28 Godly belief
29 Codgers
30 Counting everything
31 Wanderer
32 Frequent Arctic forecast
33 British refs.
37 Malaise
39 "And then . . . ?"
42 Popular camera type, for short
44 ". . . the way of a man with ___": Proverbs
47 Be half asleep
48 Not these or those
51 Window's support
52 Creme cookie
53 Actress Bonet
55 Lo ___ (noodle dish)
57 24 hours ___
58 ___-majesté
59 Centipede's multitude
61 Show showers
62 Pasture

by Manny Nosowsky

ACROSS

1 Breathless state?
6 Bach's "Mass ___ Minor"
9 1930's French P.M. Léon
13 Dixie talk
14 ___-Day vitamins
15 Ambience
16 Record company
17 "Sense and Sensibility" actor, 1995
19 Altar vow
20 Works of Homer
22 Stimulate
23 1960's–70's pop singer/actor
26 ___ Wednesday
27 Dig in
28 Codebreakers' org.
31 Hectic episodes
34 Play starter
37 Most suitable
39 End of 17-, 23-, 50- or 61-Across
42 Severe lawgiver of Athens
43 Gave temporarily
44 Sticks up
45 Disney collector's item
46 Encyclopedia unit: Abbr.
48 Ground breaker
50 Rainbow Coalition founder
56 Signal enhancer
59 Confined, with "up"
60 "___ luck?"
61 "To Kill a Mockingbird" novelist
63 Welcome one's guests, maybe
65 Korea's home
66 Ogler
67 Family girl
68 In that case
69 Word of accord
70 English county bordering London

DOWN

1 Go off script
2 Madrid museum
3 Mover and shaker
4 Lamb ma'am
5 Back streets
6 Occupied
7 Photo envelope enclosure, for short
8 Grand ___ (island near Florida)
9 Title for Münchhausen
10 Oahu wingding
11 Coffee holders
12 Chess ending
14 Cry of eagerness
18 Au ___ (how some potatoes are served)
21 "No way!"
24 Fundamental
25 Monarch's rule
28 Claudius I's successor
29 Swedish car
30 "___ Well That Ends Well"
31 Like some electric appliances
32 Potentially disastrous
33 Egg shape
35 Refs' decisions
36 Amount past due?
38 Shortstop Jeter
40 1956 Elvis hit
41 Filmmaker Coen
47 Fish hawk
49 Gas pump number
50 Sumo land
51 Blunt blades
52 Scoff (at)
53 "For goodness ___!"
54 In reserve
55 One of the original Baby Bells
56 First-rate, slangily
57 Skin problem
58 Cleveland's lake
62 Soapmaking need
64 Family girl

by Ethan Cooper and Michael Shteyman

ACROSS

1 Brutish sort
6 Picture prize
11 Phone ___
14 Vice president Stevenson
15 Seize, à la Caesar
16 Masseur's supply
17 Insect's bedtime ritual?
19 Bother
20 Hole in one
21 King in a Steve Martin song
22 1945 conference site
24 Part of a service
26 Perfumes with a joss stick, say
27 Induction motor developer
29 Very funny person
32 Game show panelist Peggy
35 Preschoolers
37 "___ Mio"
38 "Bleah!"
39 Sass from Elsie?
41 Shell mover
42 Ragú rival
44 Milton Friedman's subj.
45 Friend of Big Bird
46 ___ Club
48 Dumbstruck
50 Hand down
52 Not stop for, in a way
56 Have in one's hands
58 Test site
59 Big D.C. lobby
60 Tick off
61 Sound when a gobbler gets a joke?
64 "Y" wearer
65 Actress Eleniak
66 Oscar-winning screenwriter Robert

67 Antonym's antonym: Abbr.
68 Knocks flat
69 Aligns

DOWN

1 Raisin cakes
2 Bring out
3 Ragged Dick creator
4 Carrier to Copenhagen
5 Move quietly
6 One ___ (ball game)
7 For example
8 Kind of sole
9 They have strings attached
10 Place to stretch your legs

11 Hammer for a hopper?
12 Disney musical
13 Latch (onto)
18 Totals
23 Tres y tres
25 Whitney and others: Abbr.
26 Puss's food container?
28 Game company that originated Yahtzee
30 Steamer, e.g.
31 Medal awardee, maybe
32 Putting targets
33 Prefix with cultural
34 Rams, lambs and ewes?

36 Move with difficulty
39 Dressed like a Victorian woman
40 Sort of
43 Fat, in France
45 Slippery sort
47 Make certain
49 Some beers
51 "Hamlet" courtier
53 Public, as information
54 Bucker
55 Director Peter
56 Bakers' wares
57 Alternative to De Gaulle
58 Pastoral places
62 Hateful org.
63 Today, in Toledo

by Randolph Ross

ACROSS

1 Signs of healing
6 File folder parts
10 ___ of Capri
14 Apportion
15 Airline that serves only kosher food
16 Financial aid criterion
17 "Oh boy!"
18 Writer Ephron
19 Lotion ingredient
20 One whose name can be followed by "Esq.": Abbr.
21 Good-looking guy
23 Ho-hum
25 Sis's sib
26 W.W. II prison camp
29 China's most populous city
34 They replaced francs, marks and pesetas
35 Goatee's place
36 Hostel
37 Casual clothing item
41 Flow back
42 Business phone button
43 Nostalgic song
44 Big game on January 1, usually
47 Portray
48 Pop's partner
49 Unwakable state
50 Easy-park shopping places
55 Dressed
59 Neighbor of Afghanistan
60 Egyptian queen, for short
61 Aunt's little girl
62 Vito Corleone's creator
63 Yard sale tag
64 Silly
65 Crystal ball gazer
66 Carrot on a snowman, perhaps
67 Card game that's a hint to this puzzle's theme

DOWN

1 It's a long story
2 Coagulate
3 Plenty
4 Big hit?
5 Pork place?
6 Final frame for a bowler
7 Baseball's Moises
8 The ___ of Avon
9 Fast-paced, slangily
10 Dazed and confused
11 Prefix with defense and destruct
12 Fifth-century pope who was sainted
13 Adam's apple location?
21 Droop
22 Ornamental vase
24 Young woman
26 Passover meal
27 Sports car engine
28 Saudis, e.g.
29 Three-card monte assistant
30 Rear
31 Language in New Delhi
32 Prank
33 Atlas enlargement
35 Cornfield bird
38 Prominent shoe seller
39 Limerick, e.g.
40 "Scent of a Woman" star
45 Key of Tchaikovsky's Symphony No. 5
46 Fast-tempo jazz
47 Whoop-de-___ (big parties)
49 Tight-knit
50 Has a taste of, as wine
51 Test choice
52 Tear down
53 To boot
54 Luau necklaces
56 Plumbing problem
57 Pockmark cause
58 Bucks and does
61 Small bite

by Peter Gordon

ACROSS

1 Sheep's cry
6 On ___ (like some jobs)
10 Subject of a Sophocles tragedy
14 Video's counterpart
15 Waterfront sight
16 Standard
17 Amorous entanglement
20 Discipline that uses koans
21 Send out
22 Member of a secret order
23 Eye opening for a squint
24 Sic a lawyer on
26 Annoyance for dwellers near airports
33 Bond's "Casino Royale" foe
34 Randomizer
35 Govt. initiative
36 Subsists (on)
37 Person with a chest pad
38 String section member
39 Possible solution
40 "Just ___ thought!"
41 Acted badly
42 Clothing label designation
45 Hertz offering
46 "Of all the luck!"
47 Posthumous donation
51 Actress Pitts of old films
52 Greetings
55 Mechanical impossibility
59 Nobelist Wiesel
60 Fairy tale opener
61 With 40-Down, seat of Orange County, Calif.
62 Wildcat
63 Jab
64 Readily available

DOWN

1 Singer/activist Joan
2 Renaissance instrument
3 TV genie portrayer
4 Put on TV
5 Without inflection or feeling
6 Cheerleaders' finale, often
7 British P.M. under George III
8 Always with an apostrophe
9 Dernier ___
10 Ballet Russe star Pavlova
11 Helps, as a memory
12 Singer Guthrie
13 Marvel Comics group
18 Simple folk
19 "I agree completely!"
23 1996 horror film with sequels
24 Barbershop sound
25 Colorado native
26 Ammonia derivative
27 "Well, I ___!"
28 Campus offices: Abbr.
29 Thinks out loud
30 Fireplace tools
31 Treaded surfaces
32 "Good heavens!"
33 Boo-boo
37 Exploitative type
38 Musical artiste
40 See 61-Across
41 Fleeting muscle problem
43 Clearasil target
44 Irish port near Killarney
47 German automaker
48 Bank (on)
49 Alfred E. Neuman expression
50 Summit
51 "An Officer and a Gentleman" hero
52 Aid to the stumped
53 Smidgen
54 Say sharply
56 Blouse, e.g.
57 Game with "Draw Two" cards
58 Beachgoer's goal

by Robert Malinow

ACROSS

1 Backs, anatomically
6 Plants
11 Bouncers' requests
14 Shackles
15 Like some anesthesia
16 Rolodex no.
17 With 31-, 46- and 61-Across, comment from Franz Kafka
19 Kidnappers in 70's news
20 Body build
21 Masterful
23 Online columnist Drudge
25 Abbr. on a business letter
28 "Would ___?"
29 Fugard's "A Lesson From ___"
31 See 17-Across
34 Off-the-cuff stuff
36 Butler's request
37 Ed.'s in-box filler
38 One using a delete key
40 Hesitation sound
43 Bother no end
44 City near Bologna
46 See 17-Across
50 Checks for contraband, maybe
51 Lash mark
52 Together, musically
54 Q.E.D. part
55 Counterpart of a delete key
58 Nervous feeling
60 Umpire's call
61 See 17-Across
66 Compete
67 For a specific purpose
68 Loo sign

69 Put the kibosh on
70 Time unit?
71 Picture within a picture

DOWN

1 24 horas
2 Sun, e.g.
3 They may be pitched
4 Bull, at times
5 "___ silly question . . ."
6 Polished, languagewise
7 Part of U.C.L.A.
8 U.N. Day mo.
9 Broccoli ___ (leafy vegetable)
10 Football's Karras
11 ". . . is fear ___": F.D.R.
12 Texas border city
13 One working with heavy tiles
18 M.'s mate
22 Waterfront walk
23 Cripple
24 Poorbox filler
26 Bilked
27 Fast time?
30 Blip maker
32 Pion's place
33 Copy
35 Literally, "I forbid"
39 Strip in the news
40 Gives hope to
41 "Pure Moods" singer

42 It's rigged
43 Red-spotted critters
45 City on the Elbe
46 Jury, often
47 Self-referencing contract term
48 Walking on air
49 Subtle distinction
53 U.S.N.A. grad
56 Actor Morales
57 Cinergy Field players, once
59 Best Picture of 1958
62 Spa sounds
63 Marker letters
64 Western tribesman
65 One of a fleet fleet

by David Levinson Wilk

49

ACROSS

1 Instruments at luaus
5 Island of Napoleon's exile
9 Was in the movies
14 Man with an ark
15 Harvest
16 Stage between egg and pupa
17 "Arsenic and Old Lace" star, 1944
19 Airedale, e.g., for dogs
20 Totally
21 Scottish miss
22 Electricians, at times
23 Creditor's demand
25 Numerous
26 Colony member
27 Japanese farewell
31 Demanding
34 Knee/ankle connector
35 Trojan War hero
36 Vehicle that's hailed
37 Astound
38 Capture
39 Song for a diva
40 Capitol feature
41 Ready to hit the sack
42 Shower accessories
44 Copacabana city
45 Manage
46 Gatherings where people hold hands
50 Horrified
53 Foreboding
54 Actress Gardner
55 Emergency light
56 "Liar Liar" star
58 Life of ___
59 Fix, as copy
60 Tricks
61 Follows the leader
62 One giving orders
63 Voice above bass

DOWN

1 Open, as a bottle
2 Eucalyptus eater
3 Like the bird that catches the worm
4 Timid
5 Straying
6 Minimum
7 Outlaws
8 Fitting
9 Lacking pigment
10 Noted anti-alcohol crusader
11 Elder or alder
12 "As ___" (letter closing)
13 June honorees
18 Shuttle-riding senator
22 Oscar winner for "True Grit"
24 Top-selling vocalist of the 1990's
25 Corn
27 Phonies
28 A bit cracked?
29 Tool with teeth
30 Fired
31 Attempt
32 Skater Lipinski
33 Departure
34 Struck hard
37 Change according to circumstances
41 Crownlike headgear
43 Ambles
44 Does a double take, e.g.
46 Round after the quarters
47 "Deck the Halls," e.g.
48 Episode
49 Authority
50 Bushy do
51 Smooth-talking
52 Robust
53 Pal of Spot
56 One of the Bushes
57 Big TV maker

by Lynn Lempel

ACROSS

1 Bit of street art
6 Taken wing
11 Toast topping
14 Japanese automaker
15 Part of a TV transmission
16 Have ___ at
17 Character actor in the Cowboy Hall of Fame
19 Modern: Prefix
20 Mandlikova of tennis
21 A.A.A. suggestion: Abbr.
22 Redecorate
24 Actress Long or Peeples
26 Jelly fruit
27 After-hours pool use, maybe
32 "Phooey!"
33 Regal headdresses
34 Social misfit
36 Pentium maker
38 Fivescore yrs.
39 Enter, as data
40 No longer working: Abbr.
41 Singer Twain
43 Number cruncher, for short
44 Boo-boo
47 Cultural values
48 Big inits. on the Net
49 Like a habanero pepper
51 Nabokov novel
53 Agenda, for short
57 Dory need
58 Panhandler's request
61 Joanne of "Abie's Irish Rose"
62 Guys' prom attire, informally
63 Continental divide?

64 Shade tree
65 Minute ___ (thin cut)
66 Down and out

DOWN

1 Moonshiner's mixture
2 Bruins' sch.
3 Totally trash
4 Cardin rival
5 Pool distance
6 It's the truth
7 Gospel writer
8 Poetic homage
9 They start pitches
10 "Uh-uh!"
11 15th-century Flemish painter
12 Pulitzer winner James
13 Drop anchor
18 Farsi speaker
23 Like Dolly the clone
25 Part of IHOP: Abbr.
26 Designer Versace
27 Trig figures
28 Orchestra percussion
29 Pleasure craft
30 Most of "The Wizard of Oz"
31 Be crabby
32 Cone bearer
35 Kind of "fingerprint"

37 Designer Head
39 Green Hornet's sidekick
41 Decathlon event
42 Stern or Hayes
45 Halloween characters
46 ___-Lorraine
49 Took a tram, e.g.
50 James ___ Carter
51 Square mileage
52 Place to work
54 "Trick" joint
55 Dated expletive
56 Refuse
59 Woodcutter's tool
60 Snookums

by Bob Peoples

ACROSS

1 Kingdom east of Fiji
6 Sea plea
9 "If I ___ rich man . . ."
14 Like some suspects
15 Doll's name
16 Summing up
17 Hose part
18 Roll call call
19 See 11-Down
20 Faster than moderato
22 Not so vigorous
24 Spotted
25 "This ___" (carton label)
27 Carnival follower
28 "___ Is Born"
30 Tick off
32 Writers' references
35 Capsular, biologically
39 CARE packages, say
40 Emotionally burned out
42 Prefix with meter
43 Show shame
45 Grid official
47 Play for a sap
48 ___ nous
49 One teaspoon, maybe
52 Natural skyline former
54 Unwanted cyberads
58 Most villainous
60 Rubout
62 Not just sip
63 Blow it
65 Fail miserably
66 ___ wrench
67 Partner of Larry and Curly
68 Everything, to Einstein
69 In sorry shape
70 Landscaper's supply
71 Ebbets Field hero

DOWN

1 Yellowfin and bluefin
2 "___ Mio"
3 Loving motion
4 Lead ores
5 "Break ___!"
6 1957 Marlon Brando film
7 "The loneliest number"
8 Screw-up
9 Off the mark
10 Gives power to
11 With 19-Across, flashy display
12 Former ABC sitcom
13 On the ball
21 Many 12/26 store visitors
23 Focal point
26 By no means poured
29 Things to crack
31 Actress Winona
32 Old-time punishment need
33 Get a move on
34 Announcer Hall
36 Aunt Polly's nephew
37 Cretan peak
38 Bamboozle
41 Didn't go away
44 Fought it out, in Britain
46 Permanently attached, to a zoologist
49 Painter of ballerinas
50 Fertilization site
51 Steakhouse sound
53 Agenda entries
55 This is one
56 Van Gogh's "Bedroom at ___"
57 Reagan attorney general
59 Chooser's start
61 Off yonder
64 Kanga's kid

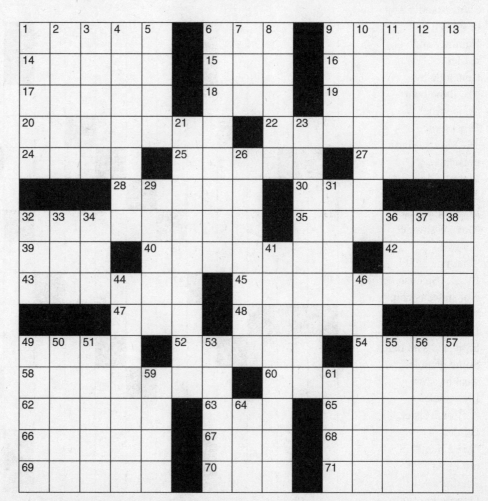

by Joel Kaplow

ACROSS

1 Furrowed part of the head
5 Cougars
10 Door fastener
14 "The ___ Ranger"
15 Basketball Hall-of-Famer Thomas
16 Hitch, as oxen
17 Start of a free call
20 "___, humbug!"
21 Hair removal brand
22 Not stand steadily
23 New York's ___ Place
25 Letter before omega
26 From ___ Z
27 Switzerland's Zug or Zurich
29 Hammer and mallet
31 Conclude by
32 "To thine own ___ be true"
33 Pepsi rival
37 1943 Mary Martin musical
40 Marquis de ___
41 Turndowns
42 Like some gases
43 Move crabwise
45 Shrewd
46 "Mamma ___!"
49 El ___ (Spanish hero)
50 Not stale, as chips
51 "O Canada," e.g.
53 Dear one, in Italy
54 Split ___ with ham
57 Some gamblers' weaknesses
60 Like books
61 A Brontë sister
62 Burden
63 "My Friend" of old radio
64 Pacifists
65 Opposed to, in "Li'l Abner"

DOWN

1 1950's horror film creature, with "the"
2 Writer Jaffe
3 Like some baseball catches
4 Tiny
5 Easy mark, slangily
6 Theater worker
7 Baseball glove
8 "How nice!"
9 Stops, as electricity
10 Jekyll's counterpart
11 Cardiologist's concern
12 ___ shooting
13 California's San ___ Bay
18 Completely
19 Astronaut Armstrong
24 Roll call at a political convention
25 Some casual shirts
27 Corporate honchos, for short
28 The "I" of "The King and I"
29 Giggle
30 Perfumes
32 Bawl out
34 Getting ahead of
35 Composer Weill
36 Villa d'___
38 Strong as always
39 Optometrist's concern
44 Bakery worker
45 Layouts
46 New Zealand native
47 Kind of tube or ear
48 1980's George Peppard series, with "The"
50 The "C" of CNN
52 "Mary ___ little lamb"
53 404, in old Rome
55 Carrier for needles and pins
56 Org.
58 Comedian Philips
59 ___ double take

by Charles E. Gersch

ACROSS

1 Deck out
6 Sign of stitches
10 Found's partner
14 Donnybrook
15 Use a whetstone on
16 Aware of
17 Strips away
18 Composer Franz Joseph's favorite 58-Across?
20 Clean-shaven
22 Ore deposit
23 Golf ball prop
24 "Woe is me!"
26 Nursling
28 Enough for former hurler Dwight?
32 Order before "Fire!"
33 Withered
34 From which gold is spun, in a fairy tale
38 Smooth-talking
40 Church council
43 Per
44 Late bloomer
46 ___-engine
48 "___ Loves You"
49 Actor Liam's younger kin?
53 Southwestern saloon
56 Bar order, with "the"
57 Champ who could "sting like a bee"
58 Go fish, e.g.
60 Sheepdog, by training
64 Presidential shaving goofs?
67 Spaghetti strainer
68 "___ plaisir"
69 Campsite sight
70 Florida keys, e.g.
71 For fear that
72 Do in
73 Stuffed item?

DOWN

1 Roadie's load
2 Judge
3 Toast topper
4 Put in fresh film
5 Snuggles down
6 Librarian's admonition
7 Kentucky resource
8 "___ home?"
9 Begin to blush
10 ___ Alamos
11 "___ a customer"
12 Beef on the hoof
13 Arcade coin
19 Efts grown up
21 Briefs brand
25 Peppy
27 Memory unit
28 Totally smitten
29 Softens, as leather
30 Pass over
31 Slowly, on a score
35 Allergy indication
36 Yearn
37 "That was close!"
39 Like the wire in a croquet wicket
41 Holds the deed to
42 Washington who sang the blues
45 Wear the crown
47 Unbeatable foe
50 Puts on the books
51 Patriot Adams
52 Meet an untimely fate
53 Gondola's place
54 Still in play
55 Puts the kibosh on
59 Sicilian smoker
61 Sub shop
62 At any time
63 Take five
65 Fall mo.
66 Slop spot

by Denise M. Neuendorf

ACROSS

1 Harasses newbies
6 Sting
10 Goya subject, nude and clothed
14 Employ, as strength
15 TV newsman Brit
16 Golf bag item
17 With 64-Across, a ticket issuer
18 Caspian feeder
19 Stitched
20 Weigh
23 Wee bit
24 Salacious look
25 Blowgun missile
28 Fine spray
31 Does 80, say
35 Aardvark's fare
37 Realtor's sale
39 One of a 22-card deck
40 Way
43 See 45-Across
44 Elbow
45 With 43-Across, leaver of a mark
46 Ready to be served
48 Starring role
50 Nonverbal communication, for short
51 Money at a casa de cambio
53 New beginning?
55 Whey
63 Fall guy?
64 See 17-Across
65 "___ Water" (Burns song)
66 Dreyfus Affair figure
67 Aptly named citrus fruit
68 Unmolested
69 Flamboyant style
70 Throw things at
71 Tie up

DOWN

1 Sailcloth fiber
2 Turnaround jump
3 Second after delta
4 At attention
5 Steady flow
6 Treat as a pariah
7 Brusque
8 Boy in a Menotti title
9 Free-for-alls
10 Villain
11 Neighborhood
12 Fleshy part
13 Elizabeth I's mother
21 Hateful disgrace
22 Biological partitions
25 Agreements
26 Habituate: Var.
27 Where "ahoy!" is heard
29 Cinch
30 Alpine region of Austria and Italy
32 Kovacs of comedy
33 People of action
34 Pharyngeal woe, for short
36 Leader
38 Young 'un
41 Concert hall
42 "That's not what I ___!"
47 Solicit, as business
49 Treat, as seawater
52 Old enough
54 Something to consider
55 Where rats race
56 Teen ___ (heartthrob)
57 Hacienda room
58 Hire for, as a position
59 Prepare to run
60 One of the Aleutians
61 Burgles
62 Hydrocarbon suffixes

by Mel Taub

ACROSS

1 "Peanuts" boy
6 Lady's man
10 Fizzling-out sound
14 Make amends (for)
15 Taj Mahal site
16 Title role for
 Peter Fonda
17 Tunneling tusker?
19 Sinn ___ (Irish
 organization)
20 Brown in the
 kitchen
21 Hurt or irritate
23 Suzanne of "Three's
 Company"
26 Sultry Hayworth
28 The "I" of T.G.I.F.
29 Fruity coolers
30 Central street
32 Brown on the
 beach
34 Basketball's
 Alcindor
35 Florida home of
 Busch Gardens
36 Not weighing much
39 Mauna Loa, e.g.
41 Bought
43 Bad breath
 cause, maybe
44 Exhaust
46 Prevaricate
47 Holiday quaff
48 New Jersey
 hoopsters
49 Clutter
50 Musician's date
52 Better ___ than
 never
54 Goodies
56 Playful child
58 Cook, as clams
60 Needle case
61 Grizzly doing a
 striptease?
66 Powder ingredient
67 Writing on
 the wall
68 Spine-tingling
69 Sailing
70 Amusement
 park lure
71 Small drinks
 of liquor

DOWN

1 Chem class
2 "How was ___ know?"
3 Common conjunction
4 Joins forces
5 One who may
 hear "Sí, sí!"
6 Yaks
7 Vain voyage?
8 Gunner's grp.
9 Fortuneteller's card
10 Bit of smoke
11 Pest that's beating it?
12 Misleading
 maneuver
13 Minds, as a bar
18 Certain meter reader
22 Result of a punch
 in the mouth
23 Artillery burst
24 Old-fashioned
 music hall
25 Big-eared blubberer?
27 Sulking
31 Quantity
33 Help
35 Snarl
37 Raise
38 Long lock
40 Dove's sound
42 "Pride and Prejudice"
 author
45 Boils over
49 Dues payer
50 Reclusive Garbo
51 Itsy-bitsy bits
53 Ann ___, Mich.
55 Showed fury
57 Typesetter's unit
59 Fork feature
62 French friend
63 End of an ___
64 Something to
 take, carefully
65 Lawyer's thing

by Norma Johnson and Nancy Salomon

ACROSS

1 Hit head-on
4 Peloponnesian War soldier
11 Milk supplier
14 Noshed
15 Awakening
16 Tankard filler
17 Great deal
18 ___ Mountains of the far West
19 Women's ___
20 37-Across, e.g.
22 Trumpet feature
24 Irish of old
25 Less verbose
26 "The Graduate" daughter
29 Metal in pennies
30 Like much writing paper
31 Big tournament
33 Soccer star Mia
37 Renaissance man
40 Jemima, e.g.
41 Contributes
42 Things
43 Wading bird
45 ___ acid
46 Talked back to
49 Worshiper of Tlaloc
51 ___ & Whitney (engine maker)
52 37-Across, e.g.
55 Epitome of slipperiness
56 In name only
58 Butter serving
60 See 2-Down
61 Cause of diminishing returns
62 Rap sheet abbr.
63 Sunbeam
64 Feasts
65 Chair part

DOWN

1 Despicable one
2 With 60-Across, 1960's TV cartoon hero
3 List of choices
4 Casa grande
5 It's a revelation
6 Assume for argument's sake
7 "Star Wars" director
8 "This ___ outrage!"
9 Bit
10 Time before midnight
11 Rings up
12 Popeye's gal
13 Composer Carl Maria von ___
21 37-Across, e.g.
23 37-Across, e.g.
25 Louise of "Gilligan's Island"
26 Vocalist Fitzgerald
27 Stead
28 In a bit
29 Alphabet ends, in Canada
31 Bookie's computation
32 Herd of seals
34 Working without ___
35 Year Queen Victoria died
36 Catchall abbr.
38 Police action
39 Quayle or Cheney: Abbr.
44 Person in a pool
45 After much delay
46 Asparagus unit
47 Field of endeavor
48 Like pretzels
49 BMW competitor
50 Boer fighters
52 Dance instructor's instruction
53 Fire ___ (gem)
54 Autumn tool
57 "___ said it before . . ."
59 Put out, maybe, in baseball

by Don West

ACROSS

1 Frightful women
5 Push
9 Greases the wheels for, say
14 Drain part
15 In the past
16 Diaper, in Britain
17 Kind of jack
18 Nurses' responsibility
19 Wood nymph
20 Short story?
23 Honey
24 "Gunsmoke" star
28 Partner
31 Rackets
33 ___-Mère-Église (Normandy invasion town)
34 Short bread?
36 Tit for ___
37 They're found in veins
38 Self-image
39 Biblical verb
40 Old master's work
41 Short stop?
45 How the St. Lawrence flows through Montreal: Abbr.
46 "Blue Moon" lyricist
47 Gentle stroke
48 Car made in Spring Hill, Tenn., once
50 Potpourri containers
51 Short change?
57 African tree snake
60 Beat badly
61 Leprechauns' land
62 Worked on Broadway
63 "Cast Away" setting
64 Let fly
65 Compote fruit
66 Dele undoer
67 Like some restaurant orders

DOWN

1 URL starter
2 Pavarotti performance
3 1982 Robin Williams title role
4 Accelerations
5 Tom turkey
6 2000 N.B.A. scoring leader for the Lakers
7 Adapter letters
8 Inkstand's site
9 Sign
10 Hitter known as The Hammer
11 Operative
12 Clean Air Act enforcer: Abbr.
13 Barrett of early Pink Floyd
21 ___ of Jericho
22 Possible drive-thru site
25 Heir cushion?
26 Suspended animation
27 Melees
28 Stirrers
29 Brand name accompanying a checkerboard logo
30 Brunch staple
31 Finger or toe
32 On-screen image
35 Fast approaching
39 Least forgiving
41 Clothes, slangily
42 Go on and on
43 Like a tanager
44 Canvas cover
49 Brownish
50 Physics unit
52 Writer Kingsley
53 Schooner part
54 Nabisco snack
55 Be a rat
56 Passionate about
57 Glove compartment item
58 Big serve
59 1959 Kingston Trio hit

by Eric Berlin

58

ACROSS

1 Lauderdale is south of it
5 Leader of pre-1917 Russia
9 Look more prominent than the rest, with "out"
12 Learn to cope
14 Loft
16 Lennon's woman
17 Literary Cather
18 Lento or largo
19 "Ladders to Fire" novelist Anaïs
20 Lousy-car buyer's protection
22 Link between nations
24 Leadership of a co.
25 Liable to make one scratch
26 Lane Kirkland of the former A.F.L.-C.I.O., e.g.
31 Lie in bed, say
32 Like some verbs
36 Latitude/longitude shower
37 Lethargy
39 Losing tic-tac-toe row
40 Let spread
42 Louse-to-be
43 Lego precursor
47 Link
49 Land bordering Greece: Abbr.
50 Long-necked instruments
51 Light that oozes
56 Links org.
57 Lucy's landlady
59 Le ___ (Paris paper)
60 Lithe swimmer
61 Late princess
62 Lower leg joint
63 Lacking moisture
64 "Let's go!"
65 Loss's opposite

DOWN

1 Loudly cry
2 Likely foil for Garfield
3 Less than 1 m.p.h., as winds
4 Level-headedness
5 "Later"
6 "Little of this, little of that" dish
7 Location for 24-hr. banking
8 Lifeguards' dangers
9 Lunch for a whale, in a Bible story
10 Like-mindedness
11 "Les Misérables" award, 1987
13 Latin dance
15 Line of mourners
21 L, e.g.: Abbr.
23 Linen color
26 Libeler, almost by definition
27 Labrador food?
28 Light purple
29 Lyre-carrying Muse
30 "Little Mermaid"
31 Loudness increaser, at a concert
33 Like a hippie's hair
34 Line on a graph
35 Ludicrous comments
37 Lutèce V.I.P.
38 Lacking faith in God
41 "Let me go!" e.g.
44 Like certain engineers: Abbr.
45 Lima animal
46 Lozenge-shaped
47 Lion's cousin
48 Lire used to be spent here
50 Lost no time
51 Letterman rival
52 Ladd or Greenspan
53 "Lonely Boy" singer Paul
54 Livy's 1,551
55 Light hammer part
58 Lunch meat

by William I. Johnston

ACROSS

1 Like a fireplace
7 Classic 1931 Wallace Beery film
15 Like some rolls
16 One opening a jail door, say
17 Had total authority
19 Connections
20 ___ Tomé
21 Fight (for)
22 Situation for rubber bullets
24 Author Birkerts
26 ___-eyed
30 Jay seen at night
31 "___ see it . . ."
32 Best conditions
34 Bug zapper sites
37 Gazetteer data
38 Where Ed Koch was once head
42 "Are you there?"
43 Ongoing story
44 Border patrol concerns
46 Tubes
47 Bonny one
51 March time
52 Early weather satellite
54 Fret
55 Actress Claire
56 Tiny point to argue
59 ___ pro nobis
60 Authority to act for another
66 Raised a rumpus
67 Anesthetic gas
68 Parting word
69 Anchored

DOWN

1 Like an eddy
2 Brimless cap
3 Workbook unit
4 Descriptive wd.
5 Mt. Olympus figure
6 Icelandic poetry collection
7 Trevi coin count
8 Throw with effort
9 Cause of strange weather
10 Give over
11 Uris novel, with "The"
12 Tempe sch.
13 Riviera waters
14 Be a snoop
18 Dishes the dirt
23 Removes from power
25 They're blue, in rhyme
26 Enjoys the boardwalk
27 Place
28 General under Dwight
29 Orient
31 Give an ___ (mark high)
33 Animal that resembles a guinea pig
35 Many millennia
36 Civil one?
38 Asian cuisine
39 In custody
40 Writer Wiesel
41 Family nickname
45 Lady of León
48 Yom Kippur observer
49 Unruffled
50 Went to and fro
53 "60 Minutes" name
55 Mashie, e.g.
57 Checklist bit
58 Dog in Oz
60 Notebooks of a sort
61 Ending with pay
62 "___ cool!"
63 Comic Philips
64 Toothpaste tube letters
65 Fraternity letter

by A. J. Santora

ACROSS

1 Hot sauce
6 Van Gogh flower
10 This for that
14 To no ___
(fruitlessly)
15 Scarf material
16 Scarf material
17 Cardplayer's
oxymoron
20 Place to stop
21 Stretched
22 Miniature
golf club
23 Misplace
24 Golfer's cry
25 Pie cutter's
oxymoron
29 School org.
32 Wanderer
33 Poem on an urn
34 Miseries
35 Unit of a molecule
36 Stares
38 Sprained, as
an ankle
39 Hawaii's ___ Coast
40 Fish eggs
41 Shampoo step
42 Work unit
43 Shuffler's oxymoron
46 Dog's favorite
part of a steak
47 Customer of
Fabergé eggs
48 Portly
51 Standard
52 "His Master's
Voice" co.
55 Polltaker's
oxymoron
58 Suffix with poet
59 Iridescent gem
60 Big bang maker
61 Socially challenged
person
62 Greek goddess
of victory
63 First American
in orbit

DOWN

1 She won a 2002
Grammy for
"Lovers Rock"
2 Shakespearean
stream
3 Extol
4 Bro or sis
5 With everything
6 Bank, to a
credit card
7 Laughfest
8 Poorly
9 Sticks on a slope?
10 Political ticket
11 Word repeated before
"Don't tell me!"
12 1/640 of a square mile
13 Nobleman
18 Slacken
19 Territory
23 Relative of a camel
24 Lose brilliance
25 Viper, for one
26 Machine powerer
27 Shirley Jackson's
"Life ___ the
Savages"
28 Wished (for)
29 Feared destination
in "Lady and
the Tramp"
30 Not wordy
31 Daisylike flower
34 Helicopter sound
36 Henry Ford II,
to Henry Ford
37 Top-notch
41 Like some charges
on a cell phone
43 Gossipy Barrett
44 "Lawrence of
Arabia" star
45 Abbr. after an
asterisk in a car ad
46 Erect
48 Tear down
49 "___ upon a time"
50 Way up a slope
51 Fargo's state: Abbr.
52 Baptism, for one
53 Common syrup
source
54 Auth. unknown
56 Prefix with gram
or center
57 Zilch

by Roy Leban

ACROSS

1 Bother
5 Be overthrown
9 Wear away
14 Square measure
15 Not in port
16 Wanders
17 Bad day for 25-Across
18 More or less follower
19 Ticket seller
20 Gridiron order
23 Egg maker
24 Take-home pay
25 Rubicon crosser
29 Armor-___
31 Grp. symbolized by an elephant
34 Sweater material
35 Thumb (through)
36 Enterprise helmsman
37 Griddle order
40 Clock sound
41 Like mellower wines
42 Stop in the Sahara
43 Band performance
44 It may give a shock on a ranch
45 French equivalent of the White House
46 Groceries holder
47 Playtex product
48 Gridley order
55 Tour of duty
57 "Purple ___" (song played at Woodstock)
58 Telegraph
59 Door part
60 Malt beverages
61 1950's British P.M.
62 Lightened (up)
63 Liquefy
64 1990 World Series champs

DOWN

1 Like some maidens of myth
2 Pakistani tongue
3 Realizes
4 "Miss America" appears on it
5 Priest's title
6 Pallid
7 Long spring
8 Turner who was called the "Sweater Girl"
9 Cleared the boards
10 Synonym compiler
11 Transmission closer
12 Lion's home
13 Superlative suffix
21 Acceptance speech word
22 Not just a tie-up
25 Business expenditures
26 Bandleader Shaw
27 Vote in
28 Drench
29 Relinquished
30 In place
31 "You'll never ___!"
32 Stan's partner in comedy
33 Sign of life
35 Plastic block maker
36 Influence
38 Bart's mom
39 Grinding tooth
44 Went in separate directions
45 One of the Gallo brothers
46 Eat to excess
47 Diagonal face of a chisel
48 $5 bills
49 Impact sound
50 Fit as a fiddle
51 Wide-mouthed pitcher
52 Assistant
53 Historic Scott
54 Desires
55 ___-wolf
56 Actress Carrere

by Steven Dorfman

ACROSS

1 Group behind a 2001 Broadway musical
5 Ready follower?
8 Big name in fireworks
14 1-Across song
16 Bacon serving
17 1-Across song
19 Painting surface
20 Vase
21 Marshall ___
22 Between assignments
24 Inebriated
25 1-Across song
30 Sped
31 Shamefaced
32 ___ school
33 Ones doing tests: Abbr.
36 "___ Queen" (1-Across song)
37 With 43-Across, description of 1-Across
39 Twisty turn
40 Born: Fr.
41 Investigate
42 1-Across song
43 See 37-Across
44 Some fund-raisers
47 Corner of a diamond
48 Where Muscat is
49 Holm of stage and screen
50 Court TV focus
55 1-Across song
59 Actually existing
60 Musical based on the songs of 1-Across
61 Calculus for canines?
62 Off-road wheels, for short
63 Not the original color

DOWN

1 Not care ___ for
2 Eliot protagonist
3 Part of some co. names
4 Tropical cuckoos
5 "Wheel of Fortune" request
6 Dictator Amin
7 Frequently abbreviated math term
8 Smile
9 "Way out!"
10 Ashe Stadium event
11 Major copper exporter
12 Wood for outdoor furniture
13 Overused humor technique
15 Difficulty
18 Mined-over matter?
22 Actress Graff and others
23 Chrysler make
24 Good-for-nothing
25 Go in the kiddie pool, maybe
26 Arab garments
27 Whips
28 Computer key
29 Safari sights
30 Go over again, as with a cloth
32 Common computer interface
33 Flintstones pet
34 V preceder
35 Talk ___
38 Scorsese, e.g.: Abbr.
42 Least wild
43 Kind of hat
44 "I see"
45 Fridge maker
46 Sonic rival
47 Word of contempt
49 Bakery employee
50 Pro ___
51 Pike
52 "___ humble opinion . . ."
53 Gérard's girlfriend
54 X-ray blocker
56 Hard-rock link
57 Writer Hentoff
58 Roman 905

by David J. Kahn

ACROSS

1 Actor Guinness
5 Frolics
10 Beatles song or movie
14 Opera star
15 Foreword, for short
16 Tarzan's raisers
17 Tied
19 New Jersey hoopsters
20 Big name in chickens
21 Most forlorn
23 Check for fit, as clothes
24 Off the correct path
26 Winemaker Ernest or Julio
28 Corn
32 Inclined path for wheelchairs
36 Dictator Amin
37 ___ bender (minor accident)
38 Disney's "___ and the Detectives"
39 "First Blood" character
41 Give a hand?
42 Starbucks orders
44 Peanut butter holder
45 Ivy League school
46 Escargot
47 Recording studio devices
49 Generic
51 NBC morning show
56 "Les Misérables" hero
59 City on the Rio Grande
60 Opera song
61 Clownish one
64 Inert element used in lights
65 Extraterrestrial
66 Columbus's home
67 Not out of one's mind
68 Lab glove material
69 Penpoints

DOWN

1 Very skilled
2 Pâté ingredient
3 "___ man for himself"
4 Enthusiastic, as an attitude
5 Religious ceremony
6 Early afternoon
7 Network with annual awards
8 Magician's word
9 Submarine detector
10 Repairman
11 Fencing sword
12 Response to "Shall we?"
13 Cousin of "ahem"
18 Belted out, as a tune
22 Honored woman
24 Emmy winner Alan
25 Brand of beef jerky
27 Broadcasts
29 Brainstorm
30 Eagerness
31 Writer ___ Stanley Gardner
32 Many wines
33 End of a prayer
34 Translucent mineral
35 Hardly a beauty
37 Duffer's cry
40 Make a cake, e.g.
43 Ice sheet
47 Capital of the Philippines
48 Pierce
50 Like a whiny voice
52 Hunter of Greek myth
53 New ___, India
54 Improvise
55 Duncan toys
56 Some car-pooling vehicles
57 Carpet buyer's calculation
58 Animal on England's shield
59 Short-tailed wildcat
62 Turned on
63 Civil War general

by Peter Gordon

ACROSS

1 Fudd of cartoons
6 Speeder's snagger
11 "The ___" (Uris novel)
14 Actress Téa
15 Carroll heroine
16 "Hooray, José!"
17 Litter in monkey cages
19 N.F.L. scores
20 U.N. Day mo.
21 Econ. yardstick
22 Solar storm
24 General Mills product
27 "What was ___ think?"
28 Toys with keys
33 Crooks crack them
36 "Now I get it!"
37 Black-tie dinner, say
38 Memorable age
39 Loafers, e.g., or a lighthearted description of 17-, 28-, 49- and 65-Across
43 Outdoor game
44 Sofer of soaps
46 Vow words
47 Actress Massey
49 Machine parts
53 Musical sense
54 More au courant
58 Colorful marble
62 Investment option: Abbr.
63 Corp. bigwig
64 D.D.E.'s predecessor
65 What clean kitchens often have
68 Versatile vehicle, for short
69 Bring joy to
70 Banks in Cooperstown

71 Scratch
72 Tapes for producers
73 Prescribed amounts

DOWN

1 Macaroni shape
2 TV host Robin
3 ___ Carlo
4 Bambi's aunt
5 Carnival game
6 Mountain-climbing technique
7 Potent potable
8 Fizzles out
9 Constitutional rights grp.
10 Astronaut Judith

11 Tough issue to handle
12 Actor Ray
13 Don't be serious
18 Indigo source
23 Party animal?
25 You ___ here
26 New York or New Orleans
29 Pi follower
30 ___ Andreas Fault
31 Oomph
32 Multigenerational story
33 Belgrade native
34 Neighborhood
35 Mail to a star
40 Truth decay?
41 Mount in Crete

42 Gave the high sign
45 "Ah, me!"
48 Timothy Leary's turn-on
50 Made 7-Down
51 Eye parts: Var.
52 Soft ball material
55 Graphic symbols
56 Like a Stephen King novel
57 Kentucky Derby prize
58 Good buddy
59 Terrier of film
60 Bush's alma mater
61 Reason to cram
66 D.D.E.'s command
67 "___ y Plata" (Montana's motto)

by Sherry O. Blackard

ACROSS

1 Dust remover
4 Shadow
9 Locker room features
14 Author Umberto
15 "The Crucible" setting
16 Pretends to get K.O.'d
17 Peacemaker?
20 To begin with
21 "Let's ___"
22 Noggin tops
23 Sacrosanct
27 Originate (from)
28 Eccentric type
30 They navigated by a star
31 Always used by a poet
32 Stocking tips
33 Accusation
35 Suavity that helps one hitch a ride?
37 It may go around the block
40 Viscount's superior
41 Canadian electees, for short
44 Butter substitute
45 Charger
47 Riverbank predator
48 Halloween display
50 Bond player, once
51 Kind of meet
52 Major British publisher
54 Like a good building developer?
58 Like two, to four
59 Oscar winner for "The Cider House Rules"
60 Diamonds, slangily
61 Meat and potatoes
62 Turn outward
63 New England catch

DOWN

1 Problem during convalescence
2 Overhead projector sheet
3 Chase
4 They open Windows
5 Pathfinder explored it
6 Part of a Rorschach test
7 Whistle-blower
8 Vermonter operator
9 1961 Newbery Medal winner Scott
10 One of many hats worn by Benjamin Franklin
11 Gametes
12 ___ room
13 Onetime streak in the sky, for short
18 Carpe ___
19 Unrevealed asset
23 Former leading light
24 Failed negotiation result
25 Humpty Dumpty
26 Conk out
28 High-quality, as a film
29 Landing craft: Abbr.
32 Opening day of the Masters: Abbr.
34 Stomach acid, symbolically
35 Backyard sight
36 ___ Bo (workout system)
37 Coiffures
38 Antlered animal
39 Buttonless shirt
41 Blah
42 Home of the Atlas Mountains
43 Like some candles
46 Debaters' needs
47 Fixed by an ed.
49 Pitchers
50 "Ahoy" recipient
52 Silvers who played Sgt. Bilko
53 Sicilian erupter
54 Amiss
55 Prefix with lithic
56 Wee hour
57 Interstice

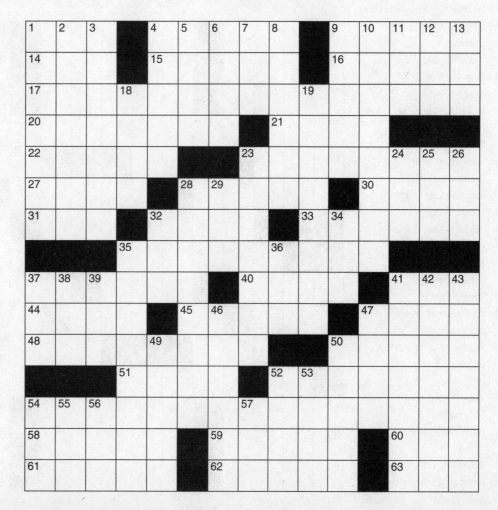

by Tyler Hinman

ACROSS

1 Place to moor a boat
5 "Pipe down!"
10 Say "%@&#!"
14 City south of Moscow
15 Rich cake
16 Poker pot primer
17 Removes squeaks from
18 Actress Samantha
19 "___ almost taste it!"
20 Elvis Presley title "corrected"
23 Suffix with percent
24 Thrilla in Manila boxer
25 Sonnets and such
27 Grand ___ National Park
29 1996 Madonna musical
33 Take to court
34 Lennon's widow Yoko
36 Environmentalist's prefix
37 Does hip-hop
38 Gershwin title "corrected"
41 Vacationers' stops
43 Hosp. units
44 "What'd I tell ya?"
45 Corn holder
46 Kennel club classification
48 Molten rock
52 Letters that don't need stamps
54 Alley-___ (basketball maneuver)
56 Nonsense
57 Fats Domino title "corrected"
62 Paul who sang "Diana"
63 Tricks
64 Start of an invention
65 One 'twixt 12 and 20
66 Like a gymnast
67 Eyeglass part
68 Dole (out)
69 Breakfast, lunch and dinner
70 After curfew

DOWN

1 Take a chill pill
2 Baltimore ballplayer
3 Luxurious fabric
4 "If all ___ fails . . ."
5 Pittsburgh product
6 Immobilize, rodeo-style
7 Craving
8 Laurel of comedy
9 Group of buffalo
10 Egypt's capital
11 He wants you
12 Bypasses bedtime
13 D.C. V.I.P.
21 Food from heaven
22 Fed. pollution monitor
26 "Absolutely!"
28 Cries at fireworks
30 Sonnets and such
31 "___ bin ein Berliner"
32 Hula hoops and yo-yos
35 Eggs ___ easy
37 Perlman of "Cheers"
38 Where many memos land
39 Before, once
40 Office subs
41 Skater's surface
42 Convention's choice
46 Sandwich, briefly
47 "Is that a fact!"
49 Like a good egg
50 "One ___, please"
51 Opposite of "Ten-hut!"
53 Absurd
55 Desert havens
58 Streetcar
59 Bigger than big
60 China's continent
61 Sledder's spot
62 $20 bill dispenser, briefly

by Harvey Estes and Nancy Salomon

ACROSS

1 Trojan War hero
5 Hawkeye's show
9 Serviceable
14 DNA carrier
15 To ___ (exactly)
16 Spoke irrationally
17 Drags along
18 Numbers to crunch
19 Fresh from the laundry
20 Keats work
21 Address book no.
22 Refrain from singing?
24 1999 Will Smith movie
27 Decay
28 Sought a seat
29 ___ von Bismarck
33 Laid-back, personalitywise
36 Unlike dirt roads
38 It's charged
39 Nightgown wearer of rhyme
42 Chowed down
43 Tom and Jerry, for two
44 "And there you are!"
45 Doesn't guzzle
47 Suffix with Manhattan
48 Teen's embarrassment
49 Modern research tool
55 Galileo ___
58 How the excited go
59 Corrida cry
60 Cara or Castle
61 Loch ___ monster
63 Pack it in
64 Exotic fruit
65 Rebuke to Brutus
66 Cancel
67 Obie candidates
68 Leak slowly
69 First couple's place

DOWN

1 Shining
2 Day after mercredi
3 Child who behaves perfectly
4 Illiterates' marks
5 Achieved success
6 In any way
7 Wimbledon unit
8 Scorching times
9 Oceanic killers
10 Get beaten by
11 Eye part
12 Navy commando
13 Poet ___ St. Vincent Millay
21 Small-time
23 Extend, as Time
25 Pulled a six-shooter
26 Emptied
30 "Kon-___"
31 Travail
32 Most qualified to serve
33 "Jabberwocky" starter
34 Hairy humanoid
35 Chick's sound
36 Drama essentials
37 Make fractions
40 France's longest river
41 Staff member?
46 Like Benny Goodman's music
48 Fastens pants, in a way
50 Dairy section selections
51 Fritter away
52 Twisted
53 Say "bo's'n," say
54 Back, as a racehorse
55 Hobbling gait
56 Asia's ___ Sea
57 Tuneful Horne
62 Summer on the Riviera
63 Can. province

by Michael Shteyman

ACROSS

1 Butts
5 BAFFIN BAY SIGHT
9 "Family Ties" mother
14 ANTLERED BEAST
15 You might get your mitts on it
16 Rifles
17 Painter Nolde
18 "Le Roi d'Ys" composer
19 Shivering fits
20 With 59-Across, what the answers to the 11 capitalized clues begin
23 San Antonio-to-Dallas dir.
24 Durham sch.
25 Arlington landmark
27 Brandy flavor
31 ___-crazy
32 Test-taker's last resort
34 Squids' kin
38 OPPOSITE OF 11-DOWN
39 MARGARINE CONTAINER
41 ANGLER'S BUY
42 Menacing look
46 Infamous W.W. I name
50 Canned
52 Ending of fame or fortune
53 More cheerful
57 One of the Bobbsey twins
58 Put on
59 See 20-Across
64 Winter Olympics athlete
66 Sch. with a branch in Berkeley
67 Seat of Allen County, Kan.
68 Atoll component
69 ___ SLAW
70 Tip or hip follower

71 Swerves
72 Whaler's direction
73 ATTEMPT A BREAK-IN

DOWN

1 White hat wearer
2 "___ Camera"
3 Hardly rosy
4 Bowling Hall of Fame location
5 Moscow theater
6 Sen. Bayh of Indiana
7 Pass again on the track
8 Folklore figures
9 Like a bungee cord
10 Journal
11 IN ONE'S SALAD DAYS

12 Pad user
13 Krupp Works city
21 Aunties' husbands
22 Within: Prefix
26 Know-how
27 Bug-eyed
28 SWAY, SO TO SPEAK
29 Fix up
30 Explosive
33 Bazooka, e.g.
35 "The Plague" setting
36 35-DOWN IS ONE
37 "And if ___ before . . ."
40 Undergrad degs.
43 Children's card game

44 Brain trust members
45 Bridle part
47 Cause of a prickly feeling
48 Jai ___
49 Brooding?
51 Count expenses when figuring taxes
53 454, in old Rome
54 IT MAY BE OPEN OR SAFE
55 Fireplace
56 Xerox competitor
60 "The Lion King" lioness
61 Baseballer Manny
62 Smart ___
63 D.E.A. agent: Var.
65 Poetic contraction

by Eric Berlin

ACROSS

1 ___ salts
6 ___-Japanese War
11 Car co. bought by Chrysler
14 Poem with 17 syllables
15 Full-length, as a movie
16 The facts of life?
17 "Beat it!"
18 World traveler from Venice
20 Nightly "NewsHour" airer
22 Skating venue
23 New York governor before George Pataki
28 Cries to bullfighters
29 Inits. on a toothpaste box
30 "___, Joy of Man's Desiring"
31 Dashboard abbr.
33 Priest's robe
34 Hands and feet
36 Like one of the two jaws
40 Some postal workers
42 Polish remover
44 Half of an audiotape
45 Croc's cousin
47 Symbol of industriousness
48 "___ Skylark" (ode)
50 Dryer buildup
51 Snarling dog
52 G.I. addresses
55 Home of the AAA Mud Hens
58 Shiploads
60 Bobby of the N.H.L.
61 By its very nature
64 Home with a dome
68 Simon and Garfunkel, once
69 Japanese port
70 Director who won his first 56-Down in 1934
71 ___ Juan (capital of 32-Down)
72 Goose eggs
73 Beginning

DOWN

1 Sounds of doubt
2 ___-Man (arcade game)
3 What to call an officer
4 Relative of a giraffe
5 Gibberish
6 Piña colada ingredient
7 Article in La Repubblica
8 Theatrical drop
9 Assistance
10 Siouan tribe
11 Buzzing with excitement
12 Winnie-the-Pooh's creator
13 Does chef's work
19 Exactly on time
21 Public row
23 Sirs' partners
24 Stevenson who lost twice for president
25 More than fervent
26 Bringing into play
27 Not at home
32 See 71-Across
35 French composer Erik
37 Hunt illegally
38 The blahs
39 Backward-looking
41 "Hurry!"
43 Time-share unit, often
46 100%
49 "Relax, and that's an order!"
52 They have pH's of less than 7
53 ___ New Guinea
54 Director Welles
56 Screen award
57 Bach instrument
59 "The Wizard ___"
62 Bout stopper, for short
63 Western treaty grp.
65 CD predecessors
66 Source of iron
67 Stable staple

by Greg Staples

ACROSS

1 Hardly high-class
6 Tiny tribesman
11 Medicine givers, for short
14 Stan's partner in comedy
15 Ham's need
16 Feed bag tidbit
17 Callisto and Europa, to Jupiter
18 Borneo critter
19 Alcott of women's golf
20 "What's up, Doc?" speaker
22 The Dow, e.g.
24 Remote button
25 Building beam
26 Take turns
29 Tweak
33 "Laugh-In" actress
34 Plants
35 Cambodia's Lon ___
36 Mamie's man
37 Less ornate
39 Brokaw's network
40 Born, in bios
41 Bizarre
42 Sandwich shop
43 Completely accurate
45 Tied fast
47 Shoots the breeze
48 Return for a buck?
49 Cornered
51 "Sufferin' succotash!" speaker
56 Phi follower
57 Fly-catching bird
59 Oarlock
60 Cigarette ingredient
61 Brain waves
62 Sent flowers to, say
63 Norm: Abbr.
64 20 Questions turn
65 Held the deed to

DOWN

1 Egyptian pyramid, e.g.
2 Moises of baseball
3 Drano target
4 Father or brother
5 "Agreed. However . . ."
6 Lying facedown
7 Tall tale
8 Aussie greeting
9 Degree div.
10 "I'm smarter than the average . . ." speaker
11 "Beep, beep!" speaker
12 With 50- and 53-Down, apt title for this puzzle
13 Charon's river
21 Sport ___ (modern vehicle)
23 ___ King Cole
25 Memo phrase
26 African charger
27 Like some old buckets
28 "I tawt I taw a puddy tat!" speaker
29 Bat one's eyelashes, say
30 Actress Skye
31 High-minded
32 Heston epic
34 Lot in life
37 "Th-th-th-that's all, folks!" speaker
38 Schleps
42 Where a boxer might be champion
44 Directions-giving org.
45 Dallas hoopster, briefly
46 Pug's combo
48 Grace word
49 Play makers?
50 See 12-Down
51 Popeye's ___'pea
52 Those for
53 See 12-Down
54 Robt. ___
55 Funny Foxx
58 College Web site suffix

by Sherry O. Blackard

ACROSS

1 Complaint
5 Singer Tori
9 Good place to be in a race
14 Turturro of "The Sopranos"
15 As it happens
16 Spanish for "fox"
17 Particular
18 They can take a yoke
19 Small amount
20 Perfect score in a certain game
23 Anago, at a Japanese restaurant
24 Pool exercise
25 Sweet treats
27 Great fear
29 IBM products
30 Vim
33 Esau and Jacob's mother
37 Coop up
38 What the perfect game consists of
42 Literary collections
43 Rugby shirts
44 Rx writers
45 Lean-___ (sheds)
46 Bullies' targets
50 1990's All-Pro linebacker Junior of the Chargers
52 Wings
55 Classified ad abbr.
56 How the perfect game is shown on the scoresheet
59 Part of a newspaper article
62 Nobelist Wiesel
63 What "++" means in Qe2++
64 Diamond flaw?
65 Diamond of note
66 Tiger or Indian, briefly
67 Dashboard display
68 Tag sale tag
69 Certain cameras: Abbr.

DOWN

1 Like fishhooks
2 Choice word
3 Channel swimmer Gertrude
4 Renown
5 Ho hi
6 Snafu
7 Bake-off needs
8 Cell phone button
9 Quetzalcoatl worshipers
10 Throng
11 Big time
12 Part of a sector
13 Female rabbit
21 Church leader
22 Potsie's pal on "Happy Days"
26 Practice one's one-two
28 Fine things?
29 Hail Mary, e.g.
31 Self-image
32 Sunday seat
34 Exquisitely wrought trinkets
35 Squeezes (out)
36 Prefix with plunk or plop
37 Four six-packs
38 When "S.N.L." wraps in N.Y.C.
39 February ___ (Groundhog Day)
40 Back talk
41 Old telecommunications name
45 Levy imposers
47 Classic drugstore name
48 Saxophonist Gordon
49 Bobby-___ (40's teenagers)
51 Praise
52 Cars' bars
53 XXI tripled
54 Skating maneuvers
57 Warrior princess of TV
58 Present day?
59 Proof letters
60 Swiss canton
61 ___ pro nobis

by Peter Gordon

ACROSS

1 Sired, biblically
6 2002 Winter Olympics locale
10 Mafia head
14 Microwave brand
15 ___ the way (lead)
16 Scent
17 Hightail it
19 In the thick of
20 Put down
21 Do a second time, as a role
23 Anniversary unit
25 Fall flower
26 Deep sleep
30 Initial phase
33 "You can say that ___!"
35 What a vacuum cleaner vacuums
36 Keats piece
39 Stop suddenly
43 Sewn edge
44 ___ china
45 Belgian city in W.W. I fighting
46 Alternative to a taco
49 Hawaiian tuber
50 Gold star
53 Frisbee
55 Running behind schedule
58 In vino ___
63 French Sudan, today
64 Change one's mind
66 Stratford's river
67 Part of the eye
68 Quaker State: Abbr.
69 Kind of conference
70 Circus sight
71 Before surgery

DOWN

1 Ali ___ and the 40 Thieves
2 Flightless flock
3 "The World According to ___"
4 Green Gables girl
5 Hang back
6 Optimistic
7 Bar bill
8 Say it's so
9 "___ goes!"
10 Not fine-grained
11 Own up to
12 Grace under pressure
13 Word after mail or money
18 Depletes, with "up"
22 Canned goods closet
24 Carrot-top
26 Direct payment
27 Undress with one's eyes
28 Sir's counterpart
29 Sharpshooter's asset
31 Crusty dessert
32 Globe
34 "___ Does It Better" (1977 Carly Simon hit)
36 Soup pod
37 Veal : calf :: venison : ___
38 "Happy Motoring" company
40 Tel. book listings
41 Blast maker
42 Suitable
46 Subway vehicles
47 Sell off
48 Riding the waves
50 Madison Avenue worker
51 Create a carpet
52 Permit
54 Germany's ___ Works
56 Give off
57 Throw down the gauntlet
59 Roman road
60 Jukebox choice
61 The New Yorker cartoonist Peter
62 Ginger cookie
65 Cousins and such

by Gregory E. Paul

ACROSS

1 New Jersey NHLer
6 Top spot
10 Environmental toxins, for short
14 Like Bo-Peep's charges
15 Heister's haul
16 Israeli dance
17 Barkeep's woe?
19 Mayberry moppet
20 Allergic reaction
21 Sweeper's accessory
23 Ignore
26 Weed killers
27 Left on a liner
30 Bygone carrier
31 In bounds
32 "No way!"
33 Geometric fig.
34 "You can say that again!"
37 Chest protector
38 Boxer's woe?
40 Sense of self
41 Thief
43 Go (for)
44 Initials may be carved in it
45 Art Deco artist
46 Get the drop on
47 Midmonth time
48 See eye to eye
50 Sake
52 War planner
54 Takes off the leash
58 Don Juan's mother
59 Stunt man's woe?
62 Wingless parasites
63 Eight, for starters
64 Where to find sweaters?
65 Mice-inspired yelps
66 Warp
67 Sheep counter's quest

DOWN

1 i lids?
2 Having neither side ahead
3 Tarzan's transport
4 Very detailed
5 TV host Gibbons
6 Politico Landon
7 Pigeon patter
8 Temperamental
9 Caesar's accusation
10 It may be checked in a security check
11 Police officer's woe?
12 Pipe material
13 French composer Saint-___
18 Relief for the stressed
22 Alan Ladd classic
24 Deep drink
25 Without exception
27 Good engine sound
28 Akron's home
29 Masseur's woe?
31 Sizzling pitch
35 Folklore fiend
36 Pans for stir-frying
38 "___ Pan"
39 Colorful fish
42 Mild currents
44 Like some lenses
48 Quick-witted
49 Wish granter
50 City division
51 Windblown soil
53 Ruckuses
55 Elisabeth of "Leaving Las Vegas"
56 German article
57 Go ballistic
60 Colorado native
61 Reaction to applause

by Nancy Salomon

ACROSS

1 Author Paretsky
5 "Mamma Mia!" group
9 Dumb bunny
14 Radical ___
15 Foundry form
16 Early sitcom star
17 Knife handle
18 Way around London, once
19 Rock bottom
20 Like second or farm
23 Stat for Clemens
24 Portfolio part, in brief
25 Dormitory annoyance
27 Incite to anger
31 Vistula River city
34 Talking bird of poetry
35 Actress Mazar
38 European erupter
39 Poetic paean
40 "Yikes!"
43 Adj. modifer
44 Lean and strong
46 Siouan people
47 "L.A. Law" lawyer
49 Best, on the links
51 Much-covered R & B song
53 Beat the draft?
56 African serpent
57 "Boola Boola" singer
59 Like wave or treatment
63 Kosher
65 Mine, in Marseille
66 Didn't have good traction
68 Slalom champ Phil
69 Reach across
70 American Theatre Wing award
71 ___ out (declined)
72 Submarine
73 Just beat

DOWN

1 Acad., e.g.
2 1956 Peck role
3 Abundant
4 When Macbeth meets his fate
5 Acela operator
6 Yawner
7 Malaise, with "the"
8 Sloganeer of sorts
9 ___ Day O'Connor
10 Song syllable
11 Like pat or still, reading down
12 Ice dancing team
13 Book before Nehemiah
21 Maine college town
22 "___ not the time!"
26 ". . . ___ he drove out of sight"
27 Search for prey
28 Contact, in a way
29 Like paper or light, reading down
30 Trim to fit
32 Actress MacDowell
33 Be uncertain
36 A star may have a big one
37 Pear variety
41 Recurring theme
42 Like Siberian winters
45 Asian capital?
48 Comeback
50 On the schedule
52 Slot spot
54 Secret supply
55 The Sun Devils' city
57 A Sesame Streeter
58 Jeté, e.g.
60 Crowd sound
61 Doofus
62 Double-decker checker
64 Tick off
67 Do colorful work

by Alan Arbesfeld

75

ACROSS

1 Klutzes
5 Ailments for which there is no known cure
10 Sharpen
14 Exchange
15 Early stage
16 London's ___ Park
17 Give a darn
18 Like chips that have been set out too long
19 The "Iliad" or "Odyssey"
20 Bristling with firepower
23 Lois Lane often needed one
24 One who's looked up to
25 Pick-up line?
28 Quick smells
32 PC key
35 ___ Strauss & Co.
37 ___ firma
38 Display contempt for
42 Apple tool
43 Feed the kitty
44 Hair colorer
45 Rob, as a stage
47 Progresso products
50 ___ of Man
52 Bitter resentment
56 Barely scrape by
61 Norwegian king
62 Rating units
63 Dog in "Beetle Bailey"
64 Where Korea is
65 Donnybrook
66 Multicolored
67 When leaves turn
68 First sign of the zodiac
69 Vaccines

DOWN

1 Prize awarded at the Kodak Theatre
2 Knowing
3 Grows crops
4 When repeated, a cry to an awardee
5 Half of a 1940's–50's comedy duo
6 Suspicious of
7 Exam for attys.-to-be
8 Indian city
9 Knights' horses
10 Cyclists pop them
11 Ballyhoo
12 Trim, as text
13 Part of M.I.T.: Abbr.
21 Expected
22 Scout's rider
26 Horne or Olin
27 Pizzeria fixtures
29 Landlord of Lucy and Ricky
30 Wear on, as the nerves
31 Fill nicely
32 Do art on metal, e.g.
33 Chase away
34 Ringlet
36 Analogy words
39 Like feudal times
40 Touch lightly
41 Emotional disorders
46 Transfusion liquid
48 Popular cooking spray
49 Busybodies
51 Go in
53 Adorable one
54 Sleek swimmer
55 "The Mary Tyler Moore Show" spinoff
56 Goof off
57 "Casablanca" woman
58 Colorado resort town
59 "The Persistence of Memory" artist
60 Shoe shaper

by Peter Sarrett

ACROSS

1 Immunizations
6 Places for tents
11 HBO rival
14 "The Planets" composer
15 Golden-___ (oldsters)
16 Ad-___
17 Nebraska's largest city
18 "Of course"
20 "Of course"
22 Memorial Day weekend event, for short
23 Fork providers?: Abbr.
24 Leather from the sea
26 Float gracefully
29 Old Mideast inits.
32 Beehives and others
33 "Honest" man
34 "Sharp Dressed Man" band
36 Spring in the Sahara
40 "Of course"
43 Dined at home
44 Holy radiances
45 Bake sale organizer, for short
46 Costa ___ Sol
48 Hectic hosp. areas
49 Letters akin to P.D.Q.
50 Asian shrines
54 Drum locale
56 Baseball's Jesus
57 "Of course"
63 "Of course"
65 Confused
66 Fraction of a joule
67 Replays may be played in it
68 Newly waxed
69 Fish eggs
70 Family car
71 Upscale hotel room features

DOWN

1 Booted?
2 Web browser button
3 Regal Norwegian name
4 Underwear top
5 Request when the national anthem is played
6 Play group
7 Malaria symptom
8 Haggard of country music
9 Victimized, with "on"
10 Speedy jet to J.F.K., once
11 Move sinuously
12 Language of Delhi
13 Future mom's doc
19 Condemn from the peanut gallery
21 Trooper maker
25 Untethered
26 "S.N.L." character Baba ___
27 Some
28 Grand banquet
30 "___ boy!"
31 Court game
34 Like land in a city
35 Petted pet's sound
37 Doesn't guzzle
38 Small quantity
39 "___ out of it!"
41 Avoided a dragnet
42 Painting holder
47 Apt to change
49 Franklin with soul
50 Harness racer
51 Oldsmobile model
52 Mountain climber's obstacle
53 Church council
55 Pile up
58 ___ mater
59 City on the Rhone
60 Like
61 Hawaiian bird
62 Simon ___
64 Ninny

by Michael Shteyman

ACROSS

1 Balance of October
6 Not ashore
10 Pal in Sydney
14 Arm of the sea
15 Pooh, for one
16 Yoked beasts
17 Hendrix biography "___ Me While I Kiss the Sky"
18 2002 Literature Nobelist Kertész
19 Decent, so to speak
20 Start of a definition of "microsecond"
23 A, in Acapulco
24 Suffix with xeno-
25 Padlock piece
28 Definition, part 2
33 Like
34 "See ya!"
35 Slender woman
36 Fam. member
37 Rhein feeder
38 Vigoda of "Barney Miller"
40 Legal conclusion?
41 Gloomy, in poetry
43 "___, Our Help in Ages Past" (hymn)
44 Twaddle
45 Definition, part 3
48 Philosophical subjects
49 "Me too"
50 "Oh, brother!"
52 End of the definition
58 "Awright!"
59 Janis's husband in the funnies
60 Runs like a deer
61 Facility
62 Creditor's claim
63 What's happening
64 "Darn it!"
65 Choice word
66 "Touched By an Angel" co-star

DOWN

1 ___ price
2 Make a small move
3 Off-color
4 What to do before a big race, maybe
5 Had a home-cooked meal
6 Rose lover?
7 Like some athletes
8 Coarse
9 Playground retort
10 Derision
11 Rod in a hot rod
12 Parts of a Victorian social schedule
13 Wrap up
21 Secret society
22 Treated badly
25 Capital of Colombia?
26 Car similar to a Grand Am
27 Oregon's capital
29 Crew tool
30 Pirates and Padres, informally
31 Kind of salts
32 Puts an edge on
34 He debuted at the Met in 1903
38 Ten-percenter: Abbr.
39 Prosperous periods
42 Army helicopters
43 Baltimore birds
46 Steamed dish
47 TV chef Lagasse
48 Smitten
51 One who hears "You've got mail"
52 Sweetheart
53 Right on the map
54 Off-white shade
55 Blunted blade
56 Gymnastic coups
57 53-Down, in Madrid
58 Kyoto currency

by Nancy Salomon and Nancy T. Shack

78

ACROSS

1 Test episode for a TV series
6 Front's opposite
10 Yen
14 Came up
15 Israeli airline
16 Actress Irene of "Fame"
17 Expensive fur
18 Christie's "Death on the ___"
19 Diplomat Abba
20 007's introduction
23 Kind of sauce
25 Shipping magnate Onassis
26 Screwball
27 Thin 1960's supermodel
29 Coil
32 ___ the Cow
33 Mathematician Descartes
34 "Invasion of the Body Snatchers" container
37 Jungle declaration
41 Main, Elm, etc.: Abbr.
42 Sicilian volcano
43 Turkic speaker
44 Flower with colorful blotches
46 "Peter Pan" playwright
47 Tasty
50 Stadium cheer
51 Where Mindy's TV friend came from
52 First line of "Moby-Dick"
57 Spoken
58 Poker payment
59 President Nasser
62 Dog on the Yellow Brick Road
63 On the double, in the O.R.
64 Get around
65 Winter forecast
66 Civil wrong
67 Spanish kids

DOWN

1 Mas' mates
2 Lyricist Gershwin
3 Capitol Hill wheeler-dealers
4 Peace Prize city
5 Adolescent
6 Cinema canine
7 Inter ___
8 Serene
9 Swiss artist Paul
10 Fridge, old-style
11 Forbidden
12 How to start up a Model T
13 Useful
21 Moistureless
22 Hit the slopes
23 What roots connect to
24 Young hooter
28 Italian actress Scala
29 Youngman of one-liners
30 "Orinoco Flow" singer
31 Sign before Virgo
33 Followers of the Pied Piper of Hamelin
34 Officer on the beat
35 Studio sign
36 Bo of "10"
38 Buddhist sect
39 Tony-winning actress for "The Country Girl"
40 Cookie holder
44 Feather-filled item
45 Navy bigwig: Abbr.
46 Crash sound
47 Glasgow residents
48 Composer Copland
49 Academy founder
50 Scarlett's love
53 Sunrise direction
54 Look ___ (study)
55 Constellation component
56 Icicle site
60 Citrus drink
61 "___ Misérables"

by Randy Sowell

ACROSS

1 Nickname in the N.B.A.
5 Part of a musical refrain
9 Hill's partner
13 "To Sir With Love" singer
14 Majestic poem
15 They hold water
17 Mine: Fr.
18 Cauldron stirrers, maybe
19 Something pushed by a trailer?
20 Drink garnish
21 "___ bin ein Berliner"
22 Treat with carbon dioxide
23 Really taut
26 Where the outboard motor goes
29 Two-time
30 "Le ___ d'Arthur"
32 Royal wish
33 Resigned remark
37 Really self-satisfied
41 Thetis bathed Achilles in it, in myth
42 Battle of Britain grp.
43 Southpaw
44 Grow old
47 Link
48 Really clever
53 Some Crimeans
54 Benzene source
55 "Hold ___ your hat!"
59 Isolated
60 Dr. ___, TV adviser on life and relationships
61 Pearl Harbor locale
62 Seaport south of Milan
63 Architect Saarinen
64 Bad spot for a nail

65 Tear
66 Formerly, formerly
67 They're sometimes candied

DOWN

1 Indication of indignation
2 "History of England" author David
3 Lotion ingredient
4 Coverlet
5 Tributary of the Delaware
6 Geronimo, e.g.
7 Really ethereal
8 Southern comforts?: Abbr.

9 Humiliate
10 "___ to the wise . . ."
11 Burton of "Star Trek: T.N.G."
12 Verdi aria
16 Appear to be
22 Unanimously
24 Like summer drinks
25 At the peak of
26 Some stage equipment
27 Construction of snow, maybe
28 City of Paris
31 Prom wear
33 Do well on
34 Garret

35 Start of a play
36 Hebrides island
38 Regions
39 ___ souci
40 Actor Baldwin
44 Two-page ad
45 Link between stories?
46 Where trade-ins are made
48 Just for men
49 More healthy
50 Make amends
51 Talked and talked
52 Weirdish
56 Mom's mom
57 ___ McAn shoes
58 Inning closers
60 ___ Dee river

by Richard Hughes

80

ACROSS

1 ___ II (razor brand)
5 A tusker
9 Guts
14 Sling
15 "Anything ___?"
16 Sociologist Durkheim
17 Where Sikkim is
18 What's left
19 Fingered
20 "Why're you acting strange?" in Delhi?
23 They bind
24 Diez x diez
25 Abaft
28 Jemima, e.g.
29 Invoice fig.
32 1922 Nobelist in physics
33 "It's all ___!"
34 Air agcy.
35 "Ya ready and able?" in Accra?
39 A.A.R.P. members
40 Professorship, e.g.
41 Actress Skye
42 It may be naked
43 Broadway debut of 10/7/82
44 Wimple wearer
46 Down in the dumps
47 Opportunity
48 "Don't even try" in Vientiane?
53 Like traditional hospital fare
55 Ottumwa's locale
56 Elders' teachings
57 Intrude, with "in"
58 December air
59 One of the Simpsons
60 Clerics' council
61 Some receivers
62 Part of a lobster pot

DOWN

1 Microwave option
2 First name in talk
3 Mezzo's tune
4 Like a bucket of bolts
5 Norway's second-largest city
6 Dairy section selections
7 ___ prof.
8 Netlike
9 Family feud
10 At full speed
11 Bean town?
12 Arena cheer
13 McCarthy quarry
21 Poitier role
22 Sheer fabric
25 Take down a peg
26 Classic board game
27 This and this
28 Sap-sucker's genus
29 In progress
30 Down East
31 30-Down product
33 Classified ad measure
36 Blocked off
37 Mover's rental
38 Makes mountain dew
44 Schools of fish
45 Cyclades island
46 A beatnik beats it
47 Lumbered, in a way
48 Tall tale
49 Wacko
50 Work like Tillie?
51 Bear that comes out at night?
52 Vegetable fuel
53 Some ammo
54 Put down

by Kumar Balani

ACROSS

1 Tony winner Minnelli
5 Not all
9 Leg bone
14 Author unknown, for short
15 List-shortening abbr.
16 Upturned, as a box
17 Direct
20 "To ___ is human . . ."
21 Seeks money damages from
22 Click and clack, e.g.
23 Nature's alarm clock
25 Attention-getter
26 Third degree?
27 Kind of rally or talk
28 Corned beef concoction
32 Alarm clock setting, perhaps
35 Boutonniere's place
37 Feed lines to
38 Town meeting site
41 Chowed down
42 What straphangers lack
43 Indian corn
44 Deliver a tirade
46 Dryly humorous
47 Hi-fi component
48 Major airports
50 "The Firm" author
54 St. Francis's home
57 Haunted house sound
58 Companion of the id
59 Surprises
62 Conjure up
63 Neighborhood
64 Gratis
65 Underground conduit
66 Lively
67 Praiseful poems

DOWN

1 Modern surgical tool
2 Conclusion's opposite
3 Famous slasher film?
4 Gasteyer of "Saturday Night Live"
5 Made a smooth transition
6 Survey choice
7 "Welcome" sites
8 Keebler cookie maker
9 Corrida de ___ (bullfight)
10 Close to personally
11 Actresses Arthur and Benaderet
12 Memo starter
13 Finds the sum
18 Narrow strip of land
19 With no assurance of payment
24 Unwanted e-mail
25 Diarist Samuel
27 Hamburger unit
29 Start of a play
30 Mideast canal
31 Roll call response
32 Unwelcome mark
33 Small amount
34 Marvel superheroes
35 They cook up whoppers
36 Animal in a mass migration
39 Beginner, slangily
40 Siestas
45 Alan of "Growing Pains"
47 Late Palestinian leader
49 Wedding party member
50 Errand runner
51 Got wind of
52 Come to terms
53 Math class figures
54 They're worth 1 or 11 points
55 Computer command
56 Put away
57 Oliver's request
60 Gullible person
61 ET's craft

by Peter Gordon

ACROSS

1 Dips in gravy
5 Typewriter type
9 Image on an old nickel
14 Site of the 9-Across on an old nickel
15 Economist Smith
16 Do penance
17 Grid great Graham
18 All-night party
19 On pitch
20 Question to a suspect
23 Pasture sound
24 Planet, poetically
25 Tom of "Newhart"
29 Sugar pie
31 Mosque V.I.P.
35 Sound from Sneezy
36 Pueblo Indians
38 Botheration
39 Question to a prospective bride
42 Make a boner
43 Great Lakes mnemonic
44 Alphabet ender
45 Need a bath badly
47 Kid-___ (children's shows)
48 Did figure eights, say
49 Big brute
51 News initials
52 Question to a speeder
59 Close to
61 Actress Sharon
62 "Phew!" inducer
63 Transported
64 Many a trucker
65 Lantern-jawed celeb
66 Say "@#$%!"
67 Call to Fido
68 Roaster's spot

DOWN

1 Pack overhead
2 "@#$%!," e.g.
3 Bread for gyros
4 Place for mail
5 Dolly who sang "Here You Come Again"
6 State with a panhandle
7 Stalactite site
8 Traitorous Aldrich
9 Ulan ___, Mongolia
10 Spanish pianist José
11 Walkman maker
12 Latish lunchtime
13 Nancy Drew's beau
21 Peanut butter choice
22 Gin's partner
25 Ham-fisted one
26 Autumn hue
27 Sandcastle site
28 How-___ (instructional books)
29 Sank, as a putt
30 Numbered work
32 "Glengarry Glen Ross" playwright
33 Old saw
34 Single-celled creature
36 Prefix with 48-Down
37 Chicago suburb
40 Hang like a chopper
41 Singer Sumac
46 Hilo honcho
48 Ball
50 Ueberroth or Ustinov
51 Out-and-out
52 Got threadbare
53 Work with acid
54 Kemo ___
55 Go out of business
56 Creative spark
57 Rice-A-___
58 Libidinous deity
59 Tummy muscles
60 Item for 58-Down

by Fred Piscop

83

ACROSS

1 Common rhyme scheme
5 Knowledge
8 Personal record
13 Winemaking county
14 Wait
15 At the right time
16 Sweater, maybe
17 Gymnastics event
19 Illegal hiring practice
21 Soda fountain drink
22 Ice cream choices
24 Cause for a handshake
27 Hydrocarbon suffix
28 Capture
29 Loser to D.D.E.
31 Year of Bush's swearing-in
32 Welcome words to a hitchhiker
34 Colloquialism
36 Possible title for this puzzle
41 Venus or Mars
42 Pool hall or neighborhood bar, for some
43 Version of a song: Abbr.
44 ___-Atlantic
47 Sgt. or cpl.
48 Simpson case judge
51 Prefix with physical
53 Spanish-American War figure
56 Trainee
58 Beverly Cleary character
59 1985 Jeff Bridges/Glenn Close film
62 Pub purchase
63 Value system
64 Honey drink
65 Actress Falco
66 Best Actress of 1990
67 Collectors' org.
68 Standings stat

DOWN

1 Home of Middle East Technical University
2 Hit loudly and repeatedly
3 Individually
4 It's a dyeing art
5 Thanksgiving gatherers, often
6 Swelling
7 The Sagebrush State
8 "Stop that!"
9 Retired for the night
10 Professor's milieu
11 Capek play
12 "You bet!"
14 Unjust verdicts
18 Different
20 Instance, for example
23 Final notice
25 Mine, on the Marne
26 Draw
30 Italian Mrs.
32 Bomb's opposite
33 Math ordinal
35 "___ & the Women" (Altman film)
36 He raised Cain
37 Richard who played 35-Down
38 Unassailable, as an alibi
39 Pend
40 Took more tricks than, possibly
45 Angered
46 Green stuff
48 1966 Mary Martin/Robert Preston musical
49 It has its faults
50 Declaims
52 1973 Rolling Stones ballad
54 Anesthetized
55 Motivate
57 Gumshoes
59 Brother of George W.
60 ___ glance
61 Rightmost pedal

by Alan Arbesfeld

ACROSS

1 "___, humbug!"
4 Funnies
10 Ed who sang "My Cup Runneth Over"
14 Prefix with puncture
15 Noah's mount
16 Telegram
17 "It's c-c-cold!"
18 Classic song from the 1913 "Ziegfeld Follies"
20 Spine-tingling
22 Hostile party
23 Mr. ___ (Shea mascot)
24 Ancient Andean
26 "My Cup Runneth Over" musical
28 Halloween decoration
33 Part of the Deep South: Abbr.
34 Prohibit
35 Performed on stage
39 Chicago phenomenon
41 Reef material
43 Sea eagle
44 Excellent buy
46 More slippery, as winter roads
48 Suffix with lemon or orange
49 Marsh light
52 Fred who played Herman Munster
55 "Get ___ writing!"
56 Live and breathe
57 Full range
61 Dark
64 "Oh, my!"
67 Shelley poem
68 Intro for boy or girl
69 Nervousness
70 Every little bit
71 Vehicle pulled by a hoss
72 Brought in, as a salary
73 Just for Men product

DOWN

1 Jesus, in the manger
2 Small farm size
3 See 11-Down
4 Bay State peninsula
5 Metallic rock
6 Wizard, old-style
7 Steel ingredient
8 Showed up
9 Frustrate
10 Bowl over
11 With 3-Down, a Florida collegian
12 Slipped up
13 Bench-clearing incident
19 Nine-headed serpent of myth
21 Tattooing fluid
25 Smart ___
27 ___ upon a time
28 1975 movie thriller with a sequel in 3-D
29 Dismounted
30 Bubbling
31 Drug agent, slangily
32 Characteristic
36 Huge quantity
37 Partner of odds
38 Bottomless
40 Sunrise
42 Where Samson slew the Philistines
45 Specialized vocabulary
47 Fixed, as a piano
50 Part of N.F.L.
51 Get the blue ribbon
52 Grand parties
53 Burning rage
54 Busybody
58 "___ Lisa"
59 Utility customer
60 Larger ___ life
62 Frivolously
63 The "T" in TV
65 Page in an appointment book
66 U-turn from WNW

by Gregory E. Paul

ACROSS

1 When new TV shows debut, traditionally
5 ___ Alaska
10 Lounge
14 Away from the wind
15 Manicurist's board
16 Impulse transmitter
17 Short passage from "Water Music"?
19 Remain unsettled
20 Schism
21 Serves, as soup
23 Snug
24 Dashboard control
25 Mickey of Cooperstown
28 Star of David, essentially
31 Greeting in Hilo
32 "___, With Love"
33 Big inits. in the record business
34 Mount from which Moses saw Canaan
35 Onetime Alaskan capital
36 ___ monde
37 A load off one's mine?
38 Rations (out)
39 "Siddhartha" author
40 Start of many classes
42 Workaholic's concern
43 Appearance
44 Poet Teasdale
45 Like "King Lear"
47 Air force unit
51 Stockings
52 Physically no match for Cain?
54 Pitcher
55 Nurmi, the Flying Finn
56 Paradisiacal place
57 Military lunchroom
58 Popular 1990's sitcom
59 Arp's art

DOWN

1 Saudi monarch, once
2 Jai ___
3 Camera attachment
4 Vietnamese official who declined a Nobel Peace Prize
5 British Honduras, now
6 Perth ___, N.J.
7 New Jersey university
8 Do wrong
9 Poor character analysis?
10 Pooch that perches
11 Lubricant for ice skates?
12 Part of DMZ
13 Certain linemen
18 ___ Gay (W.W. II plane)
22 At a distance
24 Office stations
25 Estate
26 Oldsmobile model
27 Long-winded acceptance speeches in Stockholm?
28 Monopoly purchase
29 Tickle
30 Oblique surface in carpentry
32 Sir or madam
35 Many a Winslow Homer painting
36 Foreshadowed
38 Roman 1102
39 Silent film star
41 German pistols
42 It can help you get a date
44 Balm
45 1954 horror film about giant ants
46 Brokerage house T. ___ Price
47 Prosperity
48 Slave girl of opera
49 Requirement
50 Dame ___ Everage
53 Account amt.

by Adam Cohen

ACROSS

1 Fare-beater's aid
5 Broadway dance hit of 1999
10 Soup bean
14 Cancún coin
15 Ufologist's study
16 "This ___ good as it gets!"
17 Author Jaffe
18 Prompters' utterances
19 Häagen-___
20 Start of a quip
23 One who's always buzzing off?
24 Molière's "The School for ___"
25 Like
26 Loop trains
27 Nonclerical
28 They may be running
32 Glorifies
34 Like some car headlights
36 Succulent plant
37 Middle of the quip
42 Do business
43 Brews
44 In danger
47 Old-fashioned theaters
48 Wee, to Burns
51 N.Y.C. subway overseer
52 Assn. formed in Bogotá
54 Beanie's top, perhaps
56 ___ Na Na
57 End of the quip
61 Guns
63 Throat doctor's concern
64 There's little point to it
65 Subject for Monet
66 Pocket protector brigade
67 Former Georgia senator
68 Sunday ___

69 Some of them are gray
70 Smudge

DOWN

1 Urban ___
2 New Jersey town near Teaneck
3 Anchorman's network?
4 Flip
5 Mountaineer's worry
6 This and that
7 Belt out
8 "Later!"
9 Store, as corn
10 Topper
11 Spanish queen who was given the title "the Catholic"
12 "Congratulations!"
13 One with duties
21 Port of old Rome
22 Part of a jazz combo
29 Qty.
30 Autobahn sights
31 Old anti-Communist assn.
33 Sounds of relief
34 Where heroes may be found
35 Not natural
37 1949 Tracy/Hepburn film
38 Arrive
39 Curiosity
40 Kind of time
41 60's–70's gallery hangings

45 Drinker
46 Wizard, in slang
48 Clog
49 Oscar winner for "West Side Story"
50 Dedicated
53 Cut
55 Jesse known as the "Buckeye Bullet"
58 Come-on
59 Actor Robert or Alan
60 Lip
62 Heathrow plane, now grounded

by Elizabeth C. Gorski

ACROSS

1 Simple adding devices
6 Starring role in a Menotti opera
11 Stake money (on)
14 Subaru Impreza, e.g.
15 Song from the past
16 Smeltery input
17 Surf serving #1
19 Sales at a box office, slangily
20 Sex ___
21 Sixth sense
22 Symbol in proofreading
23 Salt Lake City zone: Abbr.
24 Sink, as the sun
26 Sign ___ (accept, as a program)
28 Surf serving #2
33 Screenwriter/novelist Roald
36 Switchboard worker: Abbr.
37 Setting of a fire maliciously
38 Stage name
40 Solemn wedding words
41 Sort of way to run
42 Sundance Kid's partner, ___ Cassidy
43 Six o'clock broadcast
45 Sgts. and lts. get mail at them
46 Surf serving #3
49 Start over
50 Salvador lead-in
51 Sounds of disappointment
54 Song of praise
56 Sorority letter
59 Serious fan
61 "So ___!" ("Me, too!")
62 Surf serving #4
64 Show hosts, for short
65 Steed
66 Social blunder
67 Some advanced degs.
68 Synthetic fiber
69 Step into

DOWN

1 State in NE India
2 Sonar sounds
3 Suit to the circumstances
4 Steve ___, founder of 6-Down
5 Some payments are made thus
6 See 4-Down
7 Srta., in France
8 Stirs
9 Sizable zoo animals
10 Strasbourg article
11 Saying before a big drink
12 Sandusky's lake
13 Student's book
18 Stylish Oldsmobile
22 Sci-fi film of 1984
25 Some easy baskets
27 Sports org. with a March tourney
28 Slow down
29 Sorceress of myth
30 Searches for prey
31 Slightly, in music
32 Signs, as a contract
33 Smidgens, as of cream
34 School grad
35 Scattershot
39 Storage building
44 Smog relative
47 Strangelove or Kildare
48 Stressed out
51 Skyward
52 Stout detective Nero ___
53 Stay (clear of)
54 Soccer star Mia
55 Swimming pool site, for short
57 Sling
58 Supposing that
60 Straight ___ arrow
62 Schedule abbr. for cable viewers
63 Swamp

by Nancy Salomon and Gail Grabowski

ACROSS

1 Coffee, slangily
5 Elite
11 Western treaty grp.
14 Chem. table component
15 Uproar
16 Sis's sibling
17 Shrill
19 "The Lord of the Rings" figure
20 Ask too many questions
21 ___-Magnon
22 Tiny spot in the ocean
24 Arduous
28 1966 U.S. Open champion Fred
31 Actor Greene
32 Object trivially
33 Inopportune
37 Summer quaffs
38 Basket fiber
40 Knot
41 Soap star A ___
43 Slight color
44 ___ nous
45 Like Oreos and doughnuts, often
46 Extremely sad
50 Certain daisy
51 Eggs
52 Dessert in a pan
55 Russian fighter
56 Persuasion
61 Yale student
62 Kaput
63 ___ Romeo (sports car)
64 Sycophant's response
65 Sink to the bottom, as sediment
66 Trudge

DOWN

1 Cherokee maker
2 Apple spray
3 Extremely
4 Rock concert equipment
5 Force
6 Impresario Sol
7 Like many drugs: Abbr.
8 Biol. or chem.
9 Suffix on north or south
10 Major League player before moving to S.F.
11 ÷ symbols
12 Sen. Specter
13 Sound starting "Germany"
18 "___ Your Name" (Mamas & the Papas song)
23 Winding yarn
24 Like sore hands
25 One of Santa's team
26 Dinner bread
27 ___ Stanley Gardner
28 Trick
29 "Voilá!"
30 Completed
34 Member of an order
35 Nose (out)
36 Property title
38 Foreword: Abbr.
39 Dried up
42 Crying
43 Bluefins
45 What ÷ signifies, in math
46 Cozy
47 Force out
48 Auspices
49 Carpentry pin
52 Hardly the life of the party
53 Dope
54 "Omigosh!"
57 Parisian street
58 Cambridge sch.
59 It might make molehills out of mountains
60 Dancer's shoe attachment

by Alan Arbesfeld

ACROSS

1 Large or small, grammatically: Abbr.
4 Be next to
8 Circle in a winner's circle
14 "Tell __ story"
15 "This will __ further"
16 Have a yen (for)
17 It doesn't go full circle
18 Activity for 41-Across
20 Popular pasta
22 Place
23 Polish film, e.g.
24 Try out
25 Gluck's "__ ed Euridice"
29 Prevent
31 Three-time Indy winner Wilbur __, who introduced the crash helmet
33 Breeze (through)
34 Love, in Lima
36 Memo opener
38 New Deal letters
39 Scolding syllable
41 Subject of this puzzle
43 Hardly macho
44 News inits. beginning in 1958
45 Rain in Spain collector
46 Wine county
48 Numbskull
50 Autobahn autos
52 Stroke of the pen?
55 Cancel
57 Carpenters and harvesters
59 Fishing equipment
60 Cover when wet
62 Put in stitches
63 Activity for 41-Across
67 Hustle or bustle
68 Plane's distance recording device
69 Fishing equipment
70 Downturn
71 Beyond what's expected
72 Wall St. trading group
73 Venusians and others, for short

DOWN

1 Dumbfounded
2 Mock
3 Activity for 41-Across
4 Cabinet dept.
5 Leg up
6 Small drawers?
7 What a 41-Across does best
8 "Stop right there!"
9 Cost
10 Makes a record of
11 Wanted letters
12 Home run swatter Williams
13 Charlemagne's domain: Abbr.
19 Genetic surprise
21 Couple in a column
26 Activity for 41-Across
27 Dublin's home
28 Oil of __
30 Day spa attire
32 Bird that perches with its tail straight up
35 The __ Report (upscale magazine)
37 Big times
39 Marching band staple
40 Abreast of
42 Hammer in oil
47 Fringe benefit
49 Rob
51 Actress Dash of "Clueless"
53 "Hurray for me!"
54 Camera settings
56 Nigerian capital before Abuja
58 Pigpens
61 Globe plotter
63 Collision sound
64 __ Grande
65 Flight board abbr.
66 Roar of approval

by Manny Nosowsky

ACROSS

1 Mouthfuls of gum
5 "Fear of Flying" author Jong
10 Flying mammals
14 Side squared, for a square
15 Outdoor employee at a restaurant
16 Salt Lake City's home
17 Matt Dillon film based on an S. E. Hinton novel
19 "___ my day!"
20 Like some kisses and unlocked bikes
21 Summer in France
22 Ran, as colors
23 Pennies
25 Deer hunter's trophy
27 Airport info: Abbr.
29 Song for two
31 Word before "I told you so!"
32 Ark builder
34 Infinitesimal bit
36 Disconcert
40 "Swan Lake" garb
41 ___ lazuli
43 Poet ___ St. Vincent Millay
44 Response to "Who's there?"
46 After-bath powder
47 Give off
48 Diner sandwich
50 Kind of tolerance
52 Resident: Suffix
53 Pertains
57 Relish
59 Bog
60 Essence
62 Fruit with a peel
65 Tiny bump on a graph
66 Doofus
68 Actress Anderson
69 Swashbuckling Flynn
70 Choir member
71 Suffix with luncheon
72 "Inferno" author
73 More or ___

DOWN

1 The "W" in V.F.W.
2 Stuck in ___
3 Political descendants of Thomas Jefferson
4 Expensive fur
5 Ultimate
6 Brit. fliers
7 Tennis's Nastase
8 Jai alai equipment
9 Site of the 2004 Olympics
10 Colorful stinger
11 "___ of Two Cities"
12 Greedy one
13 Leaves hair here and there
18 Give for a while
24 Assail
26 Oolong or pekoe
27 Not pro
28 Football score of 60-0, say
30 Stone in a ring
33 Not a good thing to have to eat
35 A long way
37 Praiseworthy
38 Pique
39 Loathe
42 Game with tiles
45 Whitney of cotton gin fame
49 Got uptight
51 Like one White House office
53 Walk about
54 Jet controller
55 Not write cursively
56 Kama ___
58 Shaq of the N.B.A.
61 Scorch
63 Wacky
64 Old Testament book
67 Bon ___ (witticism)

by Randall J. Hartman

ACROSS

1 Owl's home, maybe
5 Partner of ham
10 Increase
14 ". . . __ saw Elba"
15 Jeweler's unit
16 Uncouth
17 Trip to Germany?
19 Rat-___
20 Makes beloved
21 Fudge __ ice cream
23 Martinique, par exemple
24 Ivy League buddies?
26 Informed
29 Innsbruck locale: Abbr.
30 Absorb, as a cost
31 Where people arrive to split
32 Long overcoat
34 Driver's lic. and others
37 Homeless German writer?
40 Hindu honorific
41 Cousin of a conch
42 Suffix with persist
43 Bray starter
45 Archer's asset
46 One in a cast
47 Scandinavian surveillance?
50 __ standstill
51 Metes out
52 Frontier settlement
56 Response to an insult, maybe
57 Clean B & B?
60 London gallery
61 Raring to go
62 Son of Isaac
63 Gave the once-over
64 O. Henry device
65 Cabinet div.

DOWN

1 Emmy winner Neuwirth
2 Elvis's middle name
3 Tear apart
4 Pitch-and-putt club
5 Musical arranger's work
6 Partner of means
7 Belfast grp.
8 Droop
9 Rowboat's rear
10 Italian brandy
11 One getting same-day medical service, maybe
12 1960's Interior Secretary Stewart
13 "For __ sake!"
18 Low-lying land
22 Like krypton or xenon
24 Bulletin board fastener
25 Regard highly
26 Weaponry
27 Become threadbare
28 Wipe out
29 Director Robert
32 Prefix with cycle
33 Ballpark fig.
35 Art __
36 Suffix with hip or quip
38 "__ My Heart in San Francisco"
39 Summarized, as a ball game
44 Fled and wed
46 Westernmost Aleutian
47 Take a nibble at
48 Set to rest
49 Japanese immigrant
50 Singing cowboy
52 Ready for business
53 Seine tributary
54 Lose it
55 Bolt holder
58 Kids' card game
59 Tripper's problem?

by Alan Arbesfeld

ACROSS

1 Sin city
6 Ninny
9 On the double
14 "William Tell," e.g.
15 U.S.N. rank
16 Barroom brawl
17 Spot of tea?
18 Medical rarity, these days
20 Mother deer
22 Mess kit items
23 Adds an answer (with the following space)
26 Frozen confection brand
27 Zed, stateside
28 Lake ___, source of the Mississippi
34 Dyer's need
35 Cattle count
36 Like a body temperature of 98.6°
37 Contest submission (with the following space)
39 Unconscious gaze (with the preceding space)
40 False start?
42 Romances
45 Deli fish
46 Robert and Samuel
47 Publicity
48 Sheryl Crow's "___ Wanna Do"
49 War games ammo (with the preceding space)
52 Whitey, to Yogi
57 "Shave ___ haircut"
58 Hold cheap
60 Take forcibly
63 Dirt
64 Long. crosser
65 Some lumps
66 Church assembly
67 Cabinet-level dept.
68 Sporting blades

DOWN

1 Castaway's note
2 "x" a box, say
3 Kind of office
4 Brooks Robinson, for one
5 Lions' prides?
6 Otto's "oh!"
7 Spewed forth
8 Lee side
9 "I'll say!"
10 Iron pumpers develop them
11 Kyrgyzstan range
12 An amoeba has one
13 Snigglers' catches
19 Greet and seat
21 Tag info
23 Time to quit?
24 Playground rejoinder
25 Museum-funding org.
29 Prekickoff ritual
30 Pastels, e.g.
31 Like a railroad with narrow tracks
32 King of pop music
33 Joan's "Dynasty" role
35 Stevenson fiend
38 Ukr. neighbor
41 Wayne won one in 1969
42 Listen in on
43 Windsor's prov.
44 Bourbon Street vegetable
48 Makes sense
50 Dickens title starter
51 Occupied
52 Port workhorses
53 Professor 'iggins
54 Score after deuce
55 Exec's note
56 Wilbur's horse
59 Announcement before the listing of flight connections: Abbr.
61 Actress Charlotte
62 Telephone trio

by Ron O'Hair

ACROSS

1 "The Persistence of Memory" artist
5 Powerful punch
9 Clinic complaints
14 The "A" in Chester A. Arthur
15 Lawn mower brand
16 "__ Boots Are Made for Walkin'" (1966 hit)
17 Top dog
19 Make fun of
20 Bookseller __.com
21 Liberty
23 Work station
26 Pharaoh's cross
27 Gray
31 Fat compound
33 Delivery room doctors, for short
36 Cathedral topper
37 "National Velvet" author Bagnold
38 Chew (on)
39 Drooping
40 Bird-to-be
41 Pal
42 Sound heard in a cave
43 Omar of "The Mod Squad," 1999
44 Theater worker
45 Aug. follower
46 Drop in on
47 Pricker
48 Derriere
50 Wall Street inits.
52 Tool that may be hit with a hammer
55 Burning
60 Zones
61 Top dog
64 View from an overlook
65 Do magazine work
66 Opera set in Egypt
67 Cafeteria customer
68 Using metallic dishes in a microwave, e.g.
69 Not new

DOWN

1 Comic Carvey
2 Class reunion attender
3 Dalai __
4 Don Juan's mother
5 Peach pit
6 "Skip to My __"
7 Big coffee holder
8 Play around, with "off"
9 Go to
10 Place for a peck
11 Top dog
12 Exxon predecessor
13 Look
18 Dangerfield who got "no respect"
22 Surprise attack
24 Nods off
25 Top dog
27 Complete fools
28 "The final frontier"
29 Top dog
30 As a result
32 Boar's abode
34 Pie maker
35 Avowed
38 Opposite of ooze
41 C_4H_8
43 Emerald Isle
46 Formerly all-women's college in Poughkeepsie
49 Thrill
51 __ voce
52 View from the pulpit
53 Operatic song
54 Federal agts.
56 Mrs., in Munich
57 Wading bird
58 Hitchhiker's quest
59 "Goodness gracious!"
62 "If __ say so myself"
63 Wrongdoing

by Gregory E. Paul

ACROSS

1 What rodeo horses do
5 Campus building
9 Barfly's perch
14 Workout aftereffect
15 Bread spread
16 Antilles resort
17 Not aweather
18 Exclude
19 Smelly
20 What a judo master uses to break lights?
22 Be a ham
23 Writer Kafka
24 Item in a bag
25 Texas A&M athlete
28 There are seven in a semana
30 Emulates Eminem
33 Summit
35 Work like a beaver
37 Jean-___ Picard (Patrick Stewart character)
38 I
39 Paid player
41 "I don't think so"
42 Wrath
43 Suffering
44 Hindu wrap
46 Opera set in Seville
48 Blabbed to the feds, say
50 Longings
52 Conical home
53 Little piggies
55 Shrink with fear
57 "Oh, stop your joshin'!"
59 Headline about a newly discovered refuse site?
63 Paper deliverer's plan
64 Eyes a bull's-eye, say
65 Territory
66 Playwright Rice
67 White cheese
68 Bull's-eye hitter
69 John, Paul and John Paul
70 7-6, 3-6 and 6-4, e.g.
71 Blackthorn

DOWN

1 False god
2 Bruins' sch.
3 H.S. class
4 Stay in shape
5 Whoop-de-do
6 Morsel in many a chocolate bar
7 German city famous for fairs
8 A whole bunch
9 Morley of "60 Minutes"
10 Slight quake
11 Walking despite being injured?
12 Words in passing?
13 Put on, as cargo
21 Willies
24 Asimov or Stern
25 Swears
26 Where Columbus was born
27 Sound of a golf ball landing near a hole?
29 Advice columnist Landers
31 Blender button
32 Part of a play
34 Looks inside?
36 "Supposing . . ."
40 Excavation find
45 Ask
47 Prepares to fire again
49 Col. Sanders feature
51 Meeting of leaders
54 Pitchers
56 Basilica parts
57 Get ready for an exam
58 Without help
59 Touches
60 Russia's ___ Mountains
61 Fiddling emperor, they say
62 "It's a ___!"

by Tyler Hinman

ACROSS

1 "__ magic!"
4 Give a hand
8 About 60% of the world's population
14 Place for a tack
15 Busy place
16 __ in (cozy in bed)
17 Eden exile
18 Black cat, say
19 Mountain nymphs
20 Start of a wife's lament
23 Poles, e.g.
24 Society page word
25 Egyptian cobra
28 Lament, part 2
33 Sherpa sighting, maybe
34 Brazilian port
35 One of the "north 40"
39 Slowly, on a score
42 Off the mark
43 Pickler's need
45 Snack favorite
47 Lament, part 3
53 See 60-Down
54 Chaplin title
55 Louganis feats
57 End of the lament
61 "Hogan's Heroes" setting
64 Inventor's start
65 Start of many an ode's title
66 Pull in
67 Sweetums
68 "For shame!"
69 Portable homes
70 Spanish compass point
71 Printemps follower

DOWN

1 Checkout count
2 Copenhagen park
3 Plaything for two
4 Linguist Noam
5 Car with a bar, perhaps
6 State confidently
7 Brown rival
8 Yom Kippur observer
9 Walter Reed, e.g.
10 Ensures, slangily
11 Alias letters
12 Composer Rorem
13 60's college org.
21 New Deal org.
22 Having one sharp
25 Broadway opening?
26 Cousin of a herring
27 W.W. II journalist Ernie
29 Grig, when grown
30 Western tribesman
31 Burgundy grape
32 Detroit grp.
35 "Waterloo" band
36 Central point
37 Wedding, e.g.
38 Brian of the early Roxy Music
40 Robert Morse title role on Broadway
41 Anthem contraction
44 Put in shackles
46 "Most likely . . ."
48 Long fights
49 Met display
50 Have a bug
51 Actress Mimieux
52 Show to the door
56 Outpouring
57 Court foe of Bjorn
58 Camouflage
59 Dangerous time
60 With 53-Across, a cleaver
61 Posed
62 Cremona crowd?
63 Dadaism founder

by Richard Hughes

ACROSS

1 Approach with a question or remark
7 Restaurant listings
11 Sombrero, e.g.
14 Riot participant, maybe
15 Its symbol is Fe
16 Bustle
17 Metal fusers
19 Solemn promise
20 Capital on a fjord
21 Pas' mates
22 Decorate
24 Stamp sellers
27 Crop growers
31 Greek war god
32 Sign before Taurus
33 When said three times, a dance move
34 ___ to one's word
38 Peaks
42 Rams' mates
43 Topper for 60-Across
44 Opposing group
45 River to the Caspian Sea
47 Dog or cat breed
49 Be very responsive, as a car
53 Gorge
54 Glacier composition
55 Has debts
59 Hockey great Bobby
60 Kitchen vessels
64 Lawyer's payment
65 Guitarist Clapton
66 Like many a grandparent
67 Part of F.D.I.C.: Abbr.
68 Possible result of nonpayment
69 Six-line poem

DOWN

1 Besides
2 Robbers' partner
3 "Neato!"
4 Conductor Klemperer
5 Emulate Betsy Ross
6 It's earthshaking
7 Central position
8 Before, to bards
9 ". . . see hide ___ hair of"
10 Risky
11 Mayhem
12 Worship
13 Burgs
18 Girl
23 Aloof
24 Mexican moolah
25 Home to Honolulu
26 Kukla, ___ and Ollie
27 It may be tempted
28 In ___ (aligned)
29 Red, as an apple
30 Goofs
33 Fish-and-chips fish
35 Bris or confirmation
36 États-___
37 In ___ (actually)
39 Custard dessert
40 "___ 18" (Leon Uris book)
41 It may be tall
46 Toddler's jumpsuit
47 Flexible mineral
48 Changes, as the Constitution
49 Scorn
50 Full complement of Stooges or Wise Men
51 Rowed
52 Place to do the hustle
55 Makes a choice [and one more example of this puzzle's theme]
56 "Don't go yet!"
57 Feminine suffix
58 Army N.C.O.
61 Mine find
62 Overturn
63 John ___

by Sarah Keller

ACROSS

1 Shaving products
6 Wrangler's buddy
10 Deck quartet
14 Buzzards Bay, for one
15 To ___ (exactly)
16 Classic Walt Kelly strip
17 Washington flip side
18 Monticello flip side
20 Shout of adoration
22 Monkeys, apes and such
23 Is imminent
25 Zero
26 Bad to the bone
29 Bonnet securer
31 In vitro items
34 Dunce cap-shaped
36 Fill to the gills
37 San Francisco's ___ Hill
38 Memorial flip side
41 Presidential seal flip side
43 Pub order
44 Turndowns
46 Shipbuilders' woods
47 Driveway surface
48 Shows contempt
51 12/25
52 It's found in a pound
53 Bee product?
55 A Little Rascal
59 One of the Fondas
63 Sacagawea flip side
65 Roosevelt flip side
66 Thin nail
67 It's flipped in this puzzle
68 Fuss
69 Nervous
70 Extremities
71 Grain disease

DOWN

1 Dangle poles over a pier, say
2 Not deceived by
3 Word for Yorick
4 Tinny-sounding
5 Shorthand taker, for short
6 Kind of top or party
7 Polished off
8 Makes calls on the court
9 Clear-cut
10 Fool's month
11 ___ Nostra
12 Designer von Furstenberg
13 Princes, e.g.
19 ___ domain
21 Drama with masks
24 They go around the block: Abbr.
26 Great applause
27 "There!"
28 Centerward
30 Karachi's land: Abbr.
31 A wee hr.
32 Bullshot ingredient
33 Deep pit
35 Television cabinet
39 Sullen expression
40 Bridal bio word
42 Like a close neighbor
45 Et ___ (and the following): Abbr.
49 "Venus and Adonis" painter
50 What to call a knight
52 Papa
54 Flexible, as a body
55 Singer Lane
56 Fat in a can
57 Stars and Stripes, e.g.
58 1957 Stravinsky ballet
60 Old-time sailor's drink
61 Bounceback
62 "___ does it!"
64 Topper

by John Underwood

ACROSS

1 Out of business
5 Like lions
10 Eyes
14 Singer Amos
15 Celebrity's concern
16 Tide variety
17 Pg. in a photocopier
18 Kind of chart
19 Paul feminizer
20 Thought favorably of
22 Magnate
23 Like most N.B.A. stars
24 Marzipan ingredient
25 "Prove it!"
28 Learned one
30 Leonardo da Vinci's "___ and the Swan"
31 "Heroic Stanzas," for one
37 Rainbow: Prefix
39 "Exodus" hero ___ Ben Canaan
40 TV's ___ Gillis
41 Putting the squeeze on
44 Nick at ___
45 Realm
46 Trying experience
48 Quit
52 Siouan people
53 Con ___ (lovingly)
54 Gimcracks
59 Kudrow of "Friends"
60 Fictional ringbearer
61 Ridge on a guitar neck
62 Map
63 Extend
64 Arm bone
65 Mr. of 19th-century fiction
66 Hanker (for)
67 Where the Rhone and the Saône meet

DOWN

1 Put aboard
2 Round dance
3 "Exodus" author
4 Penny pinchers
5 Was sociable at a party
6 "___ and the Night Visitors"
7 Growing alliance
8 New York archbishop Edward
9 Viña ___ Mar
10 Late bedtime
11 Like bell-bottoms
12 Conductor's wand
13 Be the opposite of 4-Down
21 "___ a Rock" (1966 hit)
22 Amalgam
24 Time in history
25 Boo-boo
26 German "Mr."
27 Cartoon dog
28 Mideast land
29 Situation favoring the server
32 Hard to find
33 Awe-inspiring
34 Theater award
35 Meter maid of song
36 It goes from stem to stern
38 River that feeds the Missouri
42 Samovar
43 Was natural and unrestrained, slangily
47 Caviar
48 Designer Lauren
49 Watson of "Gosford Park"
50 1960 Everly Brothers hit
51 Angry
52 Closer to retirement
54 Lacking plans
55 Mrs. Chaplin
56 Paris taxi destination, maybe
57 He's seen late
58 Hockey great Mikita
60 Swelter

by Alan Arbesfeld

ACROSS

1 ___ Vegas
4 Fisherman
10 Hit, as one's toe
14 AOL, e.g.: Abbr.
15 Harangue
16 Llama's land
17 Building wing
18 Iroquois Indian
19 Put up, as a picture
20 Earthquake measurer
23 Bowling target
24 Story that's "to be continued"
27 Sight-related
28 Ewe's mate
31 Five: Prefix
32 Fred Flintstone and others
35 Request after an auto breakdown
36 Carry-on bags have them
41 That: Sp.
42 See "damp" instead of "clamp," e.g.
43 Run off to wed
46 However, informally
47 Wasp homes
51 Sharp comeback
53 Christie of mystery
54 "Ahhh" and "Whew, that was close!"
58 Sentence subject, usually
60 Come by
61 Basic cleaner
62 Turnpike turn-off
63 Tiny acorn, e.g.
64 RCA and Panasonic products
65 The "B" in KB and MB
66 Rounded hills
67 Word before "Go!"

DOWN

1 Isn't straight up with
2 Catching z's
3 Broken finger support
4 Consisting of tiny bits
5 Sheer fabric
6 Actor Kinnear
7 Den
8 Icelandic literary work
9 Harvests
10 Globe
11 Attack aggressively
12 Cider server
13 Locust or beetle
21 Enliven, with "up"
22 With it, man
25 Heaps
26 Subjects of Congressional debate
28 Send in payment
29 Group in Lancaster County, Pa.
30 Washington transit system, with "the"
33 Vigor's partner
34 Scot's refusal
36 Fortuneteller
37 South Seas locale
38 Snazzy 1940's attire
39 Off-topic ramblings
40 Perfect
44 Grosse ___, Mich.
45 Work unit
48 Circus props
49 "Look What ___ Done to My Song, Ma" (1970 hit)
50 Least risky
52 Show gratitude to
53 The Little Mermaid
55 "Star Trek" weapon setting
56 "Beetle Bailey" dog
57 Take a tumble
58 Omaha's state: Abbr.
59 Prefix with acetylene

by Jim Hyres

ACROSS

1 Almanac contents
6 Book of memories, maybe
11 Big shot, for short
14 Love to bits
15 Numbers-calling game
16 67.5°, to mariners
17 Grant provider
18 Route to prison?
20 Campus locale
22 This very moment
23 Concertgoer's keepsake
25 English race place
28 Load of bunk
29 Fall (over)
30 Courts
31 Fracas
32 Like apples, say, during the fall
34 You can lend it or bend it
35 Blaster's need
36 Book in prison?
38 It's hailed
41 Rep.'s counterpart
42 Over again
44 Flies, ants and such
47 The Beatles' "Hey ___"
48 Like Nash's lama
49 Nay sayer
50 Neigh sayer
51 Track shape
52 Unofficial ticket source
54 Desperate
56 Money in prison?
59 X-rated, say
62 Wood-dressing tool
63 Grind, as teeth
64 Come after
65 Where to hear 10-Down
66 ___ Domingo
67 007, for one

DOWN

1 Furbys, once
2 Hoo-ha
3 Escape from prison?
4 Hot water, so to speak
5 Word repeated after "Qué"
6 Epitome of simplicity
7 Celestial feline
8 Pickers' instruments
9 Full-length
10 Cows' chorus
11 Of the spring
12 Shoe part
13 Nickname for a little guy
19 Out-and-out
21 Former "Family Feud" host Richard
23 "S.N.L." bit
24 T.V.A. part: Abbr.
26 "Any day now . . ."
27 Look around a prison?
31 Chess ending
33 Ideal serves
34 Go beyond the bounds of
37 Puts a stop to
38 Poetry in prison?
39 Geometric calculation
40 Period ender
41 Pink-legged bird
43 Ship's securer
44 Mathematician Blaise
45 Make cryptic
46 Quatrain or sestet
47 Michael who was five-time N.B.A. M.V.P.
50 Salon color
53 Cribbage needs
55 Light bulb's signification, in cartoons
57 World record suffix
58 P on a fraternity house
60 Winery cask
61 "Is it soup ___?"

by Tyler Hinman

ACROSS

1 Blows away
5 Turkish title
8 Apollo 15 astronaut James ___
13 Call
14 Agatha contemporary
16 Bonehead
17 Cherubic child
19 "___ funny, McGee!"
20 It may follow a bench-clearing
21 Change form
23 Water tester
24 Cavalier
27 Language suffix
28 Not sober
31 Med. readout
34 Wordsmith Webster
38 R.E.M. singer Michael
39 Imminent disaster
43 Brunei native
44 Axis leader
45 Comics scream
46 Place for an O. Henry surprise
48 Jolson and Jarreau
51 Far from buxom
57 Dian Fossey subject
59 Sub system
60 Auto option
62 Commit a deadly sin
64 Powerful politico
66 Fragrant resin
67 Father-and-daughter boxers
68 Metric prefix
69 Column type
70 Place for a FISH (which is a hint to this puzzle's theme)
71 Sets a price of

DOWN

1 First of all
2 Regaled, in a way
3 Links rarity
4 Record protector
5 Gen. Pershing's troops: Abbr.
6 Texas politico Phil
7 Major maker of beverage cans
8 "Oh, yeah?"
9 Sony rival
10 It flows to Khartoum
11 "___ expert, but . . ."
12 Sol, say
15 Mysterious: Var.
18 Fragrant rings
22 Gateway products
25 One who follows the news
26 O.C.S. relative
29 Olympics event
30 Pigeonhole's place
31 Salinger heroine
32 Skater Michelle
33 Cause of a rush
35 Frequently, in verse
36 Fuss
37 "The ___" (Uris novel)
40 Object bitterly
41 Like the Romanovs
42 Old Testament kingdom
47 Old muscle car
49 Good earth
50 Lipton rival
52 "My Way" writer
53 Leaves port
54 Tom's "Roseanne" role
55 Croupiers' gear
56 Inferior merchandise
57 Breezed through
58 Traveler to Cathay
61 M.D.'s diagnostic tools
63 British record label
65 Federal purchasing org.

by Merle Baker

ACROSS

1 Polio vaccine developer
5 "Step aside, I'll do it"
10 Unexciting
14 Have ___ to one's head
15 Bird-related
16 Where Pearl Harbor is
17 Popular cookbook author
19 "Thin" coin
20 Come into view
21 Emergency situation
23 Lock opener
24 Lock location
27 Scott Joplin's "Maple Leaf ___"
28 Lad
33 Muckety-muck
36 "Bolero" composer
37 Advance in years
38 Isn't solvent
39 Dove houses
40 What's harvested
41 Remote control abbr.
42 Filmmaker Woody
43 "If you ___" (words of deference)
44 Worked up
47 Fuel additive
48 Manipulative one
49 File folder feature
52 Excellence
56 Formally renounce
58 ___ Minor (constellation)
59 Somerset Maugham novel, with "The"
62 Mideast's Gulf of ___
63 Native Alaskan
64 Like a lime
65 Pair
66 Duke, earl, etc.
67 Three, in cards

DOWN

1 Game show host Pat
2 With mouth wide open
3 Like some gravy and mattresses
4 Midleg
5 Maze runner
6 Preceding day
7 ___ Maria liqueur
8 ___ Antony
9 Signs, as a check
10 Spanish grocery
11 Den
12 "Life is hard . . ."
13 Colored
18 Englishman in colonial India
22 Author Roald
25 Take a walk
26 Flat part of a chart line
28 ___ Alamos, N.M.
29 Occasions
30 Differentiate
31 Modest people have small ones
32 Possible result of 40-Down nonpayment
33 Exploding star
34 Delinquent G.I.
35 Carillon part
39 Nonsense
40 Auto
42 Opposing
43 Most Yugoslavs
45 Cuba, e.g.
46 Red suit
49 Elizabeth I was the last one
50 Present a case in court
51 Drunken
52 Triplet plus one
53 Language of Pakistan
54 Out of sight of shore
55 Bush's alma mater
57 Joke
60 Zuider ___
61 Your and my

by David Bunker

ACROSS

1 Passing fancies
6 Cathedral area
10 End-of-week cry
14 Greek column style
15 Fishing rod attachment
16 Roughly
17 Split
20 M.D.'s work in them
21 "Yummy!"
22 "This means ___!"
23 Home of the N.L.'s Cards
24 Sleep medication
26 Bartenders check them: Abbr.
28 Split
34 Earth tone
35 Mag. staff
36 Slap shot success
37 Not just aloof
38 Closes tight
42 Dangerous sprayer
43 Runners' units
45 601, to Nero
46 Brought on board
48 Split
52 "That means ___!"
53 Actor William of "Yanks"
54 Cooking spray brand
56 Mercury, but not Mars
58 Metal container
59 Bud's comic buddy
62 Split
66 Like poor losers
67 Itsy-bitsy bug
68 Golfer Palmer, informally
69 "The Untouchables" extras
70 Wallet padding
71 Bill from a computer company?

DOWN

1 Smart-alecky
2 Happy ___
3 Travelers' stopovers
4 Prefix with night or day
5 Runs like a rabbit
6 Coffee shop lures
7 Check endorser's need
8 Kelp and others
9 Island near Corsica
10 Unit of bricks
11 Wimbledon venue
12 "Winning ___ everything"
13 Babe in the stable
18 Arab ruler
19 Like Death Valley
24 Corrida cry
25 Something that may be hard to hold
27 Statesman Hammarskjöld
28 Gets really steamed
29 Philosopher William of ___
30 Discounter's pitch
31 Tempe sch.
32 Old sitcom maid
33 Say "Li'l Abner," say
39 One of eight Eng. kings
40 Environmental problem
41 Game "played" with answering machines
44 ___-mo
47 Suffix with Canaan
49 Gambler's need
50 Calls to mind
51 Like a skinny-dipper
54 Verbal nudge
55 It's smashed in a lab
57 BB's and bullets
59 Period of penitence
60 Something that hurts, slangily
61 Applications
63 Long time: Abbr.
64 Numbered hwy.
65 Org. for people with arms

by Nancy Salomon and Harvey Estes

ACROSS

1 Your role in this puzzle [the asterisked clues will help you crack the case]
4 *Suspected means of entry
11 No Miss America
14 Org. in Langley, Va.
15 Finders' fees
16 Chemical suffix
17 Done with a wink
18 Period in human development
19 Regular guy
20 American Beauty growth
22 Not real
24 Storage facilities
25 Big: Abbr.
27 Cause for an aspirin
28 New York cardinal
29 Major oil port
30 "Wild" one
31 Italian town with Giotto frescoes
33 Meat seasoning
35 Namesake makers: Abbr.
36 *When the break-in occurred
39 Copycat
42 This, in España
43 Stop for the night
47 Asian assassin
49 Garden with a snake
51 NASA's ___ Research Center
52 Garr of "Young Frankenstein"
53 Bag thickness
54 Port in western France
55 Nukes
58 Roofers, often
60 Lo-___
61 Site of an unwanted duty
63 Three on a clock
65 Suffering
66 Adjusts
67 Elevator ___
68 Person who does a lot of cleaning: Abbr.
69 *What the intruder accidentally left behind
70 What you may say when you crack the case

DOWN

1 Syringe amt.
2 Offshore workplaces
3 Commercial bribes
4 "Hurray!" and "Oh, no!"
5 33-Across, e.g.
6 "If asked, yes"
7 *Eyewitness's description of the intruder
8 1930's program, for short
9 Ragged part
10 Belgian river
11 Takes by force
12 Bar order
13 Old dogs
21 Kind of boom
23 ___ Paulo
24 Marine
26 Little biter
29 What a snob might put on
30 Shepherd who wrote "The Ferrari in the Bedroom"
32 Flushing site
34 Feds
37 Some thing
38 Startle
39 It may settle things
40 Spotted, as a horse
41 Matriculates
44 Its third verse begins "Let music swell the breeze"
45 Handel work
46 L.A. setting
48 "Treasure Island" boy
50 "Seinfeld" pal
54 "God ___"
56 Convention group
57 Indian garb
59 Like some verbs: Abbr.
62 Bolivian export
64 Kind of contribution

by Patrick Merrell

ACROSS

1 Sultan of ___ (Babe Ruth)
5 Gaming table stacks
9 Tease
14 Roof's edge
15 Leave out
16 Performer with a painted-on smile
17 Bygone times
18 Conceal
19 HBO deliverer
20 "You said it!"
23 September bloom
24 Royal residences
28 Knave
32 Tex-Mex snack
33 "Stop right there!"
37 Dry-as-dust
38 Short flight
39 Oceanographic charts
42 Comedian's bit
43 Currier's partner in lithography
45 "Uh-uh!"
47 Mother ___ (Nobel-winning nun)
50 Siesta sound
51 Stretchy, as a waistband
53 Notre Dame's Fighting ___
57 "I'm afraid not!"
61 Madcap
64 Seep (out)
65 Smidgen
66 Apple laptop
67 Eve's man
68 Demonic
69 Hollywood's DeVito or Glover
70 Ballfield cover
71 Byrd and Hatch, e.g.: Abbr.

DOWN

1 "Ta-ta"
2 Merchandise
3 "Halt!," at sea
4 Mosaic piece
5 Physicist Niels
6 Mideast prince
7 An almanac lists its highs and lows
8 Prepare, as tea
9 Pepsi competitor
10 Mobile home?
11 Big hunk
12 "Wise" bird
13 SSW's reverse
21 Leg shackles
22 Cave dweller
25 It goes in the hold
26 Sewing machine inventor Howe
27 Everglades grass
29 "You could've knocked me over with a feather!"
30 ___ Bator, Mongolia
31 St. ___ fire
33 Snowlike
34 It's no mansion
35 "Tosca," e.g.
36 Sign of boredom
40 Kung ___ shrimp
41 Neighbor of Israel
44 College period
46 Axis soldiers
48 Thickset
49 Lungful
52 Zagreb resident
54 1974 Tom T. Hall hit
55 Peaceful protest
56 Gets better, as a wound
58 Mentor for Luke Skywalker
59 Ivan, for one
60 Rope material
61 Grant-in-___
62 Org. for the Nets and Nuggets
63 Ship's weight unit

by Gregory E. Paul

106

ACROSS

1 Pat Boone's "___ Love"
6 Symbol of redness
10 Norway's patron saint
14 Cranberry product
15 Brand for Bowser
16 Place to stack money
17 35-Across, from 1955–61
19 Finish line, perhaps
20 Windy City trains
21 Gist
22 Hindu royal: Var.
23 35-Across in 1964
27 Syndicate head
30 Program airing
31 One who opens a can of worms?
34 Hospitalized patient's state
35 See 17-, 23-, 48- and 57-Across
41 Otherwise
42 City opposite Ciudad Juárez
43 Issues in paperback, perhaps
47 Barely managed, with "out"
48 35-Across in 1994
51 Carroll girl
52 Spawner in the Sargasso Sea
53 One way to the WWW
56 Actor Moranis
57 35-Across in 1946
61 Allot, with "out"
62 "The Morning Watch" author
63 Ear or tube preceder
64 Gofer: Abbr.
65 Marquand's Mr.
66 Approaches

DOWN

1 Court great Arthur
2 One of the Fab Four
3 Hairpieces, slangily
4 "___ bin ein Berliner"
5 Hotelier Helmsley
6 Its stakes may be a beer
7 Inventor Whitney
8 It rates m.p.g.
9 Whole bunch
10 Chief Pontiac, e.g.
11 Tropical vines
12 Trumpeter Herb
13 Admiral's force
18 Bowery ___
22 Carmaker's woe
23 Finger-in-the-socket consequence
24 Spies seek them
25 Swill
26 Fiesta Bowl site
27 Crow's sound
28 "___ number can play"
29 Links org.
32 Forever, poetically
33 Vestige
36 "It comes ___ surprise"
37 Mimicker
38 Talk, talk, talk
39 Cleveland-to-Baltimore dir.
40 Serling of "The Twilight Zone"
43 Depends (on)
44 Forces out
45 Striker, often
46 Sound system
48 Destiny
49 Napoleonic marshal
50 Spritelike
53 Visitor to Siam
54 German border river
55 Unseen "Many Tyler Moore Show" character
57 ___ and Swiss
58 Swelled head
59 Court divider
60 Common lunchtime

by Gene Newman

ACROSS

1 Santa Anna at the Alamo, e.g.
9 "Dixie" composer
15 Judge too highly
16 Like a big grin
17 Start of a comment on a popular adage
18 Cries of pain
19 Papas on the screen
20 "The Mikado" accessories
22 "What was ___ do?"
23 To be, to Bernadette
24 Comment, part 2
27 It may be raw
29 Hind, e.g.
30 C.S.A. state
33 Response to an insult
35 Hammett pooch
39 Comment, part 3
44 Rest area sight
45 Favor one side?
46 Thus far
47 "You betcha!"
51 South Vietnam's Ngo Dinh ___
53 Comment, part 4
57 Certain column
61 Just fine
62 Regarding
63 Hand warmer?
64 Ascended
66 End of the comment
69 Not so remote
70 Bombarding
71 Take stock of
72 Brunch order

DOWN

1 Alamo defender
2 Three-time Wimbledon champ
3 Setting for a famous "Les Misérables" scene
4 Smoothed (out)
5 Seaside raptor
6 Flit about
7 Hot time in Paris
8 Arrange into new lines
9 Star of France
10 Chilled dessert
11 Soft shoe
12 Set of principles
13 Certain sorority woman
14 Iron Mike
21 Oyster's home
24 Circle overhead?
25 Norwegian king
26 Part of Q.E.D.
28 Sigmoid shape
30 They may be crunched in a gym
31 Get prone
32 Usher's offering
34 Bud
36 Short
37 Pipe joint
38 Frick collection
40 45, e.g.
41 Friend of Rover
42 Send forth
43 Bad way to go?
48 Czars' edicts
49 Stair parts
50 Young newt
52 Mark with blotches
53 Zoologist's study
54 Bounds along
55 Podded plants
56 "___ fast!"
58 Like seven Ryan games
59 Marathon, e.g.
60 Conductor Koussevitzky
63 It may be hard or soft
65 Vein find
67 Resistance unit
68 "I'm impressed!"

by Ed Early

ACROSS

1 First father
5 "Voilá!"
10 Vocalized
14 Characteristic carrier
15 Pass along
16 ". . . with a banjo on my ___"
17 With 59-Across, indication of caring
19 Author Turgenev
20 ___ Deco
21 Prefix with dynamic
22 Football great Favre
23 Indication of larceny
27 Declares
29 "___ Gang"
30 Caustic chemical
31 18-wheeler
32 Test, as ore
34 Indication of detachment
41 Bing, bang or boom
42 Future attorney's hurdle: Abbr.
43 Appropriate
46 U.S. or Can. money
47 Like an oboe's sound
48 Indication of opportunity
53 Plant life
54 Quark's place
55 Place to retire
58 Jazz's Fitzgerald
59 See 17-Across
62 Like some dorms
63 Patronized, as a restaurant
64 Starting from
65 It ebbs and flows
66 Tiny poker stake
67 Having an angle

DOWN

1 Turkish title
2 Does and bucks
3 Object of loathing
4 Debussy's "La ___"
5 True's partner
6 Painter Matisse
7 Rock's ___ John
8 Stadium sound
9 Watch closely
10 Blouse accompanier
11 Show, as plans
12 With precision
13 Tamed
18 Gets some color, as they say
22 Gem mineral
24 Like the Sahara
25 ". . . off ___ the wizard"
26 1950's Communist-hunting grp.
27 Cigarette's end
28 Two-finger sign
32 Leaning
33 Sounds from a librarian
35 Delhi's land
36 It follows 11
37 Butter alternative
38 Computer company's customers
39 Father
40 Where hogs wallow
43 Have an influence on
44 Hoi ___
45 Drove (along)
47 Frolic
49 Give and take?
50 Broadway actress Uta
51 Wharton's "___ Frome"
52 Daft
56 Supply-and-demand subj.
57 Skillful
59 Perform like Salt-N-Pepa
60 Suffix with Manhattan
61 Place for beakers

by Sarah Keller

ACROSS

1 Network with an eye logo
4 Call bad names
10 High school class
14 Santa ___, Calif.
15 Twist-filled Broadway musical?
16 Vito Corleone's creator
17 Bedouin at a major waterway?
20 Not-so-secret secret language
21 Pirate rival
22 Chemical suffix
23 Cracker Jack bonus
25 Cloud's place
26 Rounded lump
29 Harshly criticize
31 Light sailboat at a hotel chain?
39 Indian prince in Mobile?
40 Tales about a 1980's singing group?
41 Actress Garr
42 ___ Flynn Boyle of "The Practice"
43 Tachometer abbr.
46 Performed
47 Magazine revenue source
49 Run for one's wife?
51 Sweetie
56 Gilda Radner character's embodiment?
59 Mideast guns
60 Paparazzo's device
61 In the past
62 Pretzel topper
63 Dissertation
64 "Help!"

DOWN

1 Andy of the comics
2 ___ B'rith
3 Turned state's evidence
4 Like some noses and numerals
5 Overjoy
6 "Veni, vidi, ___"
7 Tennis great Lendl
8 Spy novelist Deighton
9 Pitcher's stat.
10 Luxury resorts
11 Smarts
12 Arkansas's ___ Mountains
13 New Orleans sandwich
18 "Open, sesame!" speaker
19 Set down
23 Japanese floor covering
24 Missouri River city
26 Snatch
27 In ___ land
28 Neighbor of Yemen
29 Chicken
30 Missouri town where Harry Truman was born
32 Actor Aykroyd
33 Noted Italian violinmaker
34 More, in Madrid
35 Body of water between Kazakhstan and Uzbekistan
36 Hindu music form
37 Not fully shut
38 Space shuttle org.
43 Picture puzzle
44 Public square
45 Big gas brand
46 Frost relative
47 Early video game company
48 Famously temperamental singers
50 Future's opposite
51 Arrived
52 Employs
53 School orgs.
54 "Othello" villain
55 God of love
57 Play part
58 When repeated, a trombone sound

by Peter Gordon

ACROSS

1 Clipper feature
5 "Hogwash!"
10 Coventry cleaner
14 Cousin of a hawk
15 Up the ante
16 Take on
17 Improve one's golf game?
20 Marbles, so to speak
21 Jukebox favorite
22 Barely miss, as the golf cup
25 Hatcher of "Desperate Housewives"
26 Grammy-winner Black
27 Meter reading
29 Son of Cain
32 Heads downtown?
34 Sticky stuff
35 Like some noodle dishes
39 Inexperienced golfers?
42 Links rarities
43 Cheer
44 Hardly cheery
45 1996 A.L. rookie of the year
47 Composer's basis
48 Bewildered
52 First name in Polish politics
54 Mach 1 breaker
55 Common fraternity activity
56 Friend of Pooh
58 Taking one's time on the green?
63 Wanton look
64 Olympics broadcaster Jim
65 Mary Kay competitor
66 Little spin
67 Edges (out)
68 Duchamp's movement

DOWN

1 Schuss, e.g.
2 Cause of inflation?
3 Midori on the ice
4 Place for a cap
5 Kind of danish
6 Many a Swift work
7 Playing golf
8 Unhealthy-looking
9 Minute
10 "Relax, bro!"
11 Language from which "thug" is derived
12 Alan of "Gattaca"
13 PlayStation button
18 Horse operas
19 "How'm I doin'?" asker
22 Arthur Murray lesson
23 Father of Esau
24 Noncommittal response
28 Takes off
30 "That's amazing!"
31 Like Vassar, now
33 Beget
35 Brit's "Baloney!"
36 Zeroes (in on)
37 First vice president
38 ___ of Langerhans (pancreas part)
40 Rebellious Turner
41 Become wizened
45 Hemingway's Barnes
46 Rasta's music
48 iPod maker
49 Made level
50 Beyond full
51 Diary bit
53 Potter's buys
56 Trillionth: Prefix
57 Warty hopper
59 Loser to J.F.K.
60 Charlottesville sch.
61 Approval of sorts
62 Genomic matter

by James Rogers

ACROSS

1 Health resorts
5 TV series with Hawkeye and Hot Lips
9 Aspirin maker
14 N.Y.S.E. listing
15 Nabisco cookie
16 Miss Doolittle of "My Fair Lady"
17 Large section in an atlas
18 Thumbtack, British-style
20 Error
22 Office message
23 Drunkard
24 Church bell spot
26 Fall in scattered drops, as rain
28 Boot camp reply
30 Not on the road
34 Sheets and pillowcases
37 Sandwich shop
39 Restaurant chain acronym
40 Immediately, after "at"
41 Job title (giving a hint to this puzzle's theme)
42 Gooey ground
43 Hearty drink made with honey
44 Center of a Christmas display
45 Hearty steak
46 Flowering shrub
48 Water at the mouth
50 One-named Irish singer
52 Avenues
56 "What's the ___?"
59 Reps.' foes
61 Bluesman ___ Wolf
62 Well-worn
65 German "a"
66 Art stand
67 Fiction teller

68 R & B/jazz singer James
69 Beach souvenir
70 Stately trees
71 Work station

DOWN

1 Rip-offs
2 Put
3 Get up
4 Seattle landmark
5 Catwalk walkers
6 The "A" in E.T.A.: Abbr.
7 Line made by a 41-Across
8 Inventor Elias and others
9 Marathon runner Joan
10 High school math: Abbr.
11 Puppy sounds
12 Operatic singer Pinza
13 Long, angry complaint
19 Damage
21 Atop
25 Duck down?
27 White-flowered plant
29 Marry again
31 Cincinnati's home
32 Time starting at dawn
33 Fencing rapier
34 ___ Linda, Calif.
35 "Il Trovatore" soprano

36 Interscholastic sports org.
38 Lecherous looks
41 Stuck around
45 Bull in a bullring
47 Ultimate purpose
49 Additional ones
51 Walk
53 Best of the best
54 Salon jobs
55 ___ preview
56 Tableland tribe
57 Iranian "king"
58 Scots Gaelic
60 Flying jib, e.g.
63 Electric fish
64 Hit head-on

by Gregory E. Paul

112

ACROSS

1 Part of Q.E.D.
5 Contradict
10 "You can say that again!"
14 Mascara site
15 Ain't correct?
16 What the fourth little piggy got
17 Take the bait
18 Construction playthings
20 Like Mickey Mouse
22 Coup __
23 Metric measure
24 __ Solo of "Star Wars"
25 Like some suits
31 Houston-based org.
35 Bikini, e.g.
36 Way off
37 Play starter
38 Warmed the bench
39 Author connected to this puzzle's theme
42 Sushi offering
43 Verbal assault
45 Emporium event
46 Michaels of "Saturday Night Live"
48 Literary lioness
49 Shirelles hit of 1962
51 Pathet __
53 First U.S. color TV maker
54 Taxpayer's dread
57 Part of L.E.D.
62 Crow's-nest instruments
65 Lionel train layout, maybe
66 "Nana" star Anna
67 Fake jewelry
68 Declare "good" or "excellent," say
69 Drops off
70 Grace word
71 Snick and __

DOWN

1 Alabama county seat named for a European island
2 Wet forecast
3 Italian wine town
4 Teen's hangout, perhaps
5 One who's up
6 Canal of song
7 Do banker's work
8 Publicity
9 When Dijon gets hot
10 Pre-cable need
11 Like some points
12 New Age singer
13 Branch headquarters?
19 Nutritional fig.
21 On __ (doing well)
24 München mister
25 Café holder
26 Whatsoever
27 Tiny bits
28 Port near Hong Kong
29 Headed for __ (in imminent trouble)
30 Wasn't afraid
32 Sharp-tongued
33 Pool person
34 Alvin of dance
40 Flying A competitor
41 Opt
44 Bad-mouths
47 Spellbinders
50 Pigmented eye parts
52 Part of A & P: Abbr.
54 Org.
55 Until
56 Turned blue, maybe
57 To be, to Brutus
58 1969 miracle team
59 Terrible man?
60 Hoopster Archibald
61 __ club
63 Msg. sent to squad cars
64 Mineo of film

by Adam G. Perl

ACROSS

1 Not telling
4 Drink before bed, maybe
9 Belt clip-on
14 Part of a World Cup chant
15 Sister of Terpsichore
16 Squirreled-away item
17 Merkel of old movies
18 Irish symbol
20 Time off, briefly
22 Fuller than full
23 Bottom line
27 Something to draw from
30 ___ fille (French girl)
31 Society Islands island
34 Item in a thimblerig game
37 Fixes, in a way
39 Exorcist's quarry
40 Like a snap decision
44 Lines man?
45 "You've got a deal!"
46 Huge expanse
47 Tastelessly affected
49 Christina of "The Opposite of Sex"
52 Letters at a Nascar race
53 Commodity in the old South
58 Strand in winter, maybe
61 Grenoble's river
62 Informal discussion
67 Subj. of this puzzle's theme
68 Healing plants
69 Leave out, in speech
70 "Get comfy"
71 "Same here"
72 In shape
73 D.D.E.'s W.W. II command

DOWN

1 Opposite of celebrate
2 Carpi connectors
3 Stood for
4 It's the law
5 Palindrome center
6 Nutritional fig.
7 A.B.A. member: Abbr.
8 Impose (on)
9 Munich ___ of 1938
10 One to grow on?
11 Esther Rolle sitcom
12 Hosp. areas
13 12-Down staffers
19 Start angling
21 Basketball Hall of Fame nickname
24 Beach lapper
25 Condos, e.g.
26 Chicken breed
28 Make amends
29 Ship commanded by Pinzón
32 Hubbub
33 Confine, with "in"
34 Jrs.' exams
35 ___ Center
36 Cockpit aid
38 Baseball's Bud
41 Baloney
42 Montana's motto starter
43 1700
48 "The Grapes of Wrath" figure
50 Invented
51 T.G.I.F. part
54 Atlas feature
55 High-strung
56 Go around in circles?
57 "Cool!"
59 1963 role for Liz
60 Big name in petrol
62 "Batman" sound
63 Relative of -let
64 Highway warning
65 "Boy, am ___ trouble!"
66 Lofty lines

by Brendan Emmett Quigley

ACROSS

1 Put off, as a motion
6 Life stories, for short
10 Poison ivy symptom
14 Trojan War epic
15 As a twosome, musically
16 Initial stake
17 "Norma Rae" director
19 London privies
20 Extra wager
21 Tennis champ Pete
23 The "L" of L.C.D.
25 "___ to break it to you, but . . ."
26 Horticulturist who developed the Shasta daisy
31 Sky color, in Paris
32 Terra ___
33 Noted French Dadaist
37 Was remunerative
41 Princess topper
43 Writer ___ Stanley Gardner
44 1965 Roger Miller hit
48 In the midst of
50 Group of three
51 A truck may go uphill in it
53 "College" member who votes for president
58 Frist's predecessor as Senate majority leader
59 It may follow grade school
61 Ending for buck
62 Tennis score after deuce
63 City in northern France
64 Cut, as wood
65 Dems.' foes
66 Cosmetician Lauder

DOWN

1 Actors Robbins and Allen
2 Jai ___
3 Nest builder
4 After midnight, say
5 Fit to be eaten
6 Drinker's total
7 Dictator Amin
8 Surpass
9 ___ good example
10 2000 Green Party candidate
11 Polar jacket
12 Summer ermine
13 Hermann who wrote "Steppenwolf"
18 ___-do-well
22 City near Fort Lauderdale
24 "-er" or "-ing," e.g.: Abbr.
26 J.F.K.'s successor
27 Ending with sched-
28 Oolong, for one
29 Coal-mining city of West Virginia
30 Hidden means of support?
34 Former N.B.A. star Danny
35 Scott Joplin piece
36 Stick out
38 Spanish gold
39 22-Down's state: Abbr.
40 Nourished
42 Mozambique's locale: Abbr.
44 Be obsequious (to)
45 Connections
46 Ring up?
47 Channel swimmer Gertrude
48 To whom Muslims pray
49 007 player Roger
52 Barely open
54 X's, in Greece
55 Lean slightly
56 Eye amorously
57 Korean leader Syngman ___
60 Light bite

by Alan Arbesfeld

ACROSS

1 Airline to Tel Aviv
5 Soothing spots
9 Pueblo dwelling
14 Broadway Auntie
15 Strait-laced
16 Like a highway
17 Some bargains
20 ___ Sark
21 Make use of
22 Trident feature
23 Sweetie
24 Top rating, perhaps
26 ___ room
28 Diamond ___
29 Not the finest dog
31 Be an agent (for)
33 Dukes and earls
35 Prefix with graphic
37 Punk's pistol
39 Overly ominous
43 Scarsdale, e.g., to New York City
44 Dummy Mortimer
46 "Honor Thy Father" author
49 Part of S.P.C.A.: Abbr.
51 Door sign
52 Maugham's "Cakes and ___"
53 Look over
55 A bartender may run one
57 42-Down scores: Abbr.
58 Ella Fitzgerald specialty
60 "Slippery" tree
62 "___ beaucoup"
64 Reelection toast?
68 Happening
69 Devil's doings
70 Starting from
71 Turn blue, maybe
72 Cincinnati team
73 TV host who wrote "Leading With My Chin"

DOWN

1 C.P.R. expert
2 Where some suits are pressed
3 Be the equivalent of
4 Hit the road
5 More agile
6 In favor
7 "Say it ___ so!"
8 Sling mud at
9 Sitcom extraterrestrial
10 Off one's trolley
11 Tip of Massachusetts
12 Songwriter Taupin
13 Classic Fords
18 Mel of the Polo Grounds
19 Willing to try
23 Patient-care grp.
25 Associate of Gandhi
27 Yale students starting in 1969
30 Not these
32 Jury's makeup
34 Pickling need
36 Helpful
38 Monastery head
40 Compliant one
41 Cry heard in a 2-Down
42 Where Giants and Titans clash
45 Skid row woe
46 Wine expert
47 Dinette set spot
48 Flipped (through)
50 Desert ruminants
54 Bugs bugged him
56 Former Tunisian ruler
59 Cousin of an Obie
61 Pull up stakes
63 "Get ___!"
65 Western native
66 Free (of)
67 Bay area airport letters

by Richard Chisholm

ACROSS

1 Followers of Tyler and Taylor
6 One-inch pencil, say
9 To boot
13 So out it's in
14 Home to José
15 Place
16 See 48-Across
17 Hurl a barb at
18 Sacred creatures of old
19 Woodworker's own tool?
22 Oxy-5 target
23 Takes off
24 Main lines
26 Boxing Day's mo.
29 Place for a ring
30 Deliver by chute
31 Son of Aphrodite
33 City north of Nancy
35 Trash hauler
38 1990's civil war site
40 Losing purposely
42 Jam producer?
43 Voice mail prompt
45 Use binoculars, say
46 P.T.A. and N.E.A., for two
48 With 16-Across, places to pull over
50 Baseball stat
51 Slain
53 Kansas motto word
55 Cellular ___
56 Apt title for this puzzle
61 Label info
63 Visitor to Cathay
64 Talks nonsense
65 Neutral shade
66 Assist, in a way
67 Concerning
68 Letter opener
69 French possessive
70 They're verboten

DOWN

1 End of shooting
2 Epitaph starter
3 Road to old Rome
4 Llano growth
5 "Already?"
6 Home builder's tool
7 Jimmy Carter's coll.
8 City on the Tigris: Var.
9 Cookbook phrase
10 Cost of a 19th-century composer's work?
11 Brown pigment
12 Gives the boot to
14 Winter Palace throne?
20 Campbell or Judd
21 1964 Anthony Quinn role
25 They may have forks
26 Fam. tree member
27 Switch add-on
28 Undistinguished poet Pound?
32 Le ___ (Buick model)
34 Photo of the Panama Canal, once?
36 Sports stuff
37 Peak near Taormina
39 Aristotle's forte
41 Bunting places
44 Wise counsels
47 Be short with
49 "Iliad" warrior
51 Gave medicine to
52 In reserve
54 ___ acid
57 Soliloquy starter
58 Flush
59 Paradoxical Greek
60 Fast fliers, once
62 Where It.'s at

by Michael Shteyman

ACROSS

1 Strike from a manuscript
5 Gomer Pyle's org.
9 Larger than extra-large
14 Summit
15 Talk show host Dr. ___
16 Maker of the Legend
17 Mailed
18 Linoleum alternative
19 Amber or umber
20 Joseph Conrad novel
23 Slightly
24 Ballgame spoiler
25 Actress Brigitte
28 Discharge a cannon
29 Make a choice
32 Once more
33 Pitchfork part
34 0 on a phone: Abbr.
35 Balance point
38 In the past
39 Examines closely
40 Carriers of heredity
41 To the ___ degree
42 Spit four-letter words
43 Run in
44 "___ la vie"
45 Matured
46 Neither liberal nor conservative
53 Love, to Pavarotti
54 Comedian Rudner
55 Concerning
56 Stubble remover
57 Yale students
58 Turkey, businesswise
59 Antagonist
60 Religious offshoot
61 Heavy book

DOWN

1 Short run
2 Fencing weapon
3 Melodious Horne
4 Obtain, as a suspect, from another state
5 Ready for the task
6 Typewriter key
7 Not at all spicy
8 Forest gaps
9 Chan of action films
10 Storrs school, for short
11 Stubborn beast
12 Warner ___
13 Paddles
21 Steak cut
22 Not as common
25 Breakfast sizzler
26 Ticket seller
27 Salad dressing style
28 Marching band instruments
29 Share one's views
30 "For ___ sake!"
31 Secret meeting
33 Where Barbies are bought
34 Checking account woe
36 Get more mileage from
37 Be of one mind
42 Crunchy vegetable
43 Horrified
44 Modern encyclopedia medium
45 Storage area
46 Colt's mother
47 One-named supermodel
48 Take a nap
49 Dossier
50 Norway's capital
51 Unit of matter
52 Chucklehead

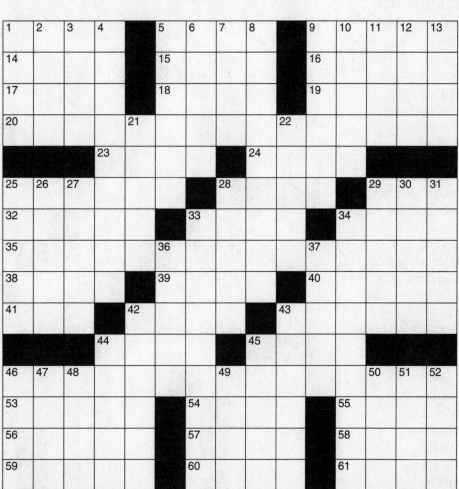

by Stanley Newman

118

ACROSS

1 Speak off the cuff
6 ___ of Commons
11 Govt. property overseer
14 Hotelier Helmsley
15 ___ salts
16 Shoemaker's tool
17 Court filings
19 Microwave, slangily
20 ". . . ___ shall die"
21 Deprived
22 It may be cut in a studio
23 Ice down again
25 ___ Reader (magazine)
27 Some ugly ducklings, so to speak
33 Scottish hillside
36 Mme., in Madrid
37 Fear
38 Spirits
40 Picnic crasher
42 End of many a college major
43 Jobs of limited duration
45 Big part of a dinosaur skeleton
47 "Much" preceder
48 Some athletes in training
51 Fencing need
52 "Stop acting up!"
56 "Roseanne" star
59 Short compositions
62 By way of
63 Eggs, in bio labs
64 Common sight after a burglary
66 Clearasil target
67 "As You Like It" woman
68 Like a sumo wrestler
69 "___ on a Grecian Urn"
70 "Yum!"
71 Commend highly

DOWN

1 ___ nothing
2 Big name in tractors
3 Computer programmer's need
4 "___ New York minute"
5 Sighter of the Pacific Ocean, 1513
6 München "sir"
7 Mayberry boy
8 Beneficial
9 Convertible type
10 CPR pros
11 Surveyor's look
12 Did one-third of a triathlon
13 Gravy Train competitor
18 Passenger safety items
22 Total
24 Ornamental shrub
26 Neighborhood that overlaps part of Greenwich Village
28 Time in history
29 What a plucker may pluck
30 Black, to poets
31 Baltic capital
32 "___ who?"
33 Low pitch?
34 Baby ___
35 Song for Sills
39 "Enough!"
41 Duty
44 Popeye's son
46 Artist Max
49 Asian nut-bearing palms
50 Antique dealer's transaction
53 Turn away
54 Sign of late summer
55 Stand for something?
56 Popular clown
57 Eager
58 Appraise
60 Military group
61 6/6/1944
64 Sept. follower
65 Wane's partner

by Christina Houlihan

ACROSS

1 Much of the back of a baseball card
6 Mac, e.g.
10 Genesis victim
14 Piece of cave art
15 Hawaii County's seat
16 Our Gang pooch
17 Yemeni thieves' hangout?
19 Keen about
20 Jockey Turcotte
21 Wrecker's job
22 Marketing lures
24 Blond hair, hot temper, etc.
26 Pouts
27 Chaucer pilgrim
29 Nebraska river
33 Fine fiddle, for short
36 Musket attachment?
38 Obie or Edgar
39 "Indeed!"
40 Sing-along syllable
41 Racer Luyendyk
42 Strengthens, with "up"
44 Schuss or wedel
45 Dish's partner in flight
46 Disassembler
48 Dwight licked him twice
50 Flinch, say
52 Give power to
56 Greek city-state
59 On vacation
60 Galley tool
61 Eggs order
62 Why the tourist departed for Africa?
65 Actress Ward
66 P.D.Q.
67 Tore to the ground
68 Quotation attribution: Abbr.
69 Shrimpers' gear
70 John of plow fame

DOWN

1 Eligible for Mensa
2 Henry VIII's house
3 Fight locale
4 Whip but good
5 Like a revealing skirt, maybe
6 Plug of tobacco
7 Suffix with fact or planet
8 Oldsmobile model
9 Get into shape
10 Actress Zadora visited Samoa's capital?
11 Out of shape
12 Kitchen annex?
13 Thirteen popes
18 Schnozzola
23 Gymnastics coach Karolyi
25 Mideast Olympic marathoner's claim?
26 African mongoose
28 Docs for dachshunds
30 Poi base
31 Rock's Cream, for instance
32 Perfect place
33 "Elephant Boy" boy
34 Some feds
35 Marsh growth
37 Fridge foray
43 "As ___ on TV!"
45 Fred played by Redd
47 Wicker material
49 Hit the road
51 X'd, as a candidate's name
53 Likker
54 Stein contents
55 Chip away at
56 ___ Nostra
57 Place for a cake
58 Move, in the realty biz
59 "So sorry!"
63 Gun moll's gun
64 ___ kwon do

by Fred Piscop

120

ACROSS

1 Other
5 Ping-Pong table dividers
9 Move like a lion
14 Ponce de ___
15 Mishmash
16 Send, as payment
17 "It is the ___, and Juliet is the sun!"
18 Movers' trucks
19 African antelope
20 Hot movie of 1981?
23 Poker pot starter
24 Head of a flock: Abbr.
25 Get satisfaction for
28 Siren luring sailors to shipwreck
32 Enchantress in Homer
33 Third-place finish
35 Bruin legend Bobby
36 Hot movie of 1974, with "The"?
40 Carmaker Ransom ___ Olds
41 Loony
42 ___ a million
43 Waltzing, say
46 2000 Olympics city
47 Suffix with meth-
48 Big furniture retailer
49 Hot movie of 1966?
56 Permit
57 Just minutes from now
58 Secluded valley
59 Late English princess
60 Run ___ (go wild)
61 Biblical twin who sold his birthright
62 Whom Truman defeated for president
63 Talks one's head off
64 Vermin

DOWN

1 The "E" in P.G.&E.: Abbr.
2 Wife of Jacob
3 Slugger Sammy
4 Beguile
5 "Nay"
6 Gladden
7 Pie containers
8 Nothing special
9 Lean toward
10 Experience again
11 Bradley or Sharif
12 Chianti or Chablis
13 Inc., in England
21 Actress Stevens of 60's TV
22 Displeased look
25 Performed
26 Quartet member
27 Field Marshal Rommel
28 Lane of "Superman"
29 Actress Sophia
30 Baseball Hall-of-Famer Banks
31 Twisted humor
33 Like a bug in a rug
34 Elev.
37 Word with strength or sanctum
38 Entry room
39 Imperil
44 Gangster known as Scarface
45 Sort of
46 They may raise a big stink
48 Macintosh laptop
49 Tennis champ Nastase
50 Cole ___
51 "Oho, dear chap!"
52 ___ cube (popular 60's–70's puzzle)
53 Ingrid's "Casablanca" role
54 Natty
55 Wildebeests
56 Do sums

by Sheldon Benardo

ACROSS

1 Punishment for a child, maybe
5 Ill-gotten gains
9 "The Lord of the Rings" figure
14 Notion
15 Bandleader Puente
16 Land colonized by ancient Greeks
17 Hoops contests since '38
18 "What's gotten ___ you?"
19 Zeal
20 "Just a moment . . ."
23 Pumps for info
24 Sparkler
25 Peter Graves's role on "Mission: Impossible"
28 It may be framed
29 Zealous
33 "You've got mail" co.
34 Martini's partner
36 Reason for not apologizing
37 Some training for a football team
40 100 bucks
41 Kind of checking
42 Albanian money
43 Did groundwork?
44 Ukr., once
45 Uses finger paints, say
47 Homer Simpson outburst
48 Battery liquid
49 Minivacation
57 Existence
58 Figure in academia
59 Anita who sang "And Her Tears Flowed Like Wine"
60 Range maker
61 Oklahoma city
62 French film
63 Angers
64 Jet set jets, once
65 Brain's site

DOWN

1 Spanish child
2 Norse deity
3 French for 65-Across
4 Land user of yore
5 Affixes with glue
6 Skid row types
7 Abbr. at the top of a memo
8 "Oh!"
9 What to do "for murder" in a Hitchcock film
10 Had on
11 Time ___ half
12 Mexican rivers
13 Subway purchase
21 Verve
22 Penthouse centerfold
25 Nicotine ___
26 "In what way?"
27 Bond on the run?
28 John Jacob ___
29 Former White House spokesman Fleischer
30 Home in Rome
31 Loafer
32 Office stations
35 Parasols
36 Early arrival, shortly: Var.
38 Cool, 60's-style
39 Falls
44 Ground cover
46 Big Apple mayor who asked "How'm I doin'?"
47 "At the Milliner's" painter
48 Expect
49 Ski lift
50 Prefix with sphere
51 Tabriz money
52 Feminizing suffix
53 Cravings
54 Falco of "The Sopranos"
55 Zola novel
56 Like Easter eggs

by Elizabeth C. Gorski

122

ACROSS

1 Airborne toy
6 "The Simpsons" storekeeper
9 Loafers holder
14 Après-ski drink
15 Zip
16 Spacious
17 Native on the Bering Sea
18 Sea lion, e.g.
20 Horseshoer's tool
21 Sports page summary
22 Purge
23 Sinuous swimmer
25 Galley tool
26 Fall off
27 Like the verb "to be"
31 Bigot
32 Society page word
33 "Step ___!"
34 Bamako's land
35 Theater receipts
37 It shouldn't be stuffed
40 Boozehound
41 Smidgens
42 Dundee denial
43 French seaport
45 Food device
47 10K, for one
48 "You stink!"
49 Right triangle part: Abbr.
50 CPR giver
51 Tune player
53 Scads
57 "Come to think of it . . ."
59 A-1
60 Pitchfork wielder
61 Actor Billy ___ Williams
62 Emerson piece
63 Excellent viewing spot
64 Comics bark
65 Transmission

DOWN

1 Part of a freight train
2 ___ nut (caffeine source)
3 Boardwalk treats
4 False top
5 Chow down
6 Zoo animals
7 Naval attire
8 Commotion
9 One-named singer from Nigeria
10 Pinafore letters
11 Organ transplants, e.g.
12 "Seinfeld" pal
13 Tree of the maple family
19 Blunder
21 Meal-to-go
24 Self-interested one
26 Mural site
27 Correspondence collector
28 Antique auto
29 Like a mirror
30 Get prone
31 W.W. II U.S. admiral nicknamed "Bull"
34 Miniature auto brand
36 It may be blown
37 Life story, in brief
38 Chinese "path"
39 Filmdom's Rocky, e.g.
41 Range part
43 Classic item in size comparisons
44 Any of several Egyptian kings
45 Spanish inn
46 Meager
48 Florida N.F.L.er
51 Become soft
52 Staff leader
54 Actress Kudrow
55 Mullah ___, former Afghan leader
56 Place for playthings
58 River inlet
59 Hard throw, in baseball

by Ron O'Hair

123

ACROSS

1 Rand McNally offering
6 Señor's emphatic yes
10 Poker stake
14 It's rubbed on a cue tip
15 Garden with forbidden fruit
16 "Gone With the Wind" plantation
17 Indoor antenna
19 Egyptian goddess
20 UFO crew
21 Charged particle
22 Sneaker
24 Swan song
25 "Jelly's Last Jam" dancer Gregory ___
26 Conductor of a sham trial
31 Ramadas and such
32 Spigot
33 Pooped out
35 "Mazel ___!"
36 Zoo bosses
39 A's opposite, in England
40 Former veep Agnew
42 Extra-wide, at the shoe store
43 Sorrows' opposites
44 Sellers in stalls
48 Mattress supports
49 Sizable sandwich
50 On the ___ (preparing for battle)
53 Poet's "eternally"
54 Mai ___ cocktail
57 Skin soother
58 Inedible mushrooms
61 The "D" in CD
62 Jane Austen classic
63 Paper size
64 Editor's "let it stand"
65 Paper purchase
66 Clear the boards

DOWN

1 Good-size field
2 "How 'bout ___?!"
3 Chem classes
4 Vatican vestment
5 Downhiller's sport
6 Witnessed
7 Actress Lupino
8 Italian film director Leone
9 On the same wavelength
10 Under debate
11 Ogden who wrote light verse
12 Duet plus one
13 Simplicity
18 So far
23 Cat chat
24 U.S.N.A. grad
25 What the starts of 17-, 26-, 44- and 58-Across all are
26 Big name in book publishing
27 Blacksmith's block
28 Sally Field's "Norma ___"
29 Gillette product
30 Deuce beaters
31 "___ show time!"
34 Football gains: Abbr.
36 Furry marsupial
37 Comics shriek
38 ___ Peanut Butter Cups
41 Look up to
43 One of the Bushes
45 Mean something
46 Where telecommuters work
47 Terrapin, e.g.
50 Rolls of bills
51 Hit the ground
52 Flower for Valentine's Day
53 Red-wrapped Dutch cheese
54 Roman robe
55 Word of woe
56 Castaway's locale
59 Doc bloc: Abbr.
60 "___ the ramparts . . ."

by Nancy Salomon and Harvey Estes

124

ACROSS

1 Hefty volume
5 Utah city
9 Hammett sleuth
14 About half of binary coding
15 Zilch
16 Noncitizen
17 God wounded in the Trojan War
18 Observed
19 Fox comedy series
20 "Hurry up!" to a person putting on a jacket?
23 French fine
24 "Timecop" actress
28 "Car Talk" airer
29 "Last one ___ a rotten egg!"
32 Short sock
33 Beyond tipsy
35 A Chaplin
36 "Hurry up!" to a person sharpening a pencil?
40 Affright
41 Peyote
42 Guinea pigs and kin
45 Under the weather
46 Attorneys' org.
49 Approached stealthily
51 Military commando
53 "Hurry up!" to a person assigning spies?
56 Island northwest of Oahu
59 Designer Gernreich
60 To be, in Tours
61 ___ fours (crawling)
62 Poker declaration
63 Cold-shoulder
64 Hostess Mesta
65 Singer k. d. ___
66 London gallery

DOWN

1 Without exception
2 Highway entry
3 More sheepish
4 Ruhr city
5 Tither's amount
6 Tanners catch them
7 Perfect place
8 Palindromic title
9 Far East boat
10 Hasbro division
11 Helping hand
12 L.A.P.D. investigator
13 Ltr. holder
21 Dimwit
22 Zadora of "Butterfly"
25 Baseball's Moises
26 Monthly bill, for many
27 ___ loss for words
30 Gossip topic
31 Monica of tennis
33 Suburban shopping area
34 Lucy's guy
36 PRNDL pick
37 Gutter site
38 Adding up, as interest
39 Senegal's capital
40 TV watchdog: Abbr.
43 Prima ballerina
44 Isuzu Rodeo, e.g.
46 Dame of mystery writing
47 Lebanon's capital
48 Actress Dahl
50 Danger
52 Bikini experiment, for short
54 Arizona city
55 Chief Norse god
56 Keystone lawman
57 Hydrocarbon suffix
58 Former Mideast alliance

by Myles Callum

ACROSS

1 Diplomat Deane
6 Lancia competitor, for short
10 Tee off
14 Prepared to be dubbed
15 Cash in Qom
16 1950's British P.M.
17 Advice to a driver, part 1
20 Hardly genteel
21 Court feat
22 Hardly genteel
23 Literary monogram
24 ___ Park (Manhattan neighborhood)
27 Barcelona title
29 One-in-a-million
30 Botanist Gray
33 Advice, part 2
37 Clear of the sea bottom
40 Moulin Rouge performance
41 Advice, part 3
45 Buck's mate
46 Long story
47 Reasons to cram
51 Garden ornamentals
54 Beer may be on it
55 Waters on stage
58 Polo Grounds legend
59 "Dumb" comics girl
60 End of the advice
64 Director Rohmer
65 Tech support caller
66 Actress Anne
67 "Why not?!"
68 Nuclear fuel holders
69 Mountain nymph

DOWN

1 Evades
2 Imbue (with)
3 Dutch cheese
4 Lotion ingredient
5 1950's–70's senator Symington, for short
6 Small toucan
7 One of the front four
8 500-pound, say
9 Apiece, in scores
10 Put in hot oil again
11 Brainchild
12 "Why not?!"
13 Son of Seth
18 "This means ___!"
19 Watchdog agcy. beginning 1887
24 Some shorthand
25 Pitching stat
26 React violently, in a way
28 Final notice
30 Sector boundary
31 Rwy. stop
32 Writer Rand
34 Write for another
35 Clotho and others
36 Jet black
37 Tag on
38 A suitor may pitch it
39 Suffix with ethyl
42 Mer contents
43 Disregarded
44 Skiers' leggings
48 A.S.A.P.
49 First first lady
50 Neutered
51 British coppers
52 Bridge guru Culbertson
53 J.D. holder: Abbr.
55 Farm females
56 Like some traffic
57 One who's got it coming
59 Shy creature
61 Start of many a Catholic church name
62 G.I. entertainer
63 Telephone interrogatory

by Ed Early

126

ACROSS

1 Book of maps
6 Lounge
10 Lounge
14 Milk purchase
15 Actress Falco
16 Word before a verb, maybe
17 Pain inside
18 Taboo
19 Not timid
20 Cruising
21 1986 Detroit debut
23 Refuses
25 Tall tale
26 E.P.A. concern: Abbr.
29 Paint over
33 Government subsidy
38 This-and-that dish
39 21-Across, e.g.
40 Bruin Bobby
41 Singer ___ James
42 Story line
43 1998 Peter Weir film, with "The"
46 Group of 100
48 "No sweat"
49 Six years, in the 46-Across
51 Period of greatest success
56 Amateurish
61 Prefix with -naut
62 Aware of
63 Without value
64 Express appreciation to
65 ___ Clayton Powell Jr.
66 Help for a detective
67 "It's the truth!"
68 Region
69 Renaissance Italian family name
70 Carried with difficulty

DOWN

1 Shades of blue
2 Oklahoma city
3 Cagney's TV partner
4 Regions
5 Narrow waterway: Abbr.
6 Late-night name
7 Olfactory stimulus
8 Dance named after an aviator
9 Dance class wear
10 Grouped
11 It may get into a jamb
12 Humdinger
13 They may be split or tight
21 An ellipse has two of them
22 "___ you sure?"
24 Take-home
27 ___ about (approximately)
28 Lash ___, who played the Cheyenne Kid in old westerns
30 Pledge
31 Concerning
32 Unfreeze
33 Openings
34 It may begin "Do not . . ."
35 Lots
36 Out
37 "___ la Douce" (1963 film)
43 Actor Stamp
44 Tennis's Arthur
45 Bill ___, TV's Science Guy
47 No. on a business card
50 Manhandles
52 "Hurray!"
53 Had control of the deck
54 Golfer Palmer, informally
55 Like farm oxen
56 Husband of Ruth, in the Bible
57 Take back
58 Funnyman Laurel
59 Oversupply
60 Peter Fonda title role
64 Explosion maker

by Alan Arbesfeld

ACROSS

1 Like a tack
6 Cape Cod town
11 Mercedes rival
14 Fencing sword
15 Tore down
16 Sculler's need
17 What to accentuate, to Bing Crosby . . .
19 Get mellower
20 Swift works
21 Gown material
23 Neat dresser's quality
27 Some radios
30 What to eliminate . . .
34 Terra ___
36 Málaga Mrs.
37 River to the Caspian
38 Home of the Jazz
39 Rocker John
41 Cost to cross
42 Abundant
43 Place to graze
44 Have a gut feeling
45 What to latch onto, with "the" . . .
49 Kobe currency
50 ___ ridgeback (hunting dog)
52 Unable to sit still
55 Pre-cable need
59 Halloween word
60 Whom not to mess with
64 Play for a sap
65 Really spooky
66 Lake ___, separating Switzerland and France
67 Mack who emceed TV's "The Original Amateur Hour"
68 Play for time
69 Bolt to unite

DOWN

1 Retired fliers from De Gaulle
2 "Good joke!"
3 Help in a heist
4 Adjust, as a brooch
5 Proportionately
6 See 32-Down
7 Squealer
8 Israeli weapon
9 Ministerial nickname
10 Ukrainian port
11 Ferry or wherry
12 Crèche trio
13 Small songbird
18 Genesis son
22 Shrewd
24 Administer the oath of office to
25 "I, Claudius" role
26 Alaska's first governor
27 Integra maker
28 Recurring theme
29 Shepherd's handful
31 O. Henry specialty
32 With 6-Down, Sibelius work
33 Popular 90's sitcom
35 Not ours
39 Patron saint of sailors
40 Heavy metal
44 Space Needle site
46 Rapper's improvisations
47 Sanford of "The Jeffersons"
48 Kudzu, for one
51 Staircase support
52 Border on
53 Cyrano's protrusion
54 Pigeon-___
56 Verne skipper
57 Kind of tide
58 ___ Boleyn, queen to Henry VIII
61 Emeritus: Abbr.
62 Nest egg letters
63 Nada

by Holden Baker

128

ACROSS

1 The Charleses' canine
5 Circus employee
10 Full of energy
14 Slick, in conversation
15 "I'd walk ___ for . . ."
16 Saharan
17 Doesn't keep
18 Hoarder's supply
19 Provide pro tem
20 Start of a quote by 53-Across, when asked to name his favorite song
23 Carbolic acid
24 Moving about
28 Quote, part 2
33 R.p.m. indicator
36 Lacks, in brief
37 Go for the gold?
38 Nickname of radio shock jock Greg Hughes
39 Monte ___
40 Chops, e.g.
41 Bobby on the ice
42 Slur over
43 Rainbows, e.g.
44 End of the quote
48 What "dis" is
49 Self-assured
53 Speaker of the quote
58 Chamber phenomenon
61 TV producer Spelling
62 Verve
63 Channel marker
64 Amount wagered
65 "Fashion Emergency" host
66 Buzzers
67 High bridge card
68 Talk back to

DOWN

1 "Get ___ on yourself!"
2 Sluggard's sin
3 Share with the church
4 Green liqueur
5 Angler's gear
6 Nanjing nanny
7 Flexible mineral
8 Like some textbook publishing
9 Item of 5-Down
10 Overshoe
11 Lode load
12 Card player's shout
13 Like all primes but one
21 Kabuki kin
22 1920's chief justice
25 Put darts into, as a garment
26 Singer Hayes
27 Carries on
29 The Andes, e.g.
30 Start to go?
31 Speck on a map
32 Rock's Brian
33 Characters in cels
34 Patriots' Day month
35 Approximately
39 Middle of the second century
40 Early shows
42 Hence
45 Relishes
46 Game one
47 H+, e.g.
50 1965 march city
51 Dutch treats?
52 Units of force
54 Talk (over)
55 Expanding grp.
56 Ollie's human friend
57 "The Mikado" character
58 Flow's partner
59 "The Hustler" prop
60 Ground breaker

by Sarah Keller

ACROSS

1 Office station
5 Arthur ___ Stadium
9 "Hurrah!," e.g.
14 School for princes William and Harry
15 Swing at a fly
16 Fool (around)
17 Bounce back
18 "Stop right there!"
19 Ringmaster
20 Judge's query
23 Foal's father
24 ___ League (56-Down's group)
25 Krazy ___
28 Bureaucratic stuff
31 "___, humbug!"
34 Cake topper
36 Little devil
37 Voice below soprano
38 Doctor's query
42 Sliver
43 18-wheeler
44 Desert spring
45 ___ Canals (Great Lakes connectors)
46 Light lager
49 Farm bale
50 Sidekick
51 See 40-Down
53 Bartender's query
59 See 8-Down
60 Beach composition
61 Shade of blue
63 Raise the curtain
64 Wings: Lat.
65 Deep ___ bend
66 Nose, slangily
67 Baby-sit
68 E-mailed

DOWN

1 Lousy grade
2 Carve in stone
3 Old warehouse district in New York
4 "Who ___ what evil . . ." (intro to "The Shadow")
5 On dry land
6 Moved to the music
7 Crown of light
8 With 59-Across, words before "Then fall, Caesar!"
9 Make ready for use, as library books
10 Warm and comfortable
11 SeaWorld whale
12 Not new
13 Titleist supporter
21 Sad song
22 Longstocking lass
25 Fuzzy fruits
26 Sneeze sound
27 Link with
29 Supermodel Cheryl
30 Morning hrs.
31 Turn red from embarrassment
32 Heart chambers
33 ___-totsy
35 Gun lobby, briefly
37 "Eureka!"
39 Dentist's tool
40 With "of" and 51-Across, a facial moisturizer
41 Religious scroll
46 ___ leather
47 Former White House speechwriter Peggy
48 Sidestepped
50 Outdoor party site
52 Foes of Rebs
53 Chirpy bird
54 Justice Black
55 Future atty.'s exam
56 New Haven institution
57 Barn topper
58 Neck and neck
59 Air rifle ammo
62 However

by Gregory E. Paul

ACROSS

1 Five Pillars of ___
6 Tobacco wad
10 Prez's backup
14 Impact sounds
15 Heavenly circle
16 Not prerecorded
17 It may bring you back to reality
19 Warts and all
20 Pail problem
21 Queried
22 Splinter group
23 Cowgirl Evans
25 Enter
27 Exit
30 Not the main office
32 Opposite of spicy
33 Replay option
34 ___-Locka, Fla.
37 Diamond ___
38 Running things
40 Part of WWW
41 NBC weekend comedy, briefly
42 Thoroughly thumps
43 Nerd
45 Lifers, e.g.
47 Like heaven's gates
48 Bee's bundle
50 Say coquettishly
51 Sailor's hail
52 Warning wail
55 Nada
59 Fancy marbles
60 Academic enclave
62 Algonquian language
63 Understands
64 Hoopster Shaquille
65 Aesop's also-ran
66 Big Board initials
67 Full of good cheer

DOWN

1 Result of a flea, maybe
2 "Get lost!"
3 Break in the action
4 Appended
5 Ed.'s pile
6 Picked out
7 Dove's opposite
8 Downwind, at sea
9 Scrabble or Boggle
10 Pickle brand
11 President whose grandson wed a president's daughter
12 Kick out
13 Trattoria topping
18 Sentry's command
24 Loud enough to hear
26 Coming
27 OPEC units: Abbr.
28 Lena of "Havana"
29 Nonmixer at a mixer
30 Ink stains
31 Column crossers
33 Go over
35 Part of a lemon
36 "Dear" advice-giver
39 Advertising lure
44 Combat area
46 Parisian palace
47 Undersized
48 Antismoking aid
49 Scarlett of Tara
50 Inherently
53 Actress Judith
54 Goes bad
56 Water pitcher
57 Spot for a spanking
58 Air France locale
61 Barnyard male

by Nancy Salomon

ACROSS

1 Composer whose music is often heard at graduations
6 Word on some diplomas
11 TV sked abbr.
14 Take for a while
15 When the Boston Marathon is held
16 It comes with a charge
17 Nondefensive military move
19 Shine, in product names
20 High dudgeon
21 Baby's ring
23 There are six of these in the middle of 17- and 56-Across and 11- and 25-Down
28 Razor brand
29 Hand or foot
30 "Well, well!"
31 Reassuring words
32 High muck-a-mucks
34 Of the flock
35 Ending of the Bible
36 Medium settings?
38 Punishment, metaphorically
41 Base tune
43 Garage figure
45 Old-hat
47 Santa ___ (hot winds)
48 "Paradise Lost," e.g.
49 Roguish
50 Jam producer
52 Scam artist
54 1995 court V.I.P.
55 Eastern way
56 "Just do it," e.g.
62 Lennon's lady
63 Sun Valley locale
64 Mirage sight
65 Theologian's subj.

66 Dot in the ocean
67 On the dot

DOWN

1 Tiny toymaker
2 Hula hoop?
3 Long-snouted fish
4 Basketball stat
5 Back in?
6 Place for a pin
7 Financing abbr.
8 Like sandpaper
9 "Just do it" shoes
10 Away from the wind
11 Fix
12 "10" music
13 Eskimo garb
18 Tour for Nicklaus
22 "Mon Oncle" star

23 1, 8 or 27
24 "Step ___!"
25 Some adult education
26 Dog star?
27 Emerging
31 Capital of old Moldavia
33 Crosby partner
34 Reveal accidentally
37 Future J.D.'s hurdle
39 Auricular
40 Knock flat
42 Connors contemporary
44 Hanukkah item
45 Flock leader
46 Like federal tax laws

47 From the heart?
50 Sweat units
51 Group values
53 Early 12th-century date
57 Leader in a beret
58 On a roll
59 ___ rule
60 Lady's man
61 Unproven ability

by Greg Staples

ACROSS

1 Voting group
5 À la ___ (with ice cream)
9 Wedding helper
14 Singer Horne
15 "Be ___!" ("Help me out!")
16 Stockholm native
17 Horse feed
18 Actress Garr
19 Spooky
20 Popular Canadian-born game show host
23 "Nope"
24 "y" ending, in superlative form
25 Dr. Frankenstein's workplace
30 The P of PRNDL
34 Enzyme suffix
35 Seize
36 Gently shift to a new topic
37 Sony Pictures Studio in Culver City, usually
41 Taboos
42 Prefix with plasm or morphic
43 Wide shoe width
44 Dele overrider
45 Use cheap materials, say
48 Stratford's stream
50 ___ culpa
51 Response to an answer
59 Jazzman Blake
60 Songwriter Bacharach
61 Sch. with generals as alums
62 Macaroni shape
63 Pricey theater section
64 Bring up, as children
65 Buildings with lofts
66 River of central Germany
67 "___ meeny miney mo"

DOWN

1 Explode, as a volcano
2 Wife of Jacob
3 Aware of
4 Vegas attraction
5 Infamous W.W. I spy
6 European auto
7 Take risks
8 Miracle drink
9 Consumers
10 Flowering vine
11 Parsley or sage
12 Singer/actress Adams
13 Stink
21 Three-stripers
22 Mystery writer Josephine
25 Suburban expanses
26 "___ in the Dark"
27 Designer Geoffrey
28 Profs' helpers, for short
29 ___ d'art
31 See eye to eye
32 Less polite
33 Conservative columnist Alan
36 Ferns reproduce with them
38 24 hours, for the earth
39 Stamped return env., e.g.
40 Counter in a car
45 Comedian Bill, familiarly
46 Lacking the skill
47 Word with "second" or "laws of"
49 Vantage points
51 Hall-of-Fame coach Ewbank
52 Belly-shaking dance
53 39-Down, e.g.
54 Part of Q.E.D.
55 Basic desire
56 "So that's what you mean"
57 Mideast's Gulf of ___
58 ___ a one (zip)

by Patrick Merrell

ACROSS

1 Sounds from a cornfield
5 Sonny who sang "Laugh at Me"
9 "Fiddlesticks!"
14 Part of a Latin 101 trio
15 "___ calling"
16 Not in dreamland
17 "You bet!"
18 They're often on their toes
20 Capital on the Hudson
22 Being broadcast
23 Poisonous plant
25 Hockey great Phil, familiarly
28 Broke a fast
29 46-Across belonged to it
30 Mentalist's claim
32 Not 'neath
33 Golf course bend
36 "Forget it!"
38 1971 Tom Laughlin cult film
41 Conductor Mehta
44 Piece of bingo equipment
46 50's nickname
47 Not swallow easily
50 Nest egg, of a sort: Abbr.
51 Uncertainties
54 Puts in writing
56 Bungled
59 Become fond of
61 Buyer
62 Bit of forensic evidence
65 Glamour rival
66 Proximate, to poets
67 Capital of Samoa
68 Marsh growth
69 "The Creation" composer

70 Classic computer game
71 Novus ___ seclorum (phrase on a dollar)

DOWN

1 Winter melon
2 Evil-repelling charm
3 Sang like a canary
4 Hoops turnover
5 Cutie pie
6 Eggs, to biologists
7 Strikeout king Ryan
8 Surfing the Net
9 ___-mutuel
10 Slop eaters
11 Waits awhile
12 Alias
13 Director Craven
19 Big times
21 Persistent, as a backache
24 Autobahn auto
26 Unimpressive brain size
27 Suffix with deposit or reposit
31 Miner's tool
34 Geisha's sash
35 Nautilus locale
37 Classic Jaguar
39 Monopoly corner square
40 Come to
41 Nada
42 Hawaiian strings
43 Fancy British wheels
45 "Batman" villain
48 Aid in crime
49 "Batman" setting
52 Gassed up
53 Big name in swimwear
55 Dieter's fare
57 Nutty as a fruitcake
58 Año starter
60 "Show Boat" composer
62 Cry from Scrooge
63 Italian article
64 Fleur-de-___

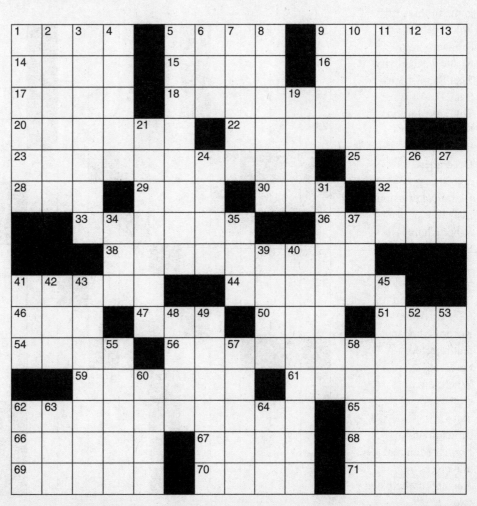

by Alan Arbesfeld

ACROSS

1 Domini preceder
5 ___ prof.
9 Aisle walker
14 Penury
15 Member of a bygone empire
16 School assignment
17 Approach the gate, say
18 Corner piece
19 Poison
20 Roman rebuke
22 Poet's Muse
23 A drawbridge spans it
24 Wrong
26 Selling very well
29 With 46-Across, an observation about the game in this grid
31 Folder labels
35 Jubilant
37 Musical sensitivity
38 That Spanish girl
39 Social
40 Tel. no. addition
41 55-Down under a flame
42 December 24 and 31, e.g.
43 Historical division
44 Instant
45 Viper's home
46 See 29-Across
48 ___-blue
49 Planning detail
51 It's 5 for B and 6 for C: Abbr.
53 Record company that rejected the Beatles
56 Where dirty clothes go
61 Sag
62 Inflict upon
63 Former Montreal player
64 Ancient marketplace
65 "So I ___!"
66 Met, for short
67 Bumpkin
68 Goes off
69 All wrapped (up)

DOWN

1 What you may do to get a hand
2 Spiffy
3 Waiting room call
4 Execration
5 Cause of a W.W. II siren
6 Porcine features
7 Sean Connery, for one
8 Cry during a duel
9 Total
10 For the immediate future
11 Prefix with -gon
12 Give off
13 Gambler's destination
21 Arena antagonist
25 ". . . ___ the fields we go"
26 Macho guys
27 Oil source
28 Colonists' annoyances
30 Bush, for one
32 Soothing plants
33 Lose a staring contest
34 Like pretzels, typically
36 Datum for college applications
40 "Monty Python" player
41 Carried
43 Woolly mama
44 Ways
47 Yak
50 Kind of court
52 Athlete Jesse
53 40's turning point
54 So
55 Prepare
57 Black, as un film
58 Wagon part
59 Erupt
60 It may be French

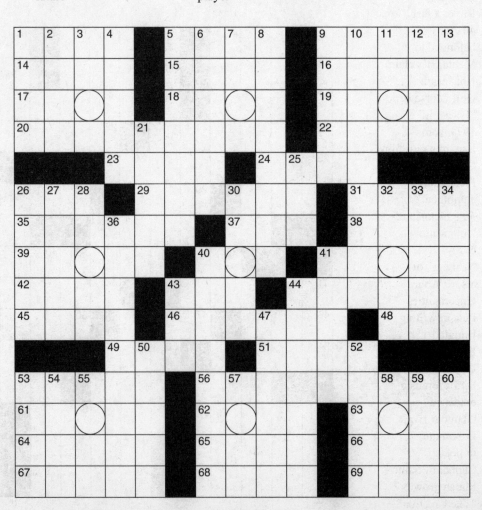

by Tyler Hinman

ACROSS

1 Home planet
6 Eurasia's ___ Mountains
10 Spy Mata ___
14 Waikiki welcome
15 Granny
16 Elderly
17 "Keep going!"
19 Season for carols
20 Hanks or Brokaw
21 Singer Kristofferson
22 Dicker over a price, say
24 Simon or Diamond
25 Supermarket section
26 Follows
28 Pie topping
32 Garlic unit
33 Prefix with scope or photo
34 Fork part
35 Retired Italian money
36 Brandish
37 Icy pellets
38 Swear to
39 Aardvarks' morsels
40 Takes an apartment
41 Pudding and pie
43 Shindig
44 Gifts to the poor
45 Scrabble piece
46 Diamond-shaped pattern
49 Jim-dandy
50 "The Sopranos" network, originally
53 Guide
54 "Keep going!"
57 ___-inflammatory
58 Armbone
59 Question with an easy answer
60 Durante's famous feature
61 Ring
62 Door holders

DOWN

1 "___ of Eden"
2 Choir voice
3 Wander
4 Your, in the Bible
5 "M*A*S*H" role
6 "___ we meet again"
7 Stadium sounds
8 Folk rocker DiFranco
9 Angry, with "up"
10 "Keep going!"
11 Wide-eyed
12 Fishing line holder
13 Not busy
18 Center of the eye
23 Foreman KO'er, 1974
24 "Keep going!"
25 Vales
26 Popeye's gal
27 Tiresome ones
28 Dates on a track team schedule
29 Midget's opposite
30 Oneness
31 Squiggly swimmers
32 Garbed
33 Slight colors
36 Practiced before playing
40 North Carolina's capital
42 Building wing
43 Unwanted engine sound
45 General Mills breakfast cereal
46 Comedian King
47 Janet in the Clinton White House
48 Gangsters' guns
49 O'Neill's "___ Christie"
50 Skirt lines
51 Run (into)
52 Unlocks, poetically
55 Spanish cheer
56 By way of

by Gail Grabowski

136

ACROSS

1 Muddy up
5 Fiber-___ cable
10 Vaulted area
14 Old Dodge
15 Wells ___
16 Envelope closer
17 Training in microscope use?
20 Primping
21 "Steppenwolf" author
22 90° from ESE
23 Elisabeth of "Leaving Las Vegas"
25 Ripken Jr. surpassed him
29 Mad rush
33 Big drink?
34 Bearded farm animal
35 Fraternity members
36 Taking an arctic vacation?
40 Timeworn
41 Museo contents
42 Caffè ___
43 Times to play or relax
46 Butter or oleo
47 School on the Thames
48 Kingston Trio hit, 1959
49 Hotpoint competitor
52 Enters
57 Why some people move to Massachusetts?
60 Crowd noise
61 River of Rome
62 Taxi charge
63 Nothing but
64 Some murder mystery suspects
65 Tibetan bovines

DOWN

1 Cavort
2 Actor Sharif
3 "Bus Stop" playwright
4 Field of work
5 In the ___ (soon to come)
6 John of first "Miracle on 34th Street"
7 H.S. math
8 Engine starter: Abbr.
9 Gear part
10 Dead to the world
11 Potpie ingredients
12 Mouth off to
13 Otherwise
18 Scorecard division
19 Pal
23 Washington, for one
24 "What ___ God wrought?"
25 "Taras Bulba" author
26 Place to learn en français
27 Swiss miss of literature
28 Managed
29 Puts into piles
30 Ham it up
31 Triangular tract
32 Pulled the plug on
34 Bridge expert Charles
37 Casino game
38 Rio Grande city
39 Garage contents
44 "Halt!" caller
45 The Beehive State
46 Beef on the hoof
48 Van company
49 Bushy do
50 Phobos, to Mars
51 Asia's ___ Sea
52 Mongolian desert
53 Far from certain
54 Final Four org.
55 Peter of the Monkees
56 Pindar volume
58 Biblical suffix
59 Fanciful story

by Janice M. Putney

ACROSS

1 "The Crucible" setting
6 Willingly
10 Chihuahua cries
14 Not merely sluggish
15 Razor brand
16 Eye rakishly
17 Start of a quip
20 Fatty treat for birds
21 Perfumer's extract
22 Wagering venue, briefly
25 Sox foes
27 Ancient Mexican
28 Rutabaga, e.g.
30 Grouch
32 Málaga Mrs.
33 Fit to serve
34 Where overreachers go
36 Middle of the quip
41 Arrow poison
42 __ B'rith
44 "Friends" network
47 Parched
48 Bikini blasts
50 Speaks like Robert Byrd
52 Unique, to Caesar
54 Painter's medium
55 Squirting flower, say
57 Talk like Daffy
59 End of the quip
64 Rock 'n' roll pioneer Freed
65 Big story
66 Where the action is
67 Model Banks
68 D.C. group
69 Off one's trolley

DOWN

1 Do some modeling
2 "Wheel of Fortune" buy
3 Science fiction writer Stanislaw
4 "__ Tu" (1974 song)
5 Honshu peak, briefly
6 Nonprofessionals
7 Social attachment?
8 European language
9 1893 Verdi opera
10 Sticks figure
11 007 and others
12 Position filler
13 Five Nations tribe
18 Axel, e.g.
19 Weather line
22 Ear: Prefix
23 Popular sandwich filler
24 Uncle Remus honorific
26 Energetic cleaner
29 Buster?
31 Classroom routine
34 Tahoe transport
35 Sticks figure

37 Diving birds: Var.
38 Goes to the mat
39 __ many words
40 Jacques of "Mon Oncle"
43 Bermuda, e.g.: Abbr.
44 For dieters
45 Rain shield, in London
46 Luxury spread
48 La Scala song
49 Discoverer of New Zealand
51 "Lovergirl" singer __ Marie
53 Guinness et al.
56 "Holy moly!"
58 Machu Picchu site

60 Kith's partner
61 Voided shot
62 Where London is: Abbr.
63 Roll-call call

by Myles Callum

138

ACROSS

1 Actress Thompson of TV's "Family"
5 Ace or jack
9 How to sing, ideally
14 Israeli airline
15 Baseball's Matty or Moises
16 Ethiopia's ___ Selassie
17 Bugs bugs him
19 "Mine!"
20 1991 Madonna hit
21 Czech-born actor Herbert
22 Discharge
23 Plummeted
28 Tierra ___ Fuego
29 Goethe character who makes a pact with the devil
30 Rock's Bon ___
31 "Vive le ___!"
33 Words of praise
35 Uncomplicated kind of question
39 Pupil
40 Expatriate
42 String after A
43 Ache (for)
44 "Silly" birds
46 Fold-up bed
49 Narrative
51 Popular clog clearer
53 Wild, wild West
54 Like some vamps
56 Horrible
59 Title hero of a Melville story
60 "La Traviata" composer
61 Repetitive learning method
62 "I've Got ___ in Kalamazoo"
63 "Humble" place
64 Years in Spain
65 Marvin of Motown

DOWN

1 Get really steamed
2 Assert without proof
3 Woman hoping for a knight in shining armor
4 Baldwin and Guinness
5 Lunch site
6 Barnard graduate
7 Endured, as a hurricane
8 It fizzles
9 Cry of terror
10 Country-singing mother
11 Medic's bag
12 ___ Lilly (Fortune 500 company)
13 "Is it soup ___?"
18 Groove
21 Beatles album after "Hey Jude"
24 Georgia and Ukraine, once: Abbr.
25 Cast a ballot
26 Fifty-fifty
27 Mile or kilometer: Abbr.
29 Wangle
31 Longtime CBS/NBC newsman
32 Bobby of the Bruins
34 Tampa Bay footballer, for short
35 Slangy assents
36 Discharge
37 ___-Soviet relations
38 R.E.M.'s "The ___ Love"
41 Excitement in the air
45 Do business with
46 Iroquois confederate
47 Sometime
48 Walk like a two-year-old
50 Clinton or Bush, collegiately
51 TV actress Susan
52 Arrange in different sacks
55 Shouts to a matador
56 Actress Gardner
57 Spider's work
58 To and ___
59 Victoria's Secret purchase

by David Ainslie Macleod

ACROSS

1 Agent Mulder's show, with "The"
7 Garment that may have advertising
13 Chef's collection
15 Pythagorean ___
16 High-spirited horse
17 Get off at the terminal
18 Starchy tuber
19 Hammer features
21 Mortise's partner
22 It rides on runners
24 Hurler's stat.
25 "___ the season . . ."
26 Acting through the skin
29 Gun, as an engine
32 "Saturday Night Fever" music
35 Rat Pack cohort of Frank
36 Tennessee team, for short
37 Queen mother, e.g.
39 Pasta with pockets
41 On the road
42 Disarrange
44 The Dow, e.g.
45 Big fat mouth
46 Nixon bested him
48 Director Van Sant
49 Ginger ___
50 "___ we forget"
54 Autocrats of old
57 One of David's compositions
59 Poke fun at
60 Event for scullers
62 Falls on the border
64 Winter cap feature
65 War of 1812 hero Stephen
66 Like porn
67 Shutterbugs' settings

DOWN

1 Dental pictures
2 Wild
3 Start of a boast from Caesar
4 P.M. William Gladstone's party: Abbr.
5 Heroic saga
6 Part of S.W.A.K.
7 Everyday article
8 Kind of tank
9 Bagel centers
10 Farsi-speaking land
11 University of Nevada locale
12 Some feds
14 Percussion instrument in a combo
15 QB's aims
20 Suffix with soft or hard
23 What spots on 1-Down show
25 Singer Turner
27 Yule quaff
28 Everglades
29 Crucifix
30 Macpherson of "Sirens"
31 Auto engine type
32 Make-or-break time
33 Corn Belt state
34 Cashless deal
36 Record albums, to collectors
38 Down Under birds
40 Contend (for)
43 Relaxing spots
46 Sell aggressively
47 Analgesic's promise
48 Some corruption
51 Poetic Muse
52 Flapjack topper: Var.
53 Skiers' lifts
54 Prehistoric predator, for short
55 Burn a bit
56 Taj Mahal site
57 Mushy food
58 PC alternatives
61 Little bit
63 Gangster's gun

by William Schaub

ACROSS

1 Winter coating
5 Big hit
10 Book before Nehemiah
14 Just
15 Phone line?
16 Sweet-talk
17 Tim of "Sister, Sister"
18 How some stocks are sold
19 In the ___ (focused)
20 Rescue Mrs. Perón's pottery?
23 Come out
24 Screen letters
28 Fill roles for a Lloyd Webber show?
33 It's hot in Paris
36 Derby prize
37 "Mamma ___"
38 Hoarse speech
39 Chips go-with
40 "___ la vie"
41 Internet address, for short
42 Get together
43 Desert sight
44 Locate cookware components?
47 Namely
48 "___ Woman" (1972 Eagles hit)
52 Misplace single fruit?
57 Cheek
60 Give off
61 Stately florae
62 Hand cream ingredient
63 Steam, e.g.
64 Unfetter
65 Kind of bust
66 File material
67 Noted vaudeville family

DOWN

1 Cowboy's companion
2 Wee hour
3 Breathing
4 Coveted golf trophy
5 Tonsorial touchups
6 Introduction to physics?
7 Skier's mecca
8 Pole, for one
9 Round dance
10 Skin condition
11 Vet's employer
12 Turned tail
13 Fire
21 "Yikes!"
22 Cong. meeting
25 High points
26 "Who's there?" response
27 Future attys.' hurdles
29 Albinism, e.g.
30 Unitas's team
31 Good thing
32 Gunpowder, for one
33 Pizza feature
34 Silent movie star?
35 Do ___ burn
39 ___-cone
40 Lets go
42 Engaged in
43 Taylor boy of 60's TV
45 Farm machine
46 Hooter's hangout
49 Mild smoke
50 Contrived
51 Toadies' replies
53 Golfer Ballesteros
54 Physical, e.g.
55 Movie extra, in brief
56 Reason to bathe
57 Short punch
58 Motivation for Manolete
59 Distress

by Alan Arbesfeld

141

ACROSS

1 Neighbor of Ecuador
5 Dressed
9 Identical
14 Firefighters' tools
15 Poison ivy reaction
16 Pulitzer-winning novelist Alison
17 Sales agents, briefly
18 This, south of the border
19 Decorates richly
20 Very bright
23 Prefix with center
24 Med. plan
25 Part of the foot
29 Actress Meryl
31 Motion while saying "Good dog!"
33 ___ mode
34 Showered
36 Mild, as weather
38 Very bright
40 Civil rights org.
42 In a sour mood
43 Build (on)
44 "Undoubtedly"
45 Mitchell of NBC News
49 Fly that carries sleeping sickness
52 ___ Beta Kappa
53 Coast Guard rank: Abbr.
54 Very bright
58 Mideast's ___ Peninsula
61 Singer Fitzgerald
62 "It's ___ to tell a lie"
63 Disdain
64 Prophet
65 Taboo
66 Like a tie game in overtime
67 Job
68 Shoelace problem

DOWN

1 Analyzes grammatically
2 Free (from)
3 Fix
4 Moscow's land, once: Abbr.
5 Famous Boston dessert
6 Rope, cowboy-style
7 "The Thin Man" dog
8 Boat on the Indian Ocean
9 Illinois city
10 Witticisms
11 Dot-com's address
12 Help
13 Parisian article
21 Silent character in "Little Orphan Annie"
22 Top-10 record
26 Towering
27 Shade tree
28 Salary
30 Rock's Clapton
31 Mexican moolah
32 Month in Israel
35 Epithet
36 Sarajevo is its capital
37 Impressed mightily
38 Walk in shallow water
39 Two-by-two vessel?
40 Singer ___ King Cole
41 TV interruptions
44 Nay opposer
46 Sanity
47 San Fernando Valley community
48 Start of a John F. Kennedy quote
50 Nicholas and Ivan, e.g.
51 Sparkle
52 Loses color
55 Part of R & R
56 Nolo contendere, e.g.
57 Aquarium
58 Former way to get to Paris
59 ___ cream
60 Negative in Normandy

by Alison D. Donald

ACROSS

1 Stranded motorist's S O S
6 Fishhook part
10 Train station
14 Set one's sights
15 Meltable spread
16 "My Friend ___" (1949 flick)
17 Showy perennials
18 Josip Broz, familiarly
19 Play, as drums
20 "Consider seriously, Bret"
23 Checkup sounds
24 Be into
25 24-hour period, in astronomy
27 Francis and Dahl
31 Novelist Umberto
32 Hotfoot it
33 "Earn straight A's, Karl"
39 Saudi or Yemeni
41 Televise
42 Final, e.g.
43 "Sing lead, Horace"
48 ___ Fail (Irish coronation stone)
49 In the style of
50 Puts in order
52 Carpet leftovers
57 Radar gun meas.
58 Bullfight bravo
59 "Stay free of discomfort, Thomas"
64 Pinocchio, for one
66 The Supremes, e.g.
67 Designer Perry
68 Sicilian smoker
69 Sloth's home
70 Brooklets
71 Brother of Cain
72 Rank above viscount
73 Final authority

DOWN

1 It's true
2 Coin in the Trevi Fountain, once
3 In a frenzy
4 Many hairlines do it
5 Cutting and pasting
6 This and that
7 Name on a police blotter
8 So out, it's in
9 Sell bathtub gin, say
10 Sis, e.g.
11 Radial pattern
12 Cornhusker's city
13 Fall guy
21 S-shaped molding
22 A pop
26 Forum city
27 Pequod captain
28 Laugh, in Lille
29 Table extender
30 "Immediately," in the O.R.
34 That guy
35 Where Tabriz is
36 Linchpin's place
37 Acid ___
38 Yule, in ads
40 It's in whole wheat
44 Norwegian saint
45 Name following "No, No"
46 Verne skipper
47 Siesta takers
51 Muse of comedy
52 Cast openings
53 Typewriter type
54 Stood for
55 ___ cotta
56 More cagey
60 Holiday tune
61 In a bad way
62 Guitarist Lofgren
63 Conoco competitor
65 "Yay, team!"

by John Greenman

ACROSS

1 Tony section of Boston
5 A chorister
9 End of a layoff
14 One of Chekhov's "Three Sisters"
15 Noggin
16 Israel's Sharon
17 Gasohol, e.g.
18 Shake up
19 Mississippi tributary
20 Mythical thing in the business world
22 Trolley sound
23 "___ you kidding?"
24 Wind dir.
26 Like some pets
30 Mexican Mrs.
31 Tom Jones hit "___ a Lady"
35 Capital of Guam, old-style
36 Restaurateur Toots
37 Butler, maid, etc.
38 Theme of this puzzle
41 French 101 verb
42 Checked out
43 One wearing a conical cap
44 Bassoonist's buy
45 1040 sender
46 Manufacturer's offer
47 Numero ___
48 Camp sack
49 "Rats!" and others
53 Coupon for the needy
59 Fictional Heep
60 Grimm beast
61 Inter ___
62 Earl or viscount
63 Astronaut Shepard
64 Like a yenta
65 Tryster's escape route, maybe
66 Hot sandwich
67 1969 Beatles hit

DOWN

1 "Keep your distance!"
2 Mr. Magoo's vision
3 "The Morning Watch" author
4 Brown rival
5 Repudiate
6 Director Sergio
7 Barber's powder
8 Like Charles Kuralt, perennially
9 Psychic Edgar
10 Asia's ___ Sea
11 Maugham's "___ of Lambeth"
12 Rocker Russell
13 In-basket stack
21 Island west of Maui
25 D.E.A. agent
26 Highlander's fling?
27 Banded stone
28 Button material
29 Signed one's name to
30 Cobblers' output
31 Yard adornment
32 Dye source
33 Vote in
34 Binge
36 Inedible peanuts
39 Düsseldorf denial
40 "Waiting for Lefty" playwright
46 Porcupine, e.g.
47 Person with a program
48 Reef buildup
49 Bushman's home
50 Nearly rainless
51 One of the Jackson 5
52 Angelic feature
54 Gawk at
55 Zingy taste
56 Medicinal plant
57 Atomizer output
58 Retribution

by Randall J. Hartman

144

ACROSS

1 Part of Miss America's attire
5 Syrian president Bashar al-___
10 When tripled, et cetera
14 4:00 socials
15 Hobbits' home, with "the"
16 Gutter locale
17 "That ___ hay!"
18 34-Down for a politician?
20 "Spare the ___, spoil . . ."
21 Fabricate, as a signature
22 Visionaries
23 34-Down for a bookkeeper?
26 Put on board
27 "As my final point . . ."
31 Japanese beer named for a city
33 Farm-related: Prefix
36 ___ de Janeiro
37 34-Down for a stenographer?
41 Bank acct. amt.
42 10 million of them equal a joule
43 Speechify
44 Dale Earnhardt org.
47 When shadows are short
48 34-Down for a dentist?
54 San Diego baseballer
57 Together
58 Prefix with sex
59 34-Down for a florist?
61 Cutlass or Delta 88
62 Additions
63 Shoelace end
64 Suspenseful
65 VCR insert
66 Wanting
67 Card above a deuce

DOWN

1 Lennon bandmate
2 "Wheel of Fortune" buys
3 Removes paint, in a way
4 D.D.E.'s predecessor
5 On land
6 Knifelike
7 Burn slightly
8 Shakespeare's Forest of ___
9 Girl at a ball
10 Watch rims
11 Loll
12 Claim
13 His's partner
19 Govt. cultural org.
21 Angry, and not going to take it anymore
24 Theda of the silents
25 Roman 152
28 Like sides of pyramids
29 Jacket buildup
30 Oxen holder
31 Norse war god
32 ___ Louise of "Gilligan's Island"
33 ___ Lingus
34 Pre-April 1 purchase
35 Monopoly quartet: Abbr.
38 Cop's collar
39 Who preceded Adam and Eve on earth
40 Sailor's rum drink
45 Cherry red
46 Downsizer
47 Nonagenarian's age
49 Not quite jumbo
50 "___ Mio"
51 Gave, as an Rx
52 Excessive
53 Moist, as the air
54 "Hey there!"
55 Color of water
56 Hauler's destination
60 Color of sand
61 Baseball's Mel

by Patrick Merrell

ACROSS

1 Direction for Greeley
5 Helen's abductor
10 Spreadsheet filler
14 Locality
15 Thomas Gray work
16 "Help ___ the way!"
17 "Poor Little Fool" singer
19 Quickly, in the I.C.U.
20 Shooting star
21 Dissertation
23 Use a Singer
25 No-nos
26 "What Kind of Fool Am I" singer
33 Met song
34 Lane co-worker at the Daily Planet
35 Norse thunder god
39 Short skirt
40 Orioles and cardinals
41 "Othello" villain
42 Genesis paradise
43 Annul
44 French airport
45 "The Fool on the Hill" bandleader
49 Dundee residents
52 "Norma ___"
53 Where bowlers may go
57 Wall Street employee
62 Tooth trouble
63 "She's a Fool" songstress
65 Perlman of "Cheers"
66 Prefix with face or faith
67 Supreme Norse deity
68 Salon job
69 Puts on the bulletin board
70 Missing

DOWN

1 Friendly
2 Cleveland's lake
3 Religious group
4 Bit of filming
5 Looked intently
6 Everybody
7 Take five
8 Dr. Frankenstein's assistant
9 "Auld Land ___"
10 Wide-angle lens concern
11 John of "The Addams Family"
12 Raise one's glass to
13 Starts a pot
18 Like a yenta
22 Word modifier: Abbr.
24 Regaining consciousness
26 Identical
27 Like the Gobi
28 Coal hole
29 Not the fringes
30 "Rigoletto" composer
31 Kind of plumbing
32 Thoroughfares: Abbr.
36 Knotty
37 Look at flirtatiously
38 Rogers and Clark
40 Prickly husk
46 Spaniard's "that"
47 Alma ___ (grads' schools)
48 Mysterious: Var.
49 Quick-witted
50 Hiding place
51 Different
54 Fast pace
55 Lotto relative
56 Fomer 44-Across sights
58 Wide-eyed
59 Knucklehead
60 Ireland, in poesy
61 Philosopher Descartes
64 Allow

by Rich Norris

ACROSS

1 Map out
5 Interfere (with), as evidence
11 Blemish, slangily
14 Cotton unit
15 Woodwind player
16 Bouncers' requests, briefly
17 Emulate Errol Flynn
19 ___ Dee River
20 Grow choppers
21 March honoree, for short
23 Ninnies
26 "___ Poetica"
28 "___ well"
29 Way back when
32 Read carefully
34 Act the blowhard
35 Six-legged soldiers
38 Indy sponsor
39 Title for this puzzle?
40 Driving hazard
43 Empty
45 New York or London district
46 Gives the cold shoulder
48 Poseidon, to the Romans
50 Pocket bread
51 Derisive laugh
54 Transnational money
55 ___ Gay
57 Gain again
60 Dict. offering
61 It's pushed in a crisis
66 Swiss canton
67 Hypnotic state
68 Leprechaun's land
69 S.F. winter hrs.
70 Steakhouse sound
71 Monopoly card

DOWN

1 "Sesame Street" channel
2 Order's partner
3 In the manner of
4 Savings for a rainy day
5 Soliloquy starter
6 Lie next to
7 Coffee order
8 Cheap so-and-so
9 Immigrant's course: Abbr.
10 Numbered rds.
11 Post office request
12 Worthy principles
13 Dreaded fly
18 "___ real nowhere man" (Beatles lyric)
22 Like a sloe
23 Priests' vestments
24 Alphabetize, e.g.
25 "Wake up!"
27 Thinly spread
30 Waterproof overshoe
31 ". . . abridging the freedom of speech, ___ the press . . ." (Bill of Rights)
33 Toronto-to-Ottawa dir.
36 Chinese food additive
37 Chinese dollar
39 U.P.S. delivery: Abbr.
41 "Horrors!"
42 Takes a turn
44 Caspian feeder
45 Checked, as growth
46 Accelerated
47 They yearn
49 Where the nuevo sol is spent
52 Ball mate
53 "57 Varieties" company
56 Rental units: Abbr.
58 Book after Proverbs: Abbr.
59 Busy as ___
62 Uris hero ___ Ben Canaan
63 Reason for overtime
64 Mine find
65 Composer Rorem

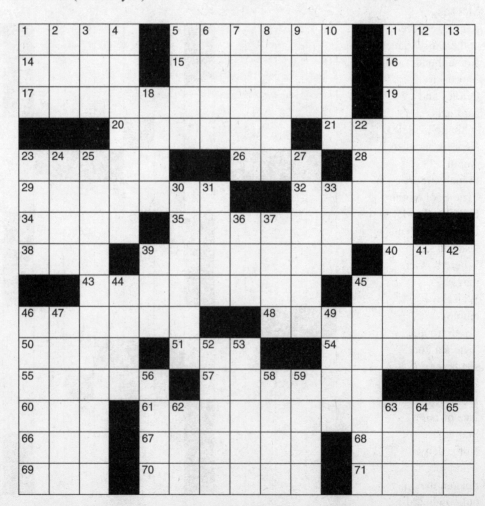

by Kelly Clark

ACROSS

1 Urban haze
5 Tests by lifting
10 What kindergartners learn
14 Ice cream holder
15 Apply, as pressure
16 Hold sway over
17 Bread maker
18 San ___, Calif.
19 "___ my way"
20 UPS alternative
23 Mediterranean fruit
24 Tiny toiler
25 Sheen
27 Boat's back
29 French composer Erik
32 Group of eras
33 "Silent" prez
35 Big galoot
36 Olympian sovereign
37 Technologically advanced
41 "___ on first?"
42 Long distance letters
43 Perfect gymnastics score
44 Unidentified John
45 Ballot caster
47 Pine sap
51 Takes effect
53 "Bali ___"
55 Carry on, as a trade
56 Cheap chat
60 Be worthy of
61 "Merrily, we roll ___"
62 Estimator's phrase
63 Supply-and-demand subj.
64 Garden "crashers"
65 Campus bigwig
66 Borscht vegetable
67 Peace Nobelist Anwar
68 Popular ice cream

DOWN

1 Treats dismissively, with "at"
2 "Shake a leg!"
3 Uptight
4 Hackman of Hollywood
5 Macho dude
6 Praises to the sky
7 Big bash
8 "Jurassic Park" menace, briefly
9 Traffic halter
10 Astrological ram
11 Inadvisable advice
12 Liquidation sale
13 V.I.P. in D.C.
21 Attacked, in a way
22 Feel regret over
26 T.L.C. givers
28 Some TV's
30 1966 Michael Caine role
31 Boy king of Egypt
34 Car buyers' protection
36 Western writer Grey
37 Common place for a knot
38 Direct, as a confrontation
39 Halloween's mo.
40 Like Halloween sounds
41 Dict. entries
45 By way of
46 Girl in a Beach Boys song
48 Dealt leniently with
49 "And how!"
50 Sheer stockings
52 Bloodhound's trail
54 Uneasy feeling
57 "Not guilty," e.g.
58 Got rid of 64-Across
59 The "C" in U.P.C.
60 Yank's foe

by Harvey Estes and Nancy Salomon

ACROSS

1 Painter Chagall
5 Suit
10 Home of Iowa State
14 Muffin topper
15 Do penance
16 "I, Claudius" role
17 Virgin Is., e.g.
18 Cheap shot?
20 Overwhelm
22 Block and tackle part
23 Use an épée
24 14 pounds, in Britain
26 Kimono accessories
29 Germ-free
33 Sosa vs. McGwire, e.g.?
37 Evidence of drunkenness
38 Necessities for pregnancies
39 Insulted, lovingly
42 Kay follower
43 Cuzco's country
45 Commotion in the commuters' terminal?
47 Watergate, e.g.
50 Israel's Abba
51 Rent again
53 Puts ice on, maybe
57 "One __ Jump"
60 "The Natural" game
63 Feature of a girls-only gathering?
65 Scottish hillside
66 Mark time
67 Sri __
68 The auld sod
69 __ off (angered)
70 Sling mud at
71 Hard to fathom

DOWN

1 Recurring theme
2 Coeur d'__, Idaho
3 Any "Seinfeld," now
4 Pipe type
5 Ali __
6 South Dakota, to Pierre
7 Links shouts
8 Bach's Mass __ Minor
9 Place to put some leaves
10 Fly-casters, e.g.
11 It may be prix fixe
12 Canal of song
13 PlayStation maker
19 Ancient letter
21 Shut out
25 Feared fly
27 Skater Midori
28 Dobbin's home
30 "__ a song go . . ."
31 Put to sleep
32 __ Stanley Gardner
33 Conks on the head
34 "__ plaisir"
35 Ancient Irish kings' home
36 Baton Rouge sch.
40 Go back
41 Musician Eddy or Allman
44 Got naked
46 Gave the cold shoulder
48 Art __
49 Ethyl and propyl, for two
52 Steak selection
54 An Osmond
55 Traffic jam noise
56 Sack out
57 News item often written in advance
58 Programmers' writing
59 Singer Lovett
61 One of the Aleutians
62 Magi guide
64 Video maker, for short

by Verna Suit

ACROSS

1 They may stand at the side of the stage
5 Twist (in)
10 Make a bundle
14 Eastern currency
15 Stag
16 Brit's cry
17 Additional guest quarters, in Massachusetts?
19 Get promoted
20 In need of changing
21 Football exec Rozelle
22 Sports figures
23 ___ Kane of "All My Children"
25 "Way to go!"
28 First name in mysteries
30 Phil Donahue and Rush Limbaugh, e.g.
34 On the double
37 Pocket Books logo
38 Fully absorbed
39 Author Calvino
41 Sail support
42 Not leave soon enough
44 Diamond features
46 Threatening sorts
47 Old Michael Jackson do
48 Chat room nonparticipant
50 Start of the 18th century
54 TV news time
57 Wine choice
59 Former Mideast inits.
60 Sailors' saint
61 Duo directed by dad, in Massachusetts?
64 "Wait ___!"
65 "___ to bed"
66 Hope to lose?
67 Do horribly, slangily
68 Uncool sort
69 Dried up

DOWN

1 "___ there yet?"
2 7-Up, sometimes
3 Page of music
4 Certain camera, for short
5 It may follow a pitch
6 Put into gear
7 Where to get a fast buck?
8 Chang's Siamese twin
9 Minute
10 A gift of fish, in Massachusetts?
11 Tibet's environs
12 In the cellar
13 Takes a gander at
18 On the side
22 Belted out
24 Middle facial mark, in Massachusetts?
26 Ring gem
27 Make copies of
29 Hang around
31 "Dies ___"
32 Suit material?
33 Adds turf to
34 Teen happening
35 Teen happening
36 Frank
37 Texas's Sen. Hutchison
40 Something to do
43 Film on ponds
45 Carrying, so to speak
47 Stir up
49 Undermine
51 1911 Chemistry Nobelist
52 Playful prank
53 Ticked off
54 Place in a box?
55 Rick's "Casablanca" love
56 Marvel superheroes
58 High-hatter
61 Smidgen
62 Vane dir.
63 MS. markers

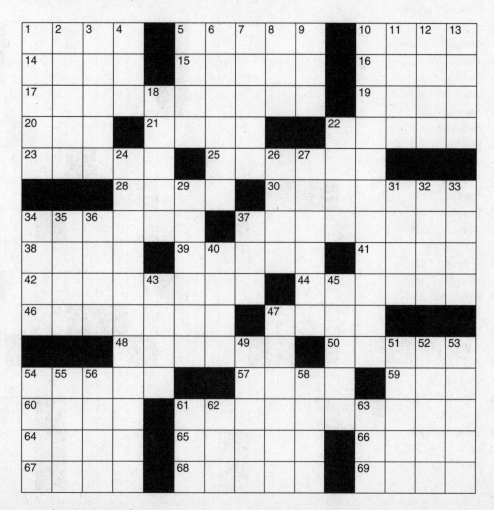

by Greg Staples

150

ACROSS

1 Enjoy the taste of
6 Log home
11 Yeshiva student
14 Baloney
15 Refrigerator brand
16 Air-quality
monitoring org.
17 Looks at lustfully
18 Incursion
at a sorority
20 Where
San Juan is
22 Formerly
23 Hospital fluids
24 Pipe player of
myth
25 ___ King Cole
27 6-4, e.g., in tennis
29 Classic Cadillac
33 ___ Na Na
36 Qaddafi's country
39 Diarist Nin
40 Media
consultant's field
43 Shoelace tip
44 Boxing venue
45 Michigan's
___ Canals
46 Wobbles on
the edge
48 Canine warning
50 Mao ___-tung
51 Pedal digit
53 Dashing style
57 "Garfield" dog
60 Colonial
silversmith
63 Substantial
entrees
65 Cut into
tiny pieces
66 Ripen
67 Likewise
68 Like the walls
at Wrigley Field
69 Moon vehicle,
for short
70 Center of a sink
71 Tears apart

DOWN

1 Comes to an end
2 Bicker
3 Nastier
4 "Falstaff"
and "Fidelio"
5 Take five
6 Frank who directed
"Mr. Deeds Goes
to Town"
7 With full force
8 Judges' seat
9 Chant
10 "Aye" canceler
11 Artist Millet
or Corot
12 Homer's "Iliad," e.g.
13 Ford a shallow
stream, say
19 Spiral pasta
21 Of the eye
26 Personification
28 Groups with influence
29 Valley
30 Neighbor
of Vietnam
31 Prefix with type
32 Old "Happy
motoring!" sloganeer
33 Petty quarrel
34 Bigger than big
35 Competent
37 Maidenform
products
38 Suffix with
saw or law
41 Envelope's contents
42 Make blood boil
47 Fix
49 Bring back
51 ___-frutti
52 Game show
announcer Johnny
who cried
"Come on down!"
54 Stalin's predecessor
55 Curve-shaped
56 Requires
57 Silica gem
58 Former Venetian
magistrate
59 Couple in a gossip
column
61 "The Thin Man"
pooch
62 Ruler of Qatar
64 Unmatched, as socks

by Janet R. Bender

ACROSS

1 TV reception problem
5 Scissors sounds
10 Breezed through, as a test
14 Make over
15 Prefix with -pathic
16 Appoint
17 Appear
18 Old-fashioned dances
19 Indigo dye source
20 Like most toy models
23 Lawyers' org.
26 Homes on wheels, for short
27 Complained bitterly
28 Fountain treat
30 Hitter of 755 home runs
32 Common meeting place
34 Wrigley Field player
37 Storm centers
38 Average guy?
39 Say "aye," say
40 Draft org.
41 Stopped by
44 Herb used in pesto
46 Cisco Kid's horse
47 Aussie lassie
50 Bacillus shape
51 Japanese moolah
52 Theme of this puzzle
56 "Picnic" playwright
57 Hang loosely
58 Disney dog
62 In the vicinity
63 Persian Gulf state
64 Solo appropriate for this puzzle
65 Lith. and Ukr., formerly
66 Mushers' vehicles
67 Abound

DOWN

1 Promgoers: Abbr.
2 Born, in bios
3 "___ to Joy"
4 Baby carrier?
5 Get dry and wrinkly
6 Christmas songs
7 "Since ___ You Baby" (1956 hit)
8 Trapper's prize
9 "My apologies"
10 Motrin alternative
11 Word with ear or Erie
12 Author Zola
13 Struck out
21 River to the Caspian
22 ___ Paulo, Brazil
23 Fire residue
24 Keeps afloat
25 Chips in
29 ___ Moines
30 Bubbling over
31 In the sack
33 Resort town near Santa Barbara
34 "I Spy" star Bill
35 Of value
36 "Don't ___ it!"
39 By way of
41 Manners
42 Worshipers
43 "Livin' la ___ Loca"
44 Those who wait
45 Pub order
47 They may get splints
48 Jazz's Earl "Fatha" ___
49 Mystery writer's award
50 Give more cushioning
53 Exam sans pencils
54 It's chopped liver
55 Blind segment
59 "All the Things You ___"
60 Run out of steam
61 Candied vegetable

by Adam G. Perl

ACROSS

1 Italian vacation spot
6 Mountain climber?
10 ___ Middlecoff, 1949 and 1956 U.S. Open champ
14 Tet observer
15 Place for a numbered flag
16 Peter Fonda title role
17 Slowly depart
19 One of the Sinatras
20 The Pointer Sisters' "___ So Shy"
21 Spiritual leader
22 Former first couple
23 Glum
24 Heartfelt
26 Its days are numbered
30 Central
31 W.W. II danger
32 503, long ago
34 Parachuting event
38 Kind of market
39 Lip-___ (doesn't really sing)
40 Hauled-away car, maybe
41 Attempt
42 Latin 101 word
43 West Wing workers
44 It may be engraved in stone
46 How lottery winners react
48 Head judges?
52 Scored on serve
53 Big picture
54 "C'mon . . . please?"
56 Luau chow
59 Schnozz
60 Reduce the area of by 50%
62 Earth, to Mahler
63 European car
64 Lugs
65 Self-help author Wayne

66 ___ II (razor brand)
67 New York city near Binghamton

DOWN

1 Payment method
2 Court legend
3 Papal name
4 W.W. II heroes: Abbr.
5 Leading
6 Bunch of sitcoms?
7 Pinhead
8 1966 song that asked, "What's it all about?"
9 Call, as a game
10 Routine
11 "Get ___!"
12 Monopoly income
13 Bakery supply
18 Glorify
22 Prefix with color
23 Negotiator's outrageous demand, e.g.
25 Ones close to le coeur
26 Denmates
27 Border on
28 "Damn Yankees" role
29 Shampoo finish
33 Like some epic poetry
35 Comic Foxx
36 European car
37 Floral arrangement
39 Leaf-turning mo.

43 Eroded
45 1-Across, e.g.: Abbr.
47 When Carmen meets Don José
48 Insert, as a code
49 Author's letter to an editor
50 Baseball news
51 Use elbow grease on
55 Alan of "Betsy's Wedding"
56 Top of the head
57 First name in fashion
58 Assuming that's true
60 "___ chance"
61 Modus operandi

by Elizabeth C. Gorski

ACROSS

1 More meanspirited
6 Elvis moved his, famously
10 Cole ___
14 Now, in Spain
15 Gaelic
16 George W. Bush's alma mater
17 Big name in weight loss
19 Sound preceding crackle and pop
20 Mornings, for short
21 "There ___ the neighborhood!"
22 Genetic anomaly
24 Inning divisions
25 Withered
26 "Take my wife . . . please!" comedian
31 Lumps of Clay?
32 Quote
33 "I do," at the altar
35 Chancellor von Bismarck
36 "Hyperion" poet
38 Baseball's Ruth
39 Poe's "The Murders in the ___ Morgue"
40 Unload, as stock
41 Took a stab at
42 "Big" director, 1988
46 Sounds of pleasure
47 Singer Redding
48 Color of Duke Ellington's "Mood"
51 Its slogan is "Where America's Day Begins"
52 Little lie
55 Medicine bottle
56 Real-life comic played in a film by Dustin Hoffman
59 Feed the kitty
60 "Heavens to Betsy!"
61 Furniture polish scent
62 Requirement
63 Scatters, as seed
64 Happening

DOWN

1 ___ California
2 Throat clearing
3 Princes, but not princesses
4 Suffix with north or south
5 Sci-fi weapons
6 Rejection of church dogma
7 Levin and Gershwin
8 Letter before omega
9 Divisions
10 Network
11 Glamorous actress Turner
12 Broadway's ___ Jay Lerner
13 Cried
18 1950's French president René
23 Press on
24 Cognizant of
25 Business attire
26 Try to get money from, slangily
27 Cosmetician Lauder
28 Florida citrus city
29 Be of use to
30 Prestigious prize
31 Supporting
34 Join in holy matrimony
36 Peepers' places
37 Shade trees
38 Playtex products
40 Glitch
41 Sewing aid
43 Caught in the act
44 Doctors make them in hospitals
45 Not leave
48 ___ the Terrible
49 Number dialed before two ones
50 July 4, 1776, e.g.
51 Chew (on)
52 Show anger
53 Bit of Windows dressing?
54 Not straight
57 Freudian topic
58 Gun, as an engine

by Randall J. Hartman

154

ACROSS

1 Very dry, as wine
5 Future blooms
9 Witch trials site
14 Minstrel's instrument
15 Put ___ writing
16 Wear away
17 Went ___ smoke
18 Foolishly enthusiastic
19 Spooky
20 Hundreds in New York, perhaps
23 Kitchen pest
24 ___ Baby
25 Russian empresses
27 Pesky e-mails
29 School of Buddhism
30 Workout site
33 Back problem
39 Ark builder
41 Floral necklace
42 Time past
43 Polynesian restaurant offering
48 Holiday drink
49 1989 General Motors debut
50 First of all
52 Inspects again
57 Lack of vigor
61 J.F.K. posting
62 House exterior choice
64 Prefix with millionaire
66 Algerian seaport
67 Forearm bone
68 Runs with minimal power
69 Whistler's whistle
70 Barely read
71 Impart knowledge
72 Sailboat feature
73 Headed for foreign ports

DOWN

1 Brief ad
2 Indian coin
3 Ancient city NW of Carthage
4 Mortise insertions
5 "So what?!"
6 Where the first transcontinental railroad was completed
7 Finger, say
8 Hitches
9 Is plenty angry
10 See 31-Down
11 System for pilots
12 City near Minneapolis
13 Runs into
21 Places for patches
22 Part of many a summer forecast
26 ___ 500
28 "___ 18" (Uris novel)
30 Econ. measure
31 With 10-Down, 1983 Lionel Richie hit
32 Traveler's guide
34 Most preferred
35 Kind of sandwich
36 Saturn model
37 Sellout indicator
38 Center of a blowout, maybe
40 Actor Grant
44 Easily irritated
45 Places
46 Lou Grant portrayer
47 Hindu princess
51 Snaky-locked woman of myth
52 "Please ___" (invoice stamp)
53 Practice piece
54 Arum lily
55 Stomachs may be in them
56 Pancake topper
58 Exploits
59 Bellybutton type
60 Brightly-colored lizard
63 Actress Wood of "Peyton Place"
65 Investigator, slangily

by Nancy Kavanaugh

ACROSS

1 Bus. bosses
5 Intermission follower, often
10 Sports "zebra"
13 "That's ___ shame"
15 Greg Evans comic strip
16 Cordoba cheer
17 Aviary timekeeper?
19 Last letters
20 Frat party dispensers
21 "___ afraid of that!"
23 Part of a geisha's attire
24 Article of Cologne
25 Abdominal anomaly
27 Whoops it up
29 Queens' Russian counterparts
31 Word before and after "de la"
32 Sounds of amazement
33 Race much shorter than a marathon
34 Aviary timekeeper?
37 Carson's predecessor
40 Swarm (with)
41 Gives a leg up
45 Out on a limb?
47 Hotel-room Bible provider
48 Persian king known as "the Great"
49 Lexicon with many citations: Abbr.
50 To and ___
51 Filthy lucre
52 Turns tail
55 Call to a shepherd
56 Sound from a 17- or 34-Across?
59 Contented sighs
60 Upper echelon
61 "Peter and the Wolf" name
62 E-mail address part
63 "Adam and Eve on a raft" site
64 "So ___ say"

DOWN

1 Guy
2 Scrounging sort
3 Get
4 Benefit
5 Old highway to Fairbanks
6 "I Spy" co-star Robert
7 Art colony near Santa Fe
8 Mag for execs
9 Blacker
10 1987 comedy based on "Cyrano de Bergerac"
11 Blissful
12 Shriner's cap
14 Rhine siren
18 Redding of R & B
22 Was obviously in pain
23 "Lord of the Rings" menace
25 "And ___ thou slain the Jabberwock?"
26 Seek an answer
28 Involve, as in an argument
29 Spa handout
30 Fraud
32 Ancient Greek theaters
35 U.S. hwys., e.g.
36 Scolders
37 Hippie's hangout
38 Algonquian Indian
39 Side by side
42 Having liberal political tendencies
43 Fast wheels
44 ___-Cone
46 ___ grouse (Pennsylvania's state bird)
47 "American Gigolo" star
49 Catchall category
52 Drops from the sky
53 Suffix with 29-Down
54 Rat-___
55 Ill-behaved
57 Actor Wallach
58 Singer Starr

by Gilbert H. Ludwig

156

ACROSS

1 Skillful
6 French friends
10 It precedes "Over here!"
14 Check recipient
15 Actress Spelling
16 Sailor's hello
17 When "S.N.L." ends in N.Y.C.
18 Beach promenade
20 Bench surrounded by pigeons?
22 1973 Rolling Stones #1 hit
23 Thin wood strip
24 WSW's opposite
25 Aesop's stories
29 Most sarcastic, as remarks
33 Writer ___ Stanley Gardner
34 Overturn, as a government
37 ___ Beta Kappa
38 Noted 19th- and 20th-century coal hauler
41 "You da ___!"
42 Places to get manicures
43 Pinnacle
44 Annoying
46 Gives 10%
48 Lincoln or Vigoda
49 British submachine gun
51 Milan's La ___
54 Pleasant sight at a supermarket checkout
59 Tariff on valuables
61 Indy competitor
62 Life sentences?
63 "___ want for Christmas . . ."
64 Gas company bought by BP
65 Alleviate

66 City on the Rhine, to locals
67 Ballplayers in pinstripes

DOWN

1 Each, in pricing
2 Comedian Carvey
3 Looker
4 Pinnacle
5 Place to observe Saturday Sabbath
6 Up, in baseball
7 Be a sponge
8 "Dies ___" (hymn)
9 Madam's mate
10 Hocked
11 Dance popularized in the 1930's
12 Songs for one
13 Young 'un
19 Book before Hosea
21 Part alphabetized in a telephone directory
24 Army volunteer
25 Physicist Enrico
26 Toward the back
27 Entry form
28 Was in front
29 The Golden Gate's is 4,200 feet
30 Notable period
31 Embarrassment
32 Ebb and others
35 Look at flirtatiously
36 No amateur
39 Weather line
40 Snitch

45 Gesture to a general
47 Where papers accumulate on a desk
49 "I ___ return"
50 Poison
51 ___ gin fizz
52 Havana's home
53 Line of rotation
54 D-Day invasion town
55 Dalai ___
56 Screen pic
57 Part of a bottle
58 God of love
60 Chatter on and on

by Jim Hyres

ACROSS

1 1930's movie dog
5 To boot
9 Couric of CBS News
14 Bleats
15 Per ___ (daily)
16 Icon
17 "Diana" crooner Paul
18 Mrs. Copperfield
19 Stocking stuff
20 American composer working at a bakery?
23 Bowler or boater
24 "To Autumn," e.g.
25 Alias initials
26 English playwright working at a press?
33 Inspiration for the Frisbee
35 Levy collector, for short
36 Koufax stat.
37 Petite desserts
38 At all
39 Blue eyes or baldness, e.g.
41 Titled Turk
42 Opposite of post-
43 Pan-fries
44 Vaudeville star working at a van company?
48 From S.F. to Las Vegas
49 "The Gold-Bug" writer
50 Scepter accompanier
53 Comedian working at an oil field?
58 Nice jacket material
59 Tide type
60 Sheltered, at sea
61 Be generous, at a bar
62 Mr. Hulot's creator
63 Actress Campbell
64 Diarist Samuel
65 Nabisco cookie
66 Turned blue, say

DOWN

1 Put to shame
2 Nick name?
3 Be a fall guy
4 "Quick!"
5 Like a postscript
6 Big name in small trains
7 Lowly worker
8 Gen. Bradley
9 Filmdom's Nastassja
10 "The Bonesetter's Daughter" writer
11 It may be spun around a campfire
12 Composer Stravinsky
13 Bard's nightfall
21 Bar mitzvah dances
22 Dinghy pair
27 Well put
28 Place for hash browns
29 Be nosy
30 Refreshment server on wheels
31 Cleveland's lake
32 Squealers
33 School grps.
34 Othello's betrayer
38 Piece by Matisse
39 Sulu portrayer on "Star Trek"
40 Boulevard crosser
42 Strip
43 Many a November birth
45 Best of times
46 Specks in the sea
47 Latest news
51 Superman player
52 Kennel club classification
53 24-karat
54 Dickens's Uriah
55 Making a hobby of
56 Affix a brand to
57 Touch the tarmac
58 Inits. at a gas station

by Norma Johnson

158

ACROSS

1 Leno, notably
5 Black key
10 Cyber-nuisance
14 The Charleses' canine
15 Suspicious
16 Place to spend euros
17 Start of a roadside verse
19 1994 Jodie Foster film
20 Animation pic
21 Tempe sch.
22 Broad scarf
23 Verse, part 2
28 Enzyme suffix
29 Lukas of "Witness"
30 Article in Hoy
33 Sacagawea, e.g.
36 Word with back or black
37 "Just ___!"
38 Verse, part 3
41 Rioter's take
42 Grates on
43 Fertile spot
44 Newswoman Compton
45 Stats for Sosa
46 S.D.I. weapon
47 End of the verse
53 Simple chord
55 Addition
56 High dudgeon
57 Library refs.
58 Provider of the verse
62 ___ greens
63 Codeine source
64 "Battle Cry" author
65 Joy Adamson's cub
66 Come home
67 Daly of "Judging Amy"

DOWN

1 Come out of one's shell?
2 Actor Milo
3 Long-legged wader
4 Road crew supply
5 French presidency, with "the"
6 Sick and tired
7 Idyllic place
8 Document ender?
9 Cobb and others
10 Brainpower
11 Quiche holders
12 Alice's chronicler in song
13 Hot sandwich
18 End of a stalk of corn
22 Focus of stomach-crunching
24 "I've ___ up to here!"
25 "Really?"
26 Lets up
27 ___ Hari
31 Brand once advertised as "Tops in taste"
32 The Red Baron and others
33 Blowout
34 Abreast of
35 Old ___ (Boston sight)
36 Like some tabloid headlines
37 Rhett's last words
39 Be in accord
40 Prestigious prizes
45 McCarthy quarry
46 Burning
48 Ziti, e.g.
49 Big bone
50 Lock site, maybe
51 Sen. Sam of Watergate fame
52 Snider teammate
53 Option for Hamlet
54 Angler's need
58 Diddley and Derek
59 It's scanned in mkts.
60 Uruguay, e.g.
61 Unfancy home

by Jerry E. Rosman

ACROSS

1 Cut with a crosscut
5 /
10 Castro's country
14 As to
15 Where Seoul is
16 Done with
17 One choosing a sweater, e.g.?
19 Let it all out
20 Sombrero, e.g.
21 Blame
22 Shoddy
24 Mrs. Harry Truman
25 One-named singer and Oscar winner
26 Item that may be connected to a car's ignition
29 Act of philanthropy
33 Opposite of out
34 Actress Tammy who won a Tony for playing Molly Brown
36 Genetic inits.
37 Recognize terrific fountain treats?
40 ___ de Cologne
41 Theater passages
42 Not straight
43 Hard-to-decide predicaments
45 Pal
46 "If ___ be so bold . . ."
47 Get together
49 Penny-pinching
52 The "shrew" in "The Taming of the Shrew"
53 Honey maker
56 Every's partner
57 Mace?
60 Riverbed deposit
61 "Goodnight ___" (1950 hit)
62 Luminous radiation
63 Do in
64 The "N" of U.S.N.A.
65 City tricked with a wooden horse

DOWN

1 Punjabi believer
2 "The King and I" tutor
3 Habeas corpus, e.g.
4 After expenses
5 Drums, in jazz lingo
6 Place
7 Boats like Noah's
8 Envision
9 Severity
10 Like C.I.A. operations
11 Part of the eye containing the iris
12 Mercedes-___
13 Painterlike
18 Robert Frost piece
23 Fido restrainer
24 Beer, say
25 Dumas's Monte Cristo, e.g.: Fr.
26 Named, as a price
27 Hawaiian island
28 Run ___ of (violate)
29 Places a call on an old phone
30 Irritated
31 Upright, as a box
32 Very unpleasant
34 Old female tabby
35 State again
38 Letter before delta
39 Border on
44 Fourscore
45 Symbol of redness
47 ___ cum laude
48 Lucy's landlady
49 Own (up to)
50 Commuting option
51 Bruins' sch.
52 Chicken ___ (dish)
53 Become hazy
54 Continental currency
55 Auctioneerless auction site
58 Gunners' org.
59 Tabby

by Mel Taub

ACROSS

1 Athens rival
7 Power glitch
12 One-dimensional
13 Best of the best
17 Basements' opposites
18 Surpasses in slyness
19 "Wow!"
21 Corp. bigwig
22 Loudness units
23 Decorative jugs
25 On vacation
28 Its cap. is Sydney
29 Alpine call
31 Strike back, say
33 Wheel's center
34 "M*A*S*H" star
37 "Wow!"
41 Env. abbreviation
42 Send via phone line
43 Salami choice
44 Chico's "ciao"
46 From ___ Z
48 Explosive inits.
49 Pine exudation
51 Magnet for a moth
53 Cereal grain
54 "Wow!"
60 War crimes trier
62 Win the heart of
63 Completely surround
64 It may be vinyl or aluminum
65 Little laugh
66 Takes a nibble of

DOWN

1 Blind strip
2 Central part
3 Opposed to
4 Jockey's straps
5 Supplement, as a bill
6 Acts investigated by insurance companies
7 Highlanders, e.g.
8 "Nah!"
9 "The Godfather" composer Nino ___
10 Supertalented
11 Environmental prefix
14 "Wow!"
15 Palm reader, e.g.
16 General ___ chicken (Chinese dish)
20 Not a lot
24 Use a loom
25 Killer whale
26 Accomplishment
27 "Wow!"
29 Bald Brynner
30 Kimono tie
32 Singer Lauper
33 Witch's work
35 Singer Celine
36 Rat-___
38 ET carrier
39 Some undergrad degs.
40 "I" problem?
45 Do harm to
46 Actress MacGraw
47 Least wild
49 Superficial teaching method
50 Bring in
51 N.J. city near the George Washington Br.
52 "Zounds!"
55 Not up or down, as a stock price: Abbr.
56 Shopper's lure
57 Not genuine: Abbr.
58 Zero
59 Work units
61 Took the bait

by Karen M. Tracey

ACROSS

1 Humane org.
5 Fibber ___ of old radio
10 Blue shade
14 Early late-night name
15 It may be red
16 Pat on the back?
17 Deli purchase
19 Parakeet's place
20 Guru's goal
21 Rhine feeder
23 Mardi Gras figure
24 With 54-Across, the theme of this puzzle [hint: New Hampshire]
25 A&E alternative
27 Giant of note
29 V-J Day pres.
30 Preserved, in a way
35 Of ___ (somewhat)
36 "Come on now!"
37 Financial page acronym
40 China ___ (showy bloom)
42 Art collectibles
43 Headshake, e.g.
45 Apple product
47 Lifesavers of a kind
49 It's like "-like"
52 Type
53 Elec. system component
54 See 24-Across
56 Garfield's master
58 Have something
60 Dublin native
62 Sailed through
64 Food experts
66 Cheesemaking byproduct
67 Be frank (with)
68 Brutus's "Behold!"
69 Ticked off
70 Clean off
71 Fan sounds

DOWN

1 Bathtub sound
2 Palette supplies
3 "As is," e.g.
4 Don't exist
5 Large openings
6 Star groups
7 Lux. neighbor
8 Like oleo vis-à-vis butter
9 Blues singer James
10 "One Life to Live" airer
11 Statistical boundary value
12 Press
13 Top spot
18 Marine dangers
22 Was a passenger
26 Bug protection
28 CD selection
31 Author Dahl
32 Misplay
33 Add-on
34 Bad: Prefix
35 Like some symmetry
37 Fuss
38 Mal de ___
39 Arrange with some effort
41 Hard rubbers
44 "Diana" singer
46 Of element no. 76
48 More unctuous
49 Home of Odysseus
50 It may make the nose wrinkle
51 Motor's power, informally
55 Willow variety
56 1975 Spielberg film
57 Word from a Spanish count?
59 Not scheduled to play
61 Stir up
63 It may be red
65 Spacewalk, for short

by Alan Arbesfeld

ACROSS

1 Bygone airline
4 Mass confusion
9 Demean
14 Roll of bills
15 Greeting
16 Rodeo participant
17 Subject of the biography "Float Like a Butterfly"
18 Home of the Blue Grotto
20 ___ of March
22 Braxton or Tennille
23 ___ Maria
24 Feed
27 Guarantees
30 Unfounded, as gossip
31 Lariat in the Southwest
32 Sheep's plaint
35 Work to get, as someone's trust
37 Outfit
40 Regular's request
44 Station
45 15-Across, in Spain
46 Full house sign: Abbr.
47 List components
50 Give a hoot
52 Ate at home
54 Smarts
58 Exiled Amin
59 Neighbor of Cambodia
61 Apiece
62 Theater guides
67 Maiden name preceder
68 Observant one
69 Hotelier Helmsley
70 Cereal grain
71 On the briny
72 Ninth mos.
73 ___ and outs

DOWN

1 "Tom Sawyer" author
2 Elusive children's book character
3 Farewell
4 "The Sweetheart of Sigma ___"
5 "For ___ a jolly . . ."
6 Sane
7 Table spread
8 Later's alternative
9 L'___ de Triomphe
10 Feathery wrap
11 Equipment
12 Deliver, as a summons
13 Great Lakes Indians
19 Speeder's penalty
21 ___ Lanka
25 Thought creatively
26 Cyrillic alphabet user
28 Large cactus
29 Sport ___ (off-road vehicles)
32 Bridge declaration
33 Beverage that's bitterer than beer
34 Mountain climbers
36 To the ___ degree
38 Egypt and Syria, once: Abbr.
39 Arafat's org.
41 Table d'___ (restaurant offering)
42 Pawning place
43 Verve
48 Pepper grinder
49 Slow movers
51 Ram's mate
52 Ross of the Supremes
53 Dunderhead
55 Vietnam's capital
56 Where the waves are
57 Sharpens
60 S-shaped molding
63 Actress Michele
64 Time in history
65 Explosive
66 KLM competitor

by Sarah Keller

ACROSS

1 An article may be written on it
5 Purse part, often
10 Cake with a kick
14 Baccarat alternative
15 Brownish gray
16 Bass products
17 Yellowstone figure
19 ___ out (barely gets)
20 "Yertle the Turtle" author
21 Rake with fire
23 "Quiet!"
24 Where cubs are raised
26 Permit
27 "I know the answer!"
30 Contract bridge tactics
33 Bother
35 Like modern clocks and recordings
36 Home on the range
38 Divine path, in Asian religions
39 Firm belief
43 Wash
46 Heat to 212°, as water
47 Where weapons are forbidden
51 Need for a keg
52 Takes too many tranqs, say
53 Peak SE of Olympus
54 "La-la" lead-in
56 Color, as a hippie's shirt
58 Breakaway country from Ethiopia
62 Other, in Oaxaca
63 Send around the bend
66 Astronaut Armstrong
67 Nonstudio film
68 Plowing unit
69 Swirl
70 Achieves perfectly
71 They're split for soup

DOWN

1 Bay Area patrollers: Abbr.
2 Carson predecessor
3 Miscalculates
4 Soda fountain choices
5 Hid
6 Catches some rays
7 Toupee, slangily
8 Copy
9 Keep going
10 1930's heavyweight champ Max
11 Acid-neutralizing compound
12 Complained
13 Selling points
18 German industrial valley
22 "Don't ___ on me"
24 Daewoo model
25 Operatic passage
27 Toward the rear
28 Tint
29 Egyptian viper
31 Blood pressure, body temperature, etc.
32 Campy 1958 sci-fi film, with "The"
34 Split-off group
37 Jetsons' lad
40 Came down with
41 Unaccounted-for G.I.
42 Saint-Moritz sight
44 Entered gradually
45 Main courses
47 Zero
48 Reworked, as text
49 Log-on name
50 Rocker Clapton
55 Fall into ___ (get caught)
57 "Last Call" host
58 Malevolence
59 Marathon
60 Pound of literature
61 Yeoman's yeses
64 Genetic info carrier
65 Uganda's Amin

by Todd McClary

ACROSS

1 Mute Marx
6 "Hop ___!"
10 Tempest in a teapot
14 The bounding main
15 "I see," facetiously
16 Charles barker
17 Don't mess with him!
20 D.C. summer setting
21 Conversant with
22 Done
23 Secret store
26 Title locale in a Cheech Marin movie
27 Don't burn them!
31 Olive with a little salt?
32 Ones foaling
33 Ticked off
35 Out of port
36 Don't make them!
38 Flat floater
42 It helps you see plays
44 "Sexy" lady of a Beatles song
45 Oberhausen "oh"
48 Don't say this!
51 Believer
53 ___ Gay (W.W. II plane)
54 Fountain favorites
55 Introduction to science?
57 Kindergarten break
60 Don't give me that!
64 Read rapidly
65 "That's right"
66 Line to the audience
67 Newcastle's river
68 Next in line?
69 Smidgen

DOWN

1 Part of HBO
2 Etcher's fluid
3 Burnout treatment
4 Butter portion
5 Low digit
6 Chiang Kai-shek's capital
7 "This can't be!"
8 Copyright page info: Abbr.
9 Low digit
10 Flatters, with "over"
11 Familiar with
12 Hard
13 Biblical footwear
18 Essen basin
19 Rib
24 Fields
25 "Survivor" network
26 Comics cries
27 Singer Sumac
28 New World grp.
29 Result of a bad shot, maybe
30 Coll. senior's test
34 Say "y'all," say
36 Refuses to
37 Te-___ cigars
39 "Oklahoma!" gal
40 Needle holder
41 Danson of "Becker"
43 Cow catcher
44 B'way sign
45 Maximally
46 Like a blackboard eraser
47 Repressed
49 Marilu of "Evening Shade"
50 Lady of "Idylls of the King"
52 "C'est moi" to us
55 Grimm villain
56 Haleakala's locale
58 Current choice
59 Cheat, in a way
61 Like a certain power
62 Perp prosecutors, briefly
63 Venom source

by Harvey Estes and Nancy Salomon

ACROSS

1 Mr. Fix-It's job
7 Diamond officials
11 Internet
   pop-ups, e.g.
14 Blake of
   "Gunsmoke"
15 "Chicago"
   star Richard
16 Note after fa
17 Marksmanship
   contest
19 It may be stubbed
20 World-weary
21 Med. plan
22 Lamb's mother
23 Ice sheets
25 Slightly sour candy
28 San ___ Obispo,
   Calif.
29 Contradict
30 Game of observation
31 Everything
32 A.M.A. members
33 "My dog ___ fleas"
35 Roar with mirth
41 Disreputable paper
42 Apropos of
43 ___ & Perrins
   (sauce brand)
44 "Dancing
   Queen" quartet
47 Rent-A-Wreck
   competitor
48 Aggressively
   publicize
49 Like a basset hound
52 Stop, Yield
   and No Passing
53 Dowsing need
54 Future C.E.O.'s deg.
55 Cosmetician Lauder
57 Bowl over
58 Survivalist's
   structure
62 Make funny faces
63 Singer Brickell
64 Rainbow color
65 Pesticide-
   monitoring grp.

66 Everything else
67 "Newhart"
   actor Tom

DOWN

1 Long-tailed pest
2 Relative of an ostrich
3 Precooks, in a way
4 Joints that
   may be twisted
5 Bright thoughts
6 Sunbathers
   catch them
7 "Eww, gross!"
8 Quaint exclamation
9 Movie trailer, e.g.
10 Attack
11 Autumn blooms
12 1950's music style

13 Not wide-awake
18 Pick
23 Opposite of muscle
24 Humdinger
26 Put into servitude
27 Piece of china
29 Magician Henning
32 ___ double-take
33 Humble homes
34 In the past
36 1-Down catcher
37 Comments to
   the audience
38 Phone answerer's cry
39 Element #10
40 Jokes that may
   be "running"
44 Steep-roofed house
45 Explode

46 Spanish grocery
47 One of the Three
   Musketeers
48 Pastures
50 Fire remnant
51 Place to live
52 Shorthand expert
56 Niña, Pinta
   or Santa María
59 "Wanna ___?"
60 Self-image
61 Harry Potter's
   best friend

by Trip Payne

ACROSS

1 One of Franklin's two certainties
6 Spielberg blockbuster
10 Library item
14 ___ Detoo of "Star Wars"
15 Economist Greenspan
16 Rich vein
17 Sports car at a deli?
19 Sportswear brand
20 Bake sale grp.
21 Amigo
22 People after whom things are named
24 Extremely
26 Lowly foot soldier, slangily
27 Muslim in Russia
29 Bewilder
33 Bell or shell preceder
36 Take ___ (try some)
38 "To your health!"
39 Elvis's middle name
40 Unseen title character in a Beckett play
42 "Gladiator" setting
43 Get through to
45 Arctic ice
46 Tabloid tidbit
47 Feeling of pity
49 Midway alternative
51 Building add-on
53 Pirate's supporter
57 Something to turn over on January 1
60 Alley ___
61 Buckeyes' sch.
62 European automaker
63 Pancake-eating senator at a deli?
66 Singer McEntire
67 Hand over (to)
68 Cathedral features
69 Netting
70 Co. medical offerings
71 2001 and 2010

DOWN

1 Extinguishes
2 Lord Byron's Muse
3 It may come out smelling like a rose
4 From A ___
5 Big to-do
6 One corner of a Monopoly board
7 Miss. neighbor
8 Addition to a concentrate
9 Grab quickly
10 Onslaught of crepe orders at a deli?
11 Leaking
12 1960's baseball All-Star Blue Moon ___
13 Some sneakers
18 Company with a "lonely repairman"
23 Burden
25 What an English student wore to a deli?
26 Traffic problems at a deli?
28 Beginning on
30 ___ suiter
31 Liberace fabric
32 K–6, as a sch.
33 Canvas cover
34 Length × width, for a rectangle
35 Part of a suit
37 Literary bear
41 Place to put bags?
44 Sharpen
48 Grab quickly
50 Slo-mo footage, perhaps
52 Violinist Zimbalist
54 "___ luck!"
55 Glacial ridge
56 Conjecture
57 Bell curve peak
58 Fencing blade
59 Spiders' work
60 Bills not stocked in A.T.M.'s
64 Tokyo of old
65 Mimic

by Peter Abide

ACROSS

1 RCA product
4 Rock singer/poet Smith
9 Drink from fermented milk
14 Pension supplement, for short
15 Fake fat brand
16 Rust, e.g.
17 Tribe related to the Fox
18 Civil War side
19 Gentleman's gentleman
20 Start of a definition of television, by 9-Down
23 Spendthrift's outing
24 Diplomat's asset
25 Some coll. exams
29 Feared flier
33 Definition, part 2
37 One with a list?
38 NATO member
39 Public image
42 Chi. setting
43 Buster?
45 Definition, part 3
47 Stopper, informally
50 "___ the Top"
51 Sit on it
53 Sit on it
57 End of the definition
63 Like ___ from the blue
64 Beatles phenomenon, e.g.
65 Tend the turf
66 He once worked for Edison
67 Follow, as a tip
68 Downed a sub?
69 Wood finish
70 Nary a soul
71 Aussie outlaw Kelly

DOWN

1 Travelers' papers
2 Writer's woe
3 Soap Box Derby entrant
4 Pays what is due
5 Baseball family name
6 Five to ten, e.g.
7 Makes lace
8 ___ water
9 Big name in early TV
10 Grandly praised
11 Plug
12 ___ fixe
13 No longer in the service: Abbr.
21 Crème ___ crème
22 Subject of a B. Kliban drawing
26 Enzyme suffix
27 Garr of "Young Frankenstein"
28 Hardly macho
30 Word with high- or low-
31 MS. enclosure
32 ___'acte
33 "Nonsense!"
34 Actor Morales
35 Engine part, for short
36 ___ avail
40 Opposite of alt, in German
41 727, e.g.
44 Violinist/composer Arcangelo ___
46 Prepared to drive, with "up"
48 Summer shade
49 Wellness grp.
52 Spin doctor
54 Eternal City dweller
55 Large bill
56 Cut down
57 "Phooey!"
58 Be a lookout for, say
59 Montgomery's Parks
60 City named for an Indian tribe
61 Within: Prefix
62 Big 22-Down

by Paula Gamache

ACROSS

1 Was in a choir
5 All-night bash
9 Tough guys
14 Award in the ad biz
15 Genesis garden
16 "To the moon, ___!" ("The Honeymooners" phrase)
17 Much modern popular music
18 Direct
20 In the offing
22 Requisite
23 Emergency message
24 Wedding ceremony, e.g.
28 Drop from the eye
29 Wandered
33 Where fighter jets touch down
38 Shareholder's substitute
39 Wrath
40 Animal hides
42 Mincemeat dessert
43 Touches down
46 Targets of football kicks
49 Stuffed shirts
51 Derrière
52 Flier at Kitty Hawk
58 Row a boat
61 Nut
62 Unearthly
63 Be a secret author
67 "Ain't Misbehavin'" star Carter
68 Musical show
69 List-ending abbr.
70 Any Poe story
71 Improve, as text
72 Lowly worker
73 Underworld river

DOWN

1 "Hightail it out of here!"
2 Island welcome
3 More friendly
4 Speedy one-seaters
5 Gridiron official, for short
6 Hubbub
7 Captain Nemo's creator
8 Computer key
9 Convertible look-alike
10 Actor Wallach
11 Russian fighter jets
12 Canyon sound
13 New Jersey hoopsters
19 Legacy receiver
21 Regimen
25 Org. for people 50 and over
26 "Peer Gynt" composer
27 Spot for a headphone
30 Swabs
31 Escape route
32 Brunette-to-redhead jobs
33 Is under the weather
34 Tehran's locale
35 Ashcroft's predecessor
36 Negotiator with Isr.
37 One of the Fab Four
41 Whole lot
44 Wall Street index, with "the"
45 Unnatural-sounding
47 Reduce, as expenses
48 Adjusts to the surroundings
50 Glacial
53 Yawn inducers
54 Merge
55 "Super!"
56 Not flat
57 Pre-Internet communication
58 Brute
59 Pause filler
60 Wander
64 Natural tanner
65 Road cover
66 Santa's helper

by Lynn Lempel

ACROSS

1 Cartographers' works
5 "I did it!"
9 Count of stars on a U.S. flag
14 Canted
15 Minute bit
16 Lavatory sign
17 Gawk
18 Catskills resort, e.g.
20 Hint at
22 Magazine number
23 Azer. or Ukr., once
24 Rich source of fossil fuel
26 Utmost degree
28 Dejected
29 Land
33 Part of a circle
36 Makeup of 18-, 24-, 53- and 64-Across
39 Ned who composed "Air Music"
42 Commotion
43 Candidate of 1992 and '96
44 Component length of 36-Across
47 Inspire respect
48 Withdraws
49 Coach Parseghian
52 Mortarboard, e.g.
53 Large real estate purchase
58 Computer key
61 Flowering shrub
63 Pago Pago's locale
64 Members of Elián González's family, e.g.
67 Highly graphic
68 Camera concern
69 Inhabitant of ancient Persia
70 Launder ending
71 All the clues in this puzzle do this with 36-Across
72 Gaelic
73 Scorch

DOWN

1 Copperfield's field
2 Mission in Texas
3 Carl Reiner film "Where's ___?"
4 Witches' recitations
5 Color on the beach
6 Arranged a dinner at home
7 Walk about with a divining rod
8 Vanderbilt and Grant
9 Risky building to be in
10 India ___
11 Complain
12 Medicinal amts.
13 Calendar's span
19 Scale unit at the post office
21 Warbler Sumac
25 Passports and driver's licenses, for short
27 Nectar-pouring goddess
29 Origin suffix
30 Incantation beginning
31 Develop
32 Medieval Italian fortress city
33 Sciences' partner
34 Investment firm T. ___ Price
35 Gator's relative
37 Makes lace
38 Orange or lemon drink
40 Major util.
41 Decorated Olympian
45 Warmish
46 Okinawa honorific
50 Interstate syst.
51 Maxims
53 Cager at the Staples Center
54 Corrosive liquids
55 Milk a scene for all it's worth
56 Arterial trunk
57 Coating
58 Flunking marks
59 Schedule position
60 Cola's beginning
62 Flimsy, as an excuse
65 Capek play
66 Married name modifier

by PAtrick MErrell

170

ACROSS
1 Fine stone
5 Pops
10 Pelée spew
14 Reunion attendee
15 It was once advertised as "Good for tender gums"
16 He gave us a lift
17 Making of handicrafts, say
20 Pivotal
21 Getaway places
22 Neutral shade
23 Latin 101 verb
24 Gone by
26 Camp sack
27 Character in a Beatles "White Album" tune
32 "Have ___" (waiting room offer)
33 Perfect, as an alibi
37 Regan's father
38 Put a strain on
40 Paris's ___ d'Orsay
41 Ballpark figure
43 Other: Fr.
44 Certain pleasure craft
47 J.F.K. regulators
50 Same old, same old
51 House member
52 Vice President Barkley
54 Eastern priest
55 Lettuce variety
58 Object formally
62 Like tights
63 Lake rental, maybe
64 Go with
65 Hard to grasp
66 "Fun, Fun, Fun" car
67 Lens type

DOWN
1 Trunk item
2 Hand cream ingredient
3 Shirkers shirk it
4 CPR giver
5 Nod, at auctions
6 Not dismissing out of hand
7 Roast spot
8 Cape ___, Mass.
9 In a blue funk
10 Give the slip to
11 Room at the top?
12 Neighbor of Leo
13 So far
18 Draw a bead on
19 It takes two nuts
23 Kind of mushroom
24 Rose's love
25 Fasten with a belt
27 Bind with haywire
28 Partakes of
29 Nifty
30 Like a candle
31 Bromine is one
34 Gumption
35 Racer of fable
36 Bireme section
38 Prohibition: Var.
39 Fighting
42 Scene of two W.W. I battles
43 Hearing-related
45 Hue and cry
46 Won easily
47 Two-timing
48 Stag
49 Paula of pop
53 Like custard
54 Actress Anderson
55 "See you later!"
56 Not fooled by
57 Originate
59 Do something
60 Urban transport
61 Woodworker's tool

by Alan Arbesfeld

ACROSS

1 Makes yawn
6 Sandwich shop
10 Backfire sound
14 Bullying, e.g.
15 With 34-Across, places to set pies to bake
16 Killer whale
17 ___ nova (60's dance)
18 Fender blemish
19 Watch face
20 "Is it soup ___?"
21 Third-place prize
24 Red roots in the garden
26 Maid's cloth
27 Grand ___ Dam
29 Five-pointed star
34 See 15-Across
35 Auditions, with "out"
36 Rowboat blade
37 Questions
38 Holy one
39 Animal caretakers, for short
40 Father's Day gift
41 Piano piece
42 On the ___ (close to defeat)
43 Pre-repair job figure
45 "Unto the Sons" author Gay ___
46 Band booking
47 Exterior
48 Southeastern Conference mascot
53 Towel stitching
56 "Hold on a moment!"
57 Barracks no-show
58 F.B.I. operative
60 Former Georgia senator Sam
61 Something passed in music class?
62 Discontinue
63 Where the Mets play
64 Royal Russian
65 Fund, as one's alma mater

DOWN

1 Diaper wearer
2 Relative of an English horn
3 Old, deteriorated ship
4 Feminine suffix
5 Landing strip constructors
6 Extinct flock
7 Smooth
8 Actress Kay of "Breezy," 1973
9 E-mail deliverer, with "the"
10 Store with taco shells
11 Like a dust bowl
12 March Madness org.
13 Effrontery
22 I-95, e.g.: Abbr.
23 Shoes are wiped on them
25 The "E" in B.P.O.E.
27 Orange container
28 Caravan's stopping point
29 Group of lions
30 German "a"
31 Venomous viper
32 Shoestrings
33 Shake, as an Etch A Sketch
35 Pulled tight
38 Like backwater
39 Shoe part that's wiped on 23-Down
41 Royal Arabian
42 Workaday world
44 Large lizard
45 Wed. preceder
47 Person likely to say "hubba hubba!"
48 Barley beards
49 "Nope!"
50 Rib or ulna
51 Deuces
52 Bit
54 ___ many words
55 Goulash
59 Tommy Franks, for one: Abbr.

by Gregory E. Paul

ACROSS

1 O'Neill's "Desire Under the ___"
5 Peak
9 Hayloft stack
14 With 23-Across, crimson
15 Horse's pace
16 Speedy train
17 The "I" of "The King and I"
18 Not limited to roads
20 "Absolutely, guaranteed"
22 Big Apple subway, with "the"
23 See 14-Across
24 Barbecuers' equipment
28 Kind of weight
30 Queen of the fairies
33 Spooky
34 Oracle
35 Directed
36 "Definitely worth getting"
39 Beats the backside of
40 "___ Yankees"
41 Like it ___
42 Award bestowed by a queen: Abbr.
43 Paper mates
44 Comfort
45 Tide alternative
46 Peter, Paul and Mary: Abbr.
47 "As a matter of fact . . ."
55 "Star Wars" weapon
56 Sporting sword
57 Wading bird
58 Self-involved
59 007
60 A bit drunk
61 Refuges
62 Raggedy fellow

DOWN

1 Cyberauction house
2 Late-night host
3 Waiter's handout
4 Attempt
5 Playing marbles
6 Flower part
7 Venus de ___
8 Caesar's words to Brutus
9 Beef ___ soup
10 Pungent
11 Browse (through)
12 Author Wiesel
13 ___ Diego
19 Goofs
21 "Oklahoma!" aunt
24 Really irk
25 Place to kick a habit
26 Singer Cara
27 They're kissable
28 Swarms
29 Check
30 ___ Carta
31 Kind of committee
32 Davis of "All About Eve"
34 Computerized photo
35 Engage in logrolling
37 Paradigms
38 Perch
43 Comely
44 Isaac and Howard
45 Early anesthetic
46 Arab chief
47 Buster Brown's four-legged friend
48 Shrek, e.g.
49 Hot rock
50 Ski lift
51 Country artist McEntire
52 Atop
53 Take care of
54 Actress Lamarr
55 Isr. neighbor

by Judy Cole

ACROSS

1 Meshed's land
5 R&B artist with the hit "Thong Song"
10 "A leopard can't change its spots," e.g.
13 Caught on a ranch
15 Baby's woe
16 Dernier ___
17 Apiarist's request on "Wheel of Fortune"?
19 Layer
20 Kind of rubber
21 Nymph of myth
23 Attention-getter
24 Land in the Seine
25 Beach memento
27 Supermodel's request on "Wheel of Fortune"?
31 Beau ___
34 Split apart
35 H⁺, e.g.
36 Ancient writing
37 Vendor's spot
39 Investor's channel
40 Sierra Madre treasure
41 Nordic saint
42 Conrad of old films
43 Ornithologist's request on "Wheel of Fortune"?
47 Arcade flubs
48 ___ judicata
49 Loop sights
52 Spyri heroine
54 This puzzle's request receiver
56 Propel, in a way
57 Cyclops' request on "Wheel of Fortune"?
60 Historic leader?
61 Sanitation worry
62 Verbal white flag
63 19th in a series
64 Shoulder muscles, briefly
65 E.R. cry

DOWN

1 Like a brogue
2 Bygone women's magazine
3 In a fitting way
4 Classic soft drink
5 Act opener
6 "Dies ___"
7 Have a bawl
8 Neighbor of N.Y.
9 Side of a pillowcase that a pillow goes in
10 Old Austrian money
11 Atlas stat
12 Empty talk
14 Go one way or the other
18 40 quarters, e.g.
22 It has its head in a glass
25 Espied
26 Flush, say
27 Resident's suffix
28 Big name in cheese
29 Stud site
30 S.A.S.E., e.g.
31 David of "Rhoda"
32 It replaced the 10-Down
33 Some are studded
37 Token taker
38 Cross shapes
39 Islet
41 Indebted
42 Bahamas' capital
44 Scholarship money
45 Partner of Porthos
46 Ballet leap
49 Cockpit button
50 Eric Clapton hit
51 Sport with traps
52 Clinton's birthplace
53 All ___
54 Trapper's trophy
55 Richards and Reinking
58 Bar stock
59 Tennessee athlete, for short

by Kelly Katharine Delevan

ACROSS

1 Vineyard fruit
6 Goes on and on
11 Pale
14 Rand McNally product
15 Cosmetician Lauder
16 Pres. Lincoln
17 Enjoy summer air-conditioning, say
19 Dieters' units: Abbr.
20 Sigma's follower
21 Right on a map
22 Frontiersman Carson
23 1970 Beatles chart-topper
27 Strikes out
29 Santa ___, Calif.
30 Cenozoic and Paleozoic
32 Brother of Cain and Abel
33 Squid's squirt
34 "Alas" and "alack"
36 Thorns' places
39 Felt bad about
41 Party list
43 The Beehive State
44 Exercise for the abs
46 African antelope
48 Southern constellation
49 ___ d'oeuvre
51 Green shade
52 Can topper
53 Washing machine cycle
56 Surgeon who pioneered the artificial human heart implant
58 Driver's need: Abbr.
59 Gymnast's feat
61 Film locale
62 "Put ___ Happy Face"
63 Be entirely satisfactory
68 "For shame!"

69 Former Chinese premier Zhou ___
70 Walkie-talkie
71 Actress Caldwell
72 Breathers
73 Guinness, e.g.

DOWN

1 Go on and on
2 Hwy.
3 Pie ___ mode
4 Page who sang "How much is that doggie in the window?"
5 Fancy homes
6 Director Spike
7 Queens's ___ Stadium
8 It precedes fast and follows farm
9 Coquettes
10 Takes up residence (in)
11 Live up to one's word
12 Hoffman who wrote "Steal This Book"
13 Hatching posts?
18 Arrogance
23 Lions' dens
24 The blahs
25 Top everything else
26 Birdie beater
28 "___, Brute?"
31 "I ___ return"
35 Not flighty
37 One of the Osmonds
38 Disreputable
40 Chad & Jeremy and others

42 Catch, as in a net
45 Suggest, as a deal
47 Big name in diamonds
50 Like ocean water
53 Fall over in a faint
54 Classic laundry detergent
55 Spikes, in volleyball
57 Up, in baseball
60 Surveyor's map
64 "___ the season . . ."
65 Altar vow
66 Lucy of "Charlie's Angels," 2000
67 Auction grouping

by Randall J. Hartman

ACROSS

1 Cone maker
4 "Don't you recognize the voice?!"
9 Give up, as a habit
13 Part of a Latin conjugation
15 Boarded
16 Prince William's school
17 Making trouble
19 Shiny gold fabric
20 Gabs and gabs
21 "Mercy!"
22 Permit
23 Cent
25 Glimpse
26 Away from the bow
29 Semi-colon?
30 One who walks a beat
33 Going to the dogs, e.g.
35 It's fit for a queen
37 "I feel great!"
41 Flash point?
42 "What's in ___?"
43 Sophs., two years later
44 Shade tree
46 Prefix with meter
47 That lady
50 Indian state
52 Birth-related
54 Ink spots
57 Making no sound
60 Ladies' man
61 Fancy duds
62 Neutral color
63 Like some cereals
64 Folk singer Guthrie
65 Delicate lock of hair
66 Unpromising
67 D.C. bigwig

DOWN

1 Regional groups of animal life
2 Stick on a stick
3 Nursery noisemaker
4 Composer Stravinsky
5 Duds
6 Not stand erect
7 Butted out?
8 Put the kibosh on
9 Green shade
10 Emphatic type: Abbr.
11 Hair straightener
12 Lower joint
14 Dog in Oz
18 Forwarding info on a letter
21 Rich, now
24 "Pretty nice!"
27 Big exams
28 Young 'un
30 Foldout bed
31 Lunch hour
32 Each
33 ___-de-France
34 Entrepreneur's deg.
36 Way to go: Abbr.
37 Syringe measures, for short
38 Paddle
39 Sounds of hesitation
40 Record producer Brian
45 Car owner's reference
47 Has the wheel
48 Fuss
49 ___ Howard, 1963 A.L. M.V.P.
50 Consumed with gusto
51 Three-card ___
53 Jessica of "Dark Angel"
54 Beer, informally
55 Venues
56 Yours and mine
58 Bean product?
59 Completed, as a putt
61 Weep

by Elizabeth C. Gorski

176

ACROSS

1 "Baywatch" beauties
6 Gulf war missiles
11 Purged
14 Water colors
15 "My Cousin Vinny" Oscar winner
16 Leb. neighbor
17 Start of a point to ponder
19 Thickness
20 Gofer
21 ". . . but is it ___?"
22 Heavenly ladle
24 Once, once
26 "That feels good!"
28 Chorus girl?
29 "The Raven" writer's monogram
31 Part 2 of the point to ponder
34 Parkinson's treatment
36 Take back
37 One waltzing Down Under
39 Now and then
43 Kind of salad
45 No-goodniks
46 Part 3 of the point to ponder
50 Point to argue
51 Half: Prefix
52 Part of E.T.A.: Abbr.
53 Strike callers
55 Medicinal syrup
57 Dander
59 Some punches
62 DVD player maker
63 End of the point to ponder
66 Perp prosecutors
67 Coffee break time, perhaps
68 Japan's second-largest city
69 Pig's pad
70 Grps.
71 She played the 10 in "10"

DOWN

1 Mexican peninsula
2 Here, in 1-Down
3 End of the line
4 Lotus-___
5 Sacramento-to-Santa Cruz dir.
6 Top banana
7 Vacation home
8 Underground org.
9 Tie
10 "Aye aye, capitán!"
11 Wee wave
12 Sea spots
13 Wood worry
18 Possesses, old-style
23 Peppermint ___ (candy purchase)
25 "Hogan's Heroes" setting
27 Five-time Derby winner
29 Nightmarish street
30 Org. for drillers and fillers
32 Chalkboard accessory
33 Country music?
35 Walk in the park, so to speak
38 Complete collapses
40 Department store department
41 Samuel's mentor
42 Retired Atl. crosser
44 Kind of violet
46 Fair portions for the Andrews Sisters
47 Cool dude, 50's-style
48 "Makes no difference to me"
49 Lamented
54 Analyze syntactically
56 Wirehair of film
58 Radiation units
60 Superior, e.g.
61 Badlands state: Abbr.
64 Seat holders
65 10's pride

by Nancy Salomon

ACROSS

1 Hollywood snooper Hopper
6 Brought to bay
11 Winter hrs. in St. Louis
14 French cinema star Delon
15 Therefore
16 Confederate soldier, for short
17 Get on board
19 Mentalist Geller
20 Pub perch
21 Early ___ (one up at 6 a.m., say)
23 Nevada town
25 "Sweet Caroline" singer
29 "___ Like It Hot"
31 Soup eater's need
32 Vegetables that roll
33 Teacher's charges
35 Designer ___ de la Renta
37 Game show originally hosted by Monty Hall
42 Opposite of fronts
43 From east of the Urals
45 Pet protectors' org.
48 Bloodhound's clue
51 Spanish girl: Abbr.
52 1990 road film starring Nicolas Cage and Laura Dern
55 With it, 50's-style
56 N.B.A.'s Shaq
57 Bullwinkle, for one
59 Genetic info dispenser
60 Planter's tool
66 Room with an easy chair
67 Online letter
68 West Pointer
69 Radical 60's campus grp.
70 Slender and long-limbed
71 Befuddled

DOWN

1 Muslim pilgrimage
2 "Xanadu" rock grp.
3 Li'l Abner's love
4 Force
5 Writer Chekhov
6 Nickname for Leo Durocher
7 ___ room (site for a Ping-Pong table)
8 Photo blow-up: Abbr.
9 Antique French coin
10 Actress Winger
11 Literary castaway
12 Venus's sister on the courts
13 Sporty Fords, informally
18 Weed whackers
22 Awe
23 Computer key: Abbr.
24 Laze
26 Peek
27 Amount of medicine
28 Peruvian Indian
30 Erik who played Ponch on TV
34 NNW's opposite
36 Nabokov novel
38 A crow's-nest is atop it
39 Keystone site
40 Bubblebrains
41 Missing a deadline
44 Quick shuteye
45 Musketeers' weapons
46 Fastened (down)
47 Gets rid of dust bunnies
49 To wit
50 1982 Jeff Bridges film
53 Author Horatio
54 Raven-haired Puccini heroine
58 Lover's quarrel
61 Doctors' org.
62 Did a marathon
63 Unkind remark
64 Fiddle-de-___
65 Airport posting: Abbr.

by Norma Johnson

178

NOTE: Sixteen answers in this puzzle have something unusual in common. What is it?

ACROSS
1 Pequod captain
5 Immense
9 Footnote abbr.
13 End of many 60's dance club names
14 Cupid
15 Bridge site
16 Sticky
17 Disgusted response
18 Did horribly on, as a test
19 "You ___ here"
20 French yeses
22 "Nerts!"
24 Lazy one, slangily
26 Make unclear
27 Trifle (with)
28 Chinese drink
32 1948 also-ran
35 Talks raucously
36 Mound builder
37 Plaintive woodwind
38 One of 18 French kings
39 Good name for a Dalmatian
40 Place for a plug
41 Courted
42 Like saltwater taffy
43 Orchestral performance
45 Any ship
46 Frenchman Descartes
47 Hamilton and Burr did it
51 Cuckoo
54 Seethe
55 Eggs
56 1997 title role for Peter Fonda
57 Hazard warning
59 Farm call
61 Welsh form of John
62 Hero
63 Moran and Brockovich
64 Puppy sounds

65 Slangy denial
66 "Not on ___!"

DOWN
1 Ancient market
2 Nonsense
3 ID info
4 "Hot-diggity-dog!"
5 Flavorless
6 Quantities: Abbr.
7 Exemplar of little worth
8 Delivery room surprise?
9 Natural
10 ___ tie
11 "Ah, yes"
12 Like a lawn at dawn

13 1946 hit "___ in Calico"
21 180° turn, slangily
23 Tints
25 To ___ (exactly)
26 Pigtail, e.g.
28 Causing to stick
29 Item for a D.J.
30 Sufficient, once
31 Lawyer: Abbr.
32 Executes
33 Web auction site
34 Bird's find
35 Pat or Daniel
38 Place of wildness, informally
39 Author Silverstein
41 "Thank heaven that's over!"

42 Onetime White House daughter
44 Primps
45 ___ generis
47 Last name in mysteries
48 Sarge's superior
49 Happening
50 During working hours
51 Chop ___
52 Ovid's 156
53 Bring in the sheaves
54 Betty ___
58 Japanese vegetable
60 Sphere

by Susan Harrington Smith

ACROSS

1 Where the mouth is
6 Offend
10 Exit, often
14 1975 Tony winner for Best Play
15 Hydrox rival
16 Alike, to André
17 Military brass?
18 Big screen name
19 Attend
20 They might require overtime
21 Theater usher's need
23 Stretch out
25 Jettison
26 See 53-Down
29 Protestant Reformation figure
33 Daily Planet chief
38 Harass
39 Skin cream ingredient
40 Suffix with Samson
41 Sea moss constituent
42 Ticket sales
43 "Anything Goes" composer
46 Alchemic mixture
48 Actor Jannings
49 Jewish month
51 Mailing supplies
56 Ox or pig
61 "There oughta be ___!"
62 "The Time Machine" people
63 Wrinkled, as a brow
64 Pernod flavoring
65 Aware of
66 Abstainer's opposite
67 Felt compassion (for)
68 Capitol topper
69 Clinton cabinet member Federico
70 Word that can follow the end of 21-, 33-, 43- or 56-Across

DOWN

1 Reasons to look for a shark?
2 Fit out
3 German gun
4 City on the Arkansas River
5 Enzyme suffix
6 Drudgery
7 "The Joy of Cooking" author Rombauer
8 Lavish meal
9 Front place?
10 Record holder
11 Eager
12 Standardized test topic
13 Represent graphically
21 Go smoothly
22 Baton Rouge sch.
24 Ironic
27 Home for Ulysses S. Grant
28 Championship
30 Sword part
31 Better chance
32 Bring up
33 Web site unit
34 Lod Airport carrier
35 French roast
36 Take another look at
37 Abound (with)
43 Get started
44 Tiresome one
45 Plug or play ending
47 Panhandle state: Abbr.
50 Dentist's request
52 Baccarat call
53 With 26-Across, 1912 Nobel Peace Prize winner
54 Emits coherent light
55 Garbo, by birth
56 More than a tiff
57 Food in a can
58 Freedom
59 Demeanor
60 Gillette product
64 "Won-der-ful!"

by Alan Arbesfeld

180

ACROSS

1 Islamic holy war
6 Channel showing Cong. hearings
11 Transatlantic flier of yore, for short
14 Pac-Man maker
15 Native whale-hunter
16 Toddler's age
17 Where horses drink
19 Tire filler
20 Tempest
21 Mount in Sicily
22 Show on which the Blues Brothers debuted: Abbr.
25 Sufficient
29 Make fun of
32 Elevates
33 The ___ Brothers of 1960's-70's R & B
34 Treaty
35 Flipping pages
42 Ostrichlike bird
43 Magazine
44 Delicacy with Champagne
47 Certain whimsical Dutch lithographs
49 It's kneaded
51 Moscow's land: Abbr.
52 It may be due on a duplex
53 Stonehenge worshiper
56 Top flier
57 Mythical pass to the underworld
63 "The Sweetheart of Sigma ___"
64 Sign before Taurus
65 Prefix with mural
66 Baseball legend Williams
67 Looks closely (at)
68 Prophets

DOWN

1 Target of a punch, maybe
2 "Give ___ rest!"
3 Derby or bowler
4 Greek war god
5 Gossip
6 Rabbit's treat
7 Replay feature
8 Little, in Lille
9 Mo. before Labor Day
10 Ultimate ordinal
11 Display on a pedestal
12 Equipment near teeter-totters
13 Synagogue scroll
18 Roman Senate wear
21 Dawn goddess
22 Skirt opening
23 "Candy / Is dandy / But liquor / Is quicker" poet
24 Lollapalooza
26 "Phooey!"
27 Individually
28 Kind of acid
30 Opal or onyx
31 Gas-electric car, e.g.
34 Org. for Tiger Woods
36 "If ___ a Hammer"
37 Poisoner of Britannicus
38 ___ Kosh B'Gosh
39 Not an abstainer
40 Knowledgeable one
41 Dame Myra
44 Christmas display
45 Poem with the story of the Trojan horse
46 Big wine holder
47 Exit
48 Avoid
49 Leaflike appendage
50 Milk giver
54 Everglades wader
55 Ready to be removed from the oven
57 Interruption
58 Prospector's prize
59 Fib
60 Western Indian
61 Dog's warning
62 Owns

by Raymond Hamel

ACROSS

1 Alternative to check or credit
5 Unrefined
10 Daedalus creation
14 Poker payment
15 "Ugh!"
16 Store sign after 9 a.m.
17 Wander
18 Really like
19 Hawaii's state bird
20 Sexologist + "The Waltons" co-star
23 Without interruption
24 Kiddy coop
28 Mtge. units
29 Short sprint
33 Picture books
34 Wish granters
36 The East
37 Film critic + "Native Son" author
41 Groceries carrier
42 Deep dislikes
43 Gap
46 "A Death in the Family" writer
47 Easter decoration
50 Third-place finisher, e.g.
52 Legend maker
54 College basketball coach + "L.A. Law" co-star
58 Pizazz
61 Scottish landowner
62 Classroom drills
63 Cockeyed
64 Refrain from children's singing?
65 Blast furnace input
66 Went really fast
67 Dummies
68 Scotch ingredient

DOWN

1 Drive-in employee
2 Sprinkle oil on
3 Union members
4 Ones who can lift heavy weights
5 Greenish blue
6 Funnyman Foxx
7 "Don't have ___, man!"
8 Deep-six
9 Aussie gal
10 Fat cat
11 Boorish brute
12 ___ state (pleasant place to be)
13 From K.C. to Detroit
21 Threw in
22 1960 chess champion Mikhail
25 Midwife's instruction
26 Broadcast
27 Code-breaking org.
30 Alicia of "Falcon Crest"
31 ___-Japanese War
32 Ibsen's Gabler
34 Become familiar with
35 Great gulp
37 Racetrack fence
38 Historic periods
39 Wish undone
40 "That is to say . . ."
41 Chinese tea
44 Samovar
45 Took a cruise
47 Writer Welty
48 Grimm girl
49 Most mirthful
51 Marsh of mystery
53 Data holder
55 Went very fast
56 The Stooges, for instance
57 Hullabaloos
58 Keebler cookiemaker
59 Chat room chuckle
60 Biggest diamond

by Norma Johnson and Nancy Salomon

ACROSS

1 "___ Poetica"
4 Build (on)
7 Money set aside
13 Doo-wop syllable
14 Wimbledon five-peater
16 Nigerian novelist Chinua ___
17 Tap-dancing without taps
19 Move unsteadily
20 Jewish month
21 Reinking on Broadway
22 Actually, legally
23 A von Trapp
25 Like paradise
27 Post-E.R. destination, maybe
28 Increase, with "up"
29 Hopscotch player's buy
33 Fla. vacation spot
36 Necessary: Abbr.
38 Tell a whopper
39 Sportage maker
40 Scalia colleague, once
42 "Solaris" author
43 Like some verbs: Abbr.
44 Former Bush adviser Karl
45 Get a little teary
47 Grade of tea
49 Mo. named for an emperor
51 Southern Conference sch.
52 Like many models
54 Chair designer Charles
57 Containing cracks, maybe
60 Liquor in a shot
62 Block brand
63 Detection devices
64 "Not to mention . . ."
66 Ultimatum words
67 Pope, 1513–21

68 Suffix with boff, in old slang
69 Comic Howie
70 "Citizen Kane" studio
71 Joined

DOWN

1 State of India
2 1970's comedy spinoff
3 Zoo alternative
4 Crunch targets
5 Qatar's capital
6 Yawn-inducing speaker
7 Have a home-cooked meal
8 Coastal highway, say
9 Marin of comedy
10 Soaks, as flax
11 U.K. awards
12 "___ #1!"
15 Like "waitperson"
18 Jiffy
24 Cassette deck feature
26 Squared
30 Worst ever
31 Stead
32 1996 veep hopeful
33 Go past
34 Get jaded
35 "Foucault's Pendulum" author
37 Iranian city
41 Picture frame shape
46 Like some talk
48 Warren Report name
50 It blows off steam
53 Detroit dud
55 Tied, as a French score
56 "Alas!"
57 Memo word
58 "___ Croft: Tomb Raider" (2001 flick)
59 Yemen's Gulf of ___
61 "Star Wars" creature
65 Prefix with skeleton

by Leonard Williams

ACROSS

1 Fashionable
5 Where bats "hang out"
9 Triangular traffic sign
14 Sweep under the rug
15 Like droughty land
16 Typo
17 Neck and neck
18 Lion's locks
19 Popular dip for 48-Down
20 Gain wealth opportunely, in a way
23 "Two Mules for Sister ___" (1970 film)
24 Three, on a sundial
25 "That feels good!"
28 Snake that may warn before it strikes
31 Harper Valley grp., in song
34 Lock of hair
36 "___ was saying . . ."
37 Any day now
38 Nickname in James Fenimore Cooper tales
42 Artist Warhol
43 Vintner's tank
44 Cruise ship
45 Put into words
46 Hot pepper
49 Give it a whirl
50 Little League field surface, probably
51 Stethoscope holders
53 She played TV's Amanda Woodward
61 Shake hands (on)
62 Per person
63 ___ Major
64 More vigorous
65 Suffix with buck
66 Appearance

67 Be head over heels about
68 Prospectors' receptacles
69 Tiptop

DOWN

1 Bake-off figure
2 Honey factory
3 "The very ___!"
4 Piggy bank filler
5 Tourist's take-along
6 Where Noah landed
7 Chianti or Soave
8 Place of bliss
9 Boot camp affirmative
10 Tehran resident
11 Writer ___ Stanley Gardner
12 Profit's opposite
13 "Darn!"
21 Severe
22 "Old MacDonald" refrain
25 World Almanac section
26 Madison Square Garden, e.g.
27 Exciting
29 One of the senses
30 "Saving Private Ryan" craft: Abbr.
31 Score unit
32 Laser printer powder
33 Hopping mad
35 Hog's home
37 Go downhill fast?
39 Dodge
40 Element of hope?
41 Pencil pusher
46 Stick together
47 Converted liberal, informally
48 Mexican snacks
50 Beef animal
52 Losing streak
53 "That is so funny"
54 "Goodness gracious!"
55 Guthrie who sang at Woodstock
56 Harvest
57 Zhivago's love
58 New York's ___ Canal
59 Toward the big waves
60 Captain, e.g.

by Gregory E. Paul

184

ACROSS
1 An American in Paris, maybe
6 "By ___!"
10 Sch. groups
14 Edwin in Reagan's Cabinet
15 "Excuse me . . ."
16 Pathetic
17 Stupefied
18 Superman's mother
19 Board member, for short
20 Summer retreat
23 Silhouette
24 Annoyance
25 With deliberate hamminess
28 Player's club?
29 N.Y.C. subway
32 More slippery, perhaps
33 Break bread
34 Middling
35 Summer retreat
39 Author Dinesen
40 "I want my ___!" (1980's slogan)
41 Sword handles
42 ___ Paul guitars
43 Gossip
44 Mocks
46 Shoveled
47 Initial venture
48 Summer retreat
54 Promotable piece
55 Fictional detective Wolfe
56 Dangerous gas
57 Babysitter's headache
58 Perón and Gabor
59 Work often read before the "Odyssey"
60 Compos mentis
61 Lone
62 Euro fractions

DOWN
1 Actor Jannings
2 TV's leather-clad princess
3 Busiest
4 At this very moment
5 Bit of summer attire
6 Bucket of bolts
7 Midway alternative
8 "Billy Budd" captain
9 Grossly underfeed
10 Naval Academy freshman
11 Travel before takeoff
12 "Right on!"
13 Very short wait, in short
21 Film producer Roach
22 Workmanship
25 Polite
26 Build ___ against (work to prosecute)
27 Layered minerals
28 Bit of luggage
29 Cries one's eyes out
30 Sporty Mazda
31 Romantic rendezvous
33 Letter container: Abbr.
34 Story that might include a dragon
36 Conceives of
37 Gambling site, briefly
38 Flamboyantly overdone
43 Astronaut Grissom
44 Humorous
45 Suffix with ranch
46 "Inferno" poet
47 Not domesticated
48 Poet Teasdale
49 McGregor of "Down With Love"
50 "Whip It" band
51 Tennis score after deuce
52 Bearded animal
53 Leaves off
54 "Nova" network

by Karen M. Tracey

ACROSS

1 Sidelines shout
4 One appearing between numbers
9 Greek marketplace
14 "___ pig's eye!"
15 Old Pisa dough?
16 Deadly snake
17 Definition of 41-Across
20 Joshes
21 Jones of the Miracle Mets
22 Bib. prophet
23 Definition of 41-Across
27 Sweater material
29 Caffeine source
30 Actor Wallach
31 Pleasing view
35 Doofus
39 Mountains crossed by Hannibal
41 Theme of this puzzle
43 Property claim
44 Corrective eye surgery
46 Straight from the keg
48 Cross shape
49 Berlin Airlift grp.
51 Foes of Carthage
53 Definition of 41-Across
59 W.W. II sphere: Abbr.
60 Hard to get to know
61 Neighbor of Minn.
64 Definition of 41-Across
68 Josh
69 "He's ___ nowhere man . . ." (Beatles lyric)
70 Beehive State native
71 Eagerness
72 Gossipmonger
73 No-show's test score

DOWN

1 Classic Parker Brothers game
2 Prefix with lock or knock
3 Travails
4 Tarzan portrayer Ron
5 Near the center of
6 "Photographs & Memories" singer
7 Quarter back?
8 Ruhr Valley city
9 Pennsylvania and others
10 Jazz arranger Evans
11 Microscope lens
12 Witherspoon of "Legally Blonde"
13 Tapestry
18 Where pomelos grow
19 Derisive shout
24 Louis ___, the Sun King
25 Source of embarrassment
26 Table salt formula
27 Banquet
28 ___ podrida
32 Jack of "Barney Miller"
33 Wine cask
34 Lizard's nibble
36 Like commando raids
37 Bad-tempered
38 ___ probandi (burden of proof)
40 Beget
42 Mend
45 Person with a paddle
47 Detachable craft
50 Tab site
52 Like 1950's recordings
53 Hostess Perle
54 Lupine : wolf :: lutrine : ___
55 "WarGames" setting
56 "Forget it!"
57 Orléans's river
58 A lot
62 When the witches first appear in "Macbeth"
63 Ship's backbone
65 Equal: Prefix
66 Magician's prop
67 Where I-10 and I-95 meet: Abbr.

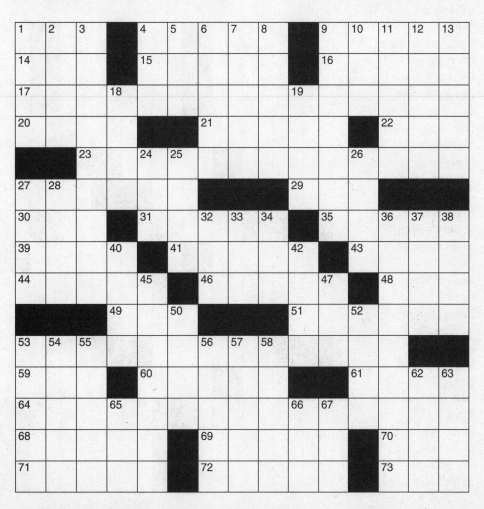

by Barbara Olson

ACROSS

1 Karate blow
5 Microscope part
9 Separates, as flour
14 Super-duper
15 Baseball's Moises or Felipe
16 Dunderhead
17 Poker holding lower than three-of-a-kind
18 Oscar winner Patricia
19 Big
20 Punish action star Norris?
23 Superlative suffix
24 "Anchors Aweigh" grp.
25 CPR expert
26 "Moby Dick" whaler
28 Lipton competitor
30 Hurrying
33 Parts of gowns that go over the shoulders
36 Detroit baseballer
37 Titled lady
40 Massage
42 Fast jets, briefly
43 Alex Haley saga
45 River in a Strauss waltz
47 Spills clumsily
49 Big name in small planes
53 Close by
54 Letters before an alias
55 Balloon filler
56 High-jumper's hurdle
58 Rely on comic Keaton?
62 In the sky
64 Delhi dress
65 "Well done!"
66 Roast host
67 The dark force
68 Miners' finds
69 Worker with autumn leaves
70 Dicker
71 Toward the sunset

DOWN

1 Kid's pistol
2 Like laryngitis sufferers
3 Whopper toppers
4 Lima's locale
5 Acquire slugger McGwire?
6 Put into office
7 Biblical ark builder
8 "Star Trek" navigator
9 Formal headgear
10 Actress Lupino
11 Dismiss gangster Moran?
12 Clothing
13 Proofreader's "leave it"
21 Hair removal brand
22 Jail, slangily
27 Crops up
29 Fearsome fly
30 "No man ___ island . . ."
31 Ready
32 "48___" (Nick Nolte film)
34 "No ifs, ___ or buts!"
35 Sweet ___ (flower)
37 E.R. workers
38 "You've got mail" co.
39 Drop drawers on actor Hudson?
41 Avoid President Clinton?
44 Break into bits
46 Boyfriend
48 Goof up
50 Lampoon
51 Sisters' daughters
52 Collar
54 Skylit lobbies
56 30's boxing champ Max
57 ___ mater
59 Like Goodwill goods
60 Prepare for a rainy day
61 Falling flakes
63 Membership charge

by Nancy Salomon and Harvey Estes

ACROSS

1 Civil rights org.
6 Madame Bovary
10 Choice on "Let's Make a Deal"
14 Come to pass
15 Castle defense
16 Henry VIII's second or fourth
17 1954 movie starring 25- and 44-Across
20 Storm center
21 Kelly's possum
22 "I swear!"
23 Worth a C
24 Half of a sawbuck
25 Half of a famous comic duo
29 Tibetan priest
33 Jennifer Garner spy series
34 Bachelor's last words?
35 Rah-rah
36 Some auction bids
37 Arsonist, e.g.
39 Grin from ear to ear
40 Blunted blade
41 William Halsey, e.g.: Abbr.
42 Marilyn Monroe's real first name
43 Virgin Is., e.g.
44 Half of a famous comic duo
47 Sheepcote
48 Beanery sign
49 Source of mohair
53 Diner handout
54 ___ alai
57 1956 movie starring 25- and 44-Across
60 Kind of page
61 Skin soother
62 It comes from the heart
63 Desires
64 A bit less than a meter
65 Steadfast

DOWN

1 Musical mark
2 "___ Breaky Heart" (1992 hit)
3 Farm measure
4 Pool tool
5 Takes care of charges ahead of time
6 Political refugee
7 Like early LP's
8 Periodical, for short
9 Kansas town famous in railroad history
10 Mend, in a way
11 Story starter
12 Burden of proof
13 Musical mark
18 Muddy up
19 Charged particle
23 "George of the Jungle" star Brendan
24 Generic pooch
25 A singing Jackson
26 Run off to wed
27 Bill tack-on
28 One of the Flintstones
29 Hercules had 12
30 Turn away
31 Orange Bowl city
32 Jingle writer
37 Backward-moving basketball shot
38 Delightful place
42 Musical mark
45 Had to have
46 ___-war bird
47 Act the snoop
49 "Hey, sailor!"
50 "Uh-uh"
51 Campbell of country
52 GM line, once
53 Othello was one
54 Trial group
55 "The Thin Man" dog
56 Emphatic type: Abbr.
58 Plug or pay ender
59 Ghost's cry

by Roy Leban

188

ACROSS

1 Fermentation receptacle
4 Aromatic salves
9 Rough, as a car engine
14 Rabin's land: Abbr.
15 Enjoyed immensely
16 Loosen, as laces
17 Long-ago battle protection
19 Klutzy
20 Annual July sports event with the world's largest live audience
22 Cookbook author Rombauer et al.
23 ___ sauce
24 Co. badges
27 Playing dirty tricks
28 Should, with "to"
31 Part of a parcel
32 "Peter Pan" dog
33 Shortly
35 Lance Armstrong, e.g.
39 Batman's home
40 Daredevil Knievel
41 End-of-the-week cry
42 Slowly merged (into)
44 Moves it, informally
48 Key futilely pushed after a computer freeze
49 Kind of hand
50 One must be quick to join it
51 Winner's prize, in 20-Across
55 Ruler of a hive
58 "Janie's Got a Gun" rock band
59 UPS shade
60 Catches
61 From Okla. City to Houston
62 Pantywaist
63 "Uncle Tom's Cabin" girl
64 Novelist Josephine

DOWN

1 Muggee, e.g.
2 Toward the beach
3 Emotional damage
4 Cigar wraps
5 "Look ___!"
6 Table extender
7 ___ Woods National Monument
8 Big media to-do
9 Like good oranges
10 Feminine suffix
11 31-Down plan: Abbr.
12 Laotian money
13 So far
18 Ayatollah's land
21 Saw
24 SALT topic
25 Job for a plumber
26 Match unit
28 Hot bowlful
29 Prefix with sphere
30 Pool and darts
31 Driver's aid: Abbr.
32 Big lobby in D.C.
34 Montreal is in it: Abbr.
35 Frequent San Francisco conditions
36 Related to: Suffix
37 Channels 2–13, briefly
38 Last moment to prepare
39 Old inits. in telecommunications
43 Cry after a long wait
44 Start of an idea
45 More than urge
46 Sub-Saharan pest
47 Willie Mays phrase
49 Copper
50 Unkempt
51 Fir trees
52 Wine: Prefix
53 Shawl, e.g.
54 Bends, as in a river
55 Gridiron V.I.P.'s
56 Mentalist Geller
57 Canon camera model

by Patrick Merrell

ACROSS

1 Spellbound
5 Homer epic
10 Early baby word
14 Ibiza, e.g., to Spaniards
15 Mother-of-pearl
16 Not new
17 Extended family
18 Unique
20 Chilling out
22 Behind a wrecker, say
23 Actor with the catchphrase "I pity the fool!"
24 Picks out in a lineup, for short
27 In-flight info
28 Eight: Prefix
32 Uncle of old TV
34 Boneless chicken pieces
37 Wise ___ owl
38 Satisfying close . . . or what 20- and 55-Across have in common?
41 Gazillions
42 Port of southern Italy
43 Some French Impressionist paintings
46 Nothin'
47 Life story
50 "Indeed!"
51 Notes after dos
53 Moves like a dragonfly
55 Not going anywhere
59 1950's–60's adolescent
62 Same, in Somme
63 Augury
64 "Breakdown ahead" warning
65 "Good shot!"
66 Metal in some batteries
67 Wards (off), as an attack
68 Brown quickly

DOWN

1 1980's–90's hitmaker Lionel
2 Leaning
3 Farms with banana trees
4 Fiery ballroom dance
5 Home ___ (near)
6 Singer k. d. ___
7 Reykjavik's home: Abbr.
8 Forster's "___ With a View"
9 Bend out of shape
10 John Wayne nickname
11 "Just ___ suspected!"
12 TV room
13 Do sums
19 Spumante region
21 "Forget it!"
24 "Nothing to worry about . . ."
25 Corner-to-corner: Abbr.
26 Capitol V.I.P.: Abbr.
29 401, to Nero
30 Change for a 20
31 Radio City Music Hall fixture
33 Reclined
35 Suffix with Rock
36 Actress Ward
38 Polar bear's transport?
39 Actor Beatty
40 Alternative to a volunteer army
41 "Little Women" woman
44 Chicago paper, for short, with "the"
45 Trigger
48 Cornell's home
49 Horse farm hand
52 "Lifted"
54 They may be placed on a house
55 In ___ (coordinated)
56 Classic supermodel
57 Dweeb
58 Some coll. tests
59 Dickens's pen name
60 French friend
61 London's Big ___

by Elizabeth C. Gorski

ACROSS

1 Lettuce variety
5 "La Vie en Rose" singer Edith
9 From way back
14 Available to serve
15 Fruit with wrinkled skin
16 Zellweger of "Chicago"
17 Fruit plate item
19 Saltine brand
20 Buys off
21 Jackson 5 member
23 Coffee-to-go need
24 Whom a coach coaches
25 Overcharge
26 Diner sign
27 Broth shortcut
30 States further
33 Humor magazine since 1952
34 Word reference pioneer
35 ___-Magnon
36 Spike Lee's "Summer of ___"
37 Mom-and-pop grp.
39 Medical plan, for short
40 Transcribers' goofs
42 Battery size
43 British gun
44 Ben & Jerry's offering
48 Blow off steam
49 Fitzgerald forte
50 Snigglers' prey
53 Roth ___
54 Saxophonist Stan
55 Fix in a cobbler's shop, say
57 Impression
59 Theme of this puzzle, so to speak
61 Between the lines
62 Golden rule word
63 2002 Eddie Murphy film
64 Inuit transports
65 "Hey you!"
66 Place-kickers' props

DOWN

1 Long, high pass
2 Not active, chemically
3 Contradict
4 African trees with thick trunks
5 Bars of Avon
6 Foot store chain inits.
7 In sum
8 Befitting a son or daughter
9 Petite pasta
10 Contingency ___
11 Blitz
12 1960 Everly Brothers hit
13 Determined to have
18 Verne's reclusive captain
22 Ali vs. Liston outcome, 1964
25 Thailand, once
26 Prefix with management
28 Thurman of "Pulp Fiction"
29 Gun rights org.
30 They've got issues
31 Corn flakes or raisin bran
32 Atone
36 Ukr. or Lith., once
37 Treaty
38 Lao-tzu's "___ Te Ching"
41 Columbus Day mo.
42 Hippolyta's warriors
43 Deems it appropriate (to)
45 Language suffix
46 Goes haywire
47 Cry out for
51 Freewheeling
52 Ski run
54 Comes down with
55 Urban disturbance
56 Häagen-Dazs alternative
58 Half brother of Tom Sawyer
60 Capt.'s inferiors

by Harvey Estes

ACROSS

1 Word in many farm names
6 [Look over here!]
10 "___ Apart" (2003 film)
14 Bear market direction
15 Like some league games
16 Singer Horne
17 Quickly, to an egotist?
20 Not on board, maybe
21 Poverty
22 Zero
23 One in a suit
25 Determines the age of
27 It may be sealed
30 Put away
31 Fail to stop on a dime?
33 Garfield's foil
35 Kind of party
40 Toast made by an egotist?
43 Fell back
44 ___ lily
45 May event, for short
46 Cheer competitor
49 Ham, to Noah
50 Used a fruit knife
53 ___-Roman
55 Summer cooler
56 "Back in the ___"
59 Bursts
63 Egotist's favorite person?
66 Deep-six
67 Uncreative learning method
68 Move (over)
69 Clinches, as a victory
70 Class identification
71 Brains

DOWN

1 Where SARS originated
2 Reasons to vote no
3 Crime novelist Rendell
4 Underlying character
5 Everest guide, often
6 Pen ___
7 Pen group
8 Lucid
9 Young 'un
10 1936 candidate Landon
11 Intended
12 Meg's "Sleepless in Seattle" role
13 Things at one's fingertips?
18 Flatfoot's circuit
19 Rare find
24 Second-in-command
26 "See you 'round"
27 Danish physicist Niels
28 ___ fixe
29 Tabloid fodder
31 Breaking pitch
32 Many wedding guests
34 Spooky
36 Lyric poem
37 Barroom sticks
38 Jason's ship
39 Heraldic beast
41 Parody
42 Beside oneself
47 Natural breakwater
48 On the opposite bank
50 Page of music
51 Temporary, as a committee
52 Baseball's Pee Wee
53 Actress Garbo
54 Shot glass capacity, roughly
57 Nimble
58 ___ gin
60 Lowly laborer
61 General ___ chicken
62 Net-surfer's stop
64 Dunderhead
65 "___ the glad waters of the dark blue sea": Byron

by Norm Guggenbiller

ACROSS

1 Kiss
6 Tool building
10 Butcher's or bakery
14 Process in a blender
15 Sampras or Rose
16 Place to see 20th-century paintings in N.Y.
17 Philanthropist Brooke __
18 Grad
19 Sign on a store door
20 "Royal" action film, 2002
23 "__ Haw"
24 Yo-yo or Slinky
25 Corsage flower
29 Brother of Abel
31 "Camelot" president, for short
34 U.S. Grant's foe
35 Angel's headgear
36 Prefix with commuting
37 "Royal" Bogart/Hepburn film, 1951
40 Knife handle
41 Grades 1–12, for short
42 Let loose, as pigs
43 No longer used: Abbr.
44 Over hill and __
45 Like bread dough
46 Brief instant
47 Hurry
48 "Royal" film based on a classic children's story, 1974
57 Maui dance
58 Nest eggs for seniors: Abbr.
59 Bottled water from France
60 Egyptian fertility goddess
61 On-the-hour radio offering

62 Extremely successful, slangily
63 Old Iranian leader
64 Heredity carrier
65 Deuce takers

DOWN

1 Small fight
2 Sled dog command
3 Johnson of TV's "Laugh-In"
4 Corporate heads, for short
5 Woman's head cover
6 Extra
7 Aid
8 Needle case
9 Drop from major to captain, say

10 Great __ Mountains National Park
11 Pueblo Indian
12 Augur
13 Sharp pain, as from hunger
21 Multivolume ref.
22 Oui's opposite
25 Right: Prefix
26 Addict's program, in short
27 Heads of staffs?
28 Furnace output
29 Hidden stash
30 Jai __
31 Army vehicles
32 Navy unit
33 Singer Rogers
35 San Francisco's Nob __

36 Sandwich fish
38 Responding (to)
39 Most odd
44 Agnus __
45 Puppy sound
46 /
47 "Steppenwolf" author
48 1950's TV's "__ Is Your Life"
49 Silence
50 Director Kazan
51 Elm or oak
52 Place for an Easter egg hunt
53 Songwriter Novello
54 Kindly
55 Like dry mud
56 Genesis grandson

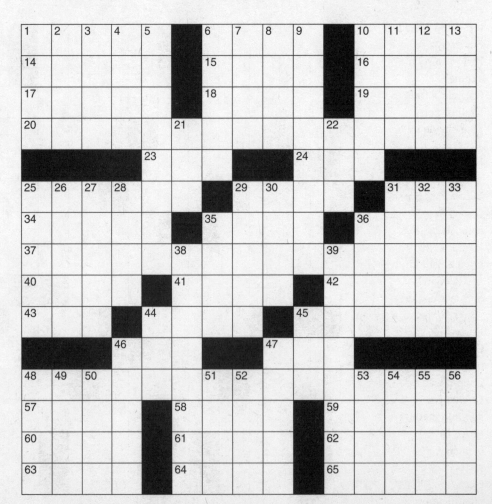

by Andrea Carla Michaels

ACROSS

1 Letters that lack stamps
6 Johnny ___, "Key Largo" gangster
11 Bar bill
14 Circulation mainstay
15 Acquired relative
16 Yale Bowl rooter
17 Mistreated vegetable?
19 Zip
20 Make well
21 Choppers, so to speak
22 Mount Rushmore locale: Abbr.
23 Summer Games org.
25 Cupcake brand
27 Mistreated spice?
32 Author Rand
33 Castor or Pollux
34 A to E, musically speaking
37 Start over
39 Three, in a saying
42 Writer Ephron
43 Intimidate, with "out"
45 "Cold one"
47 Arles assent
48 Mistreated spread?
52 Wrinkly-skinned dog
54 In the past
55 Leprechaun's land
56 Select group
59 Words of woe
63 Speed limit abbr.
64 Mistreated meat?
66 Wall St. debut
67 Have a feeling
68 Jeweler's unit
69 Impresario Hurok
70 Coin words
71 Worshiped ones

DOWN

1 Price word
2 "Encore!"
3 Neck of the woods
4 Right-leaning?
5 Hasty escape
6 Tilt-A-Whirl, e.g.
7 Story starter
8 Dress
9 Drive-in server
10 Part of B.Y.O.B.
11 Greenhorn
12 Rap sheet handle
13 Swindles
18 "Yada, yada, yada . . ."
22 45-Across holder
24 Gives the go-ahead
26 Tanning lotion letters
27 Be a kvetch
28 Some whiskeys
29 Pop art icon
30 Patriotic women's org.
31 Space explorer
35 In alignment
36 Salon sweepings
38 Earthy pigment
40 Tie the knot
41 Discuss pros and cons
44 In fashion
46 Toupee, slangily
49 Bird with a showy mate
50 Pier's support
51 "What a shame"
52 They're weighed at weigh stations
53 Zoo heavyweight
57 ___ facto
58 Made tracks
60 Sizable sandwich
61 "Square" thing
62 New newts
64 Popular CBS drama
65 601, in old Rome

by Steven Kahn

194

ACROSS

1 List ender
5 Line crosser?
9 Brief argument
14 1984 Peace Nobelist
15 It might need two hands to be removed from a shelf
16 Work, in a way
17 "Topaz" author
18 Bearded bloom
19 Traffic sign
20 Flying an SST?
23 Pandora's boxful
24 Varnish ingredient
25 "Everyone welcome"
29 Kind of rule
30 Mattress problem
33 Bowser
34 What "that" ain't
35 Certain something
36 Missouri baby carriers?
40 French 101 verb
41 Before, before
42 Sight along the Mississippi
43 ___-devil
44 See 13-Down
45 Comedians, e.g.
47 Icarus' undoing
48 Porkpie feature
49 Cost of a certain grain?
56 Sleep disturbance
57 1980's TV police comedy
58 Queens's ___ Stadium
59 This puzzle's theme
60 Bit of roofing
61 Scuttle filler
62 Pope's writings
63 "No ifs, ___ . . ."
64 Breaks off

DOWN

1 Place for pins
2 Go sour
3 Working away
4 W. C. Fields persona
5 Squelch
6 Marine deposits
7 Out of whack
8 First-place
9 1970's space station
10 Pioneering 1940's computer
11 Numerical suffix
12 Raconteur's offering
13 With 44-Across, handyman's task
21 Skater's figure
22 Artful dodges
25 Church areas
26 Far from eager
27 Nantes's river
28 Result of an oil surplus?
29 Part of spring in France
30 Urbane
31 Ordnance supplier
32 Some are inert
34 Cry's partner
35 Mars' counterpart
37 Sierra ___
38 Eyeball
39 Roly-poly
44 Plantation libations
45 Noted traitor
46 Department store section
47 Take a powder
48 Niger neighbor
49 Bring to ruin
50 Knot
51 Loser to VHS
52 5K or 10K
53 "The heat ___"
54 Part of a punch ballot
55 Some are shockers
56 Gullible one

by Ed Early

ACROSS

1 Take out of the freezer
5 Whole lot
9 Nuclear weapon, in old headlines
14 Atmosphere
15 Fish in a salad
16 Confederate general, for short
17 Customer
18 Battery fluid
19 Momentary flash
20 "Pshaw!"
23 The Amish, e.g.
24 Spanish king
25 Show the effects of weight
28 Coffee container
31 "___ your age!"
34 Pick up the tab for
36 "In what way?"
37 Like rush hour traffic
38 "Pshaw!"
42 Gift on a first date, maybe
43 Can metal
44 Pilot light
45 She sheep
46 Kitchen set
49 End a fast
50 Cul-de-___
51 Warlike god
53 "Pshaw!"
61 Knock for ___
62 Sen. Bayh of Indiana
63 Lumber source
64 Wait on
65 Blend
66 Composer Stravinsky
67 Four-bagger
68 Whom a hunter hunts
69 Verne captain

DOWN

1 Tightly strung
2 "Pipe down!"
3 Vicinity
4 ___ and all (including faults)
5 Laundry stiffener
6 Transparent plastic
7 "National Velvet" author Bagnold
8 Dry riverbed
9 States one's case
10 "Button" site
11 Miscellany
12 Restaurant posting
13 "All ___ are off!"
21 Bench-clearing incident
22 Not leave enough room
25 Blank look
26 Cupid's projectile
27 Silly ones
29 German wine valley
30 Fashionable, in the 60's
31 Pond buildup
32 Pause indicator
33 Sound from a nest
35 Favorable vote
37 Weekend TV show, for short
39 City east of Syracuse
40 Family
41 #1 Beatles hit "___ Fine"
46 Certain piano pedal
47 Tex-Mex treat
48 Hip
50 Hotpoint appliance
52 Fine blouse material
53 Salt amount
54 Butter alternative
55 Typical amount
56 Dole's running mate, 1996
57 At any time
58 Press upon
59 Subj. with circles and such
60 Person with a medal, maybe

by Gregory E. Paul

196

ACROSS

1 Window base
5 One-tenth: Prefix
9 Within reach
14 Operatic solo
15 Dash
16 Children's
   song refrain
17 Al Capp parody
   of Dick Tracy
20 Octad plus one
21 Princely initials
22 On the sheltered side
23 Examines
   a passage
24 A prospector
   may stake one
26 Midwest hub
28 B westerns
33 Repair tears
36 MasterCard rival
38 Salman Rushdie's
   birthplace
39 User of air
   abrasion to
   clean teeth
43 Bewildered
44 Exam taken
   in H.S.
45 Pipe joint
46 African
   bloodsucker
48 It's given to
   a waiter
51 Breathing room
53 Reggae fan,
   often
57 Play divisions
61 Actor Wallach
62 Shoe part
63 Muscleman's
   garment
66 "Careless Hands"
   singer Mel
67 List-ending abbr.
68 Otherwise
69 Fess up
70 Wall St.
   trading center
71 Prognosticator

DOWN

1 Equipped with
   air bags, say
2 Castle of dance
3 Tropical vine
4 "Streets of ___"
   (cowboy song)
5 Exploit
6 Golfer Ernie
7 What credit
   cards may bring
   about, eventually
8 Prefix with structure
9 "For ___ a jolly . . ."
10 Verdi opera
11 Filmmaker Jordan
12 They show their
   faces in casinos
13 Oxen's harness
18 Whip
19 The Buckeye State
24 Like new
   dollar bills
25 Common street name
27 ___ Maria
29 Big blast maker
30 Make changes to
31 Soufflés do it
32 Glut
33 Squabble
34 Food, slangily
35 Sage
37 How a prank may
   be done, after "on"
40 Mosquito protection
41 Edinburgh girl
42 J.F.K.
   approximation
47 Sporting blade
49 Shore birds
50 Diaper wearers'
   woes
52 ___ wrench
54 Subway station
   device
55 To the point
56 More inclined
57 "The Thin
   Man" dog
58 Lump of dirt
59 Contract
   stipulation
60 Big rig
62 Castaway's home
64 One who
   looks Rover over
65 Swedish carrier

by Ed Early

ACROSS

1 Soda fountain purchases
6 Street fleet
10 Guest bed, maybe
14 Parting word
15 "We'll tak ___ o' kindness yet"
16 Iran is a mem. of it
17 W
20 Publicity
21 When doubled, start of a cheer
22 "What foolishness!"
23 Rattrap
24 Valuable green stuff
25 Island near Corsica
27 X
34 Swedish exports
35 Strauss's "___ Rosenkavalier"
36 DVD menu option
37 Part of E.T.A.: Abbr.
38 What detectives follow
40 Sue Grafton's "___ for Evidence"
41 Turkish generals
43 Chronic misbehaver
44 Bag lunch eater?
46 Y
50 Sizable vessels
51 100-cent unit
52 Metro stop: Abbr.
55 Its hub is in Copenhagen
56 Actor Vigoda
57 At most, informally
60 Z
64 Violinist Leopold
65 "___ Brockovich"
66 Spoonful, say
67 Burro's cry
68 Wds. of similar meaning
69 Mr. Bean on the screen

DOWN

1 "___ help?"
2 God who rides an eight-legged horse
3 Gun's recoil
4 Cry of mock horror
5 Wide-brimmed chapeaux
6 Vacationer's vehicle
7 It isn't returned
8 Hit by strong winds
9 Sports car features
10 Blubber
11 Major work
12 Love or song ending
13 Like flu victims
18 White House staffer
19 Some Antietam combatants
24 Triangular sail
26 Piece of sound equipment
27 Esau's father
28 Florida's Key ___
29 Merlin Olsen, once, for short
30 Show flexibility
31 Wide-awake
32 Employee's request
33 Radio Hall of Fame inductee Kay
38 Chemical bonds
39 Go-between
42 Wee, to Burns
44 Opening of a toast
45 Lennon's love
47 ___ Minor
48 Pines
49 San Juan Hill site
52 One who crosses the line?
53 Promote an album, possibly
54 Sailing
57 Shoot past, e.g.
58 ___ saxophone
59 2000 sci-fi film
61 Test
62 Apéritif choice
63 "You'll go ___!"

by Alan J. Weiss

ACROSS

1 Games nobody wins
5 Small, medium or large
9 Green fruit drink flavor
13 West Coast gas brand
14 Shoelace problem
15 Get ___ a good thing
16 "Well, I'll be!"
19 Out for the evening, maybe
20 Gymnast Comaneci
21 Yogi or Smokey
23 Quart divs.
24 "Sesame Street" skills
28 Get-up-and-go
30 Folklore meanie
33 Overly, informally
35 ___-Cat (off-road vehicle)
37 Motor City labor org.
38 "If only . . ."
41 Advice columnist Landers
42 Broadway hit letters
43 Cat that catches rodents
44 No longer on active duty: Abbr.
46 "Dumb" girl of old comics
48 Fourposters, e.g.
49 Got together
51 007
53 Photo tint
55 Port in "The Marines' Hymn"
60 "Stupid of me not to know"
62 Defeat decisively
63 Handle roughly
64 ___ gin fizz
65 ___-bitty
66 Stuff to the gills
67 Weigh station units

DOWN

1 Tex-Mex snack
2 Wrinkle remover
3 Quito's country: Abbr.
4 Auctioneer's closing word
5 Kid's wheels
6 Scared (of)
7 Animal house
8 English prep school
9 Deceived
10 Wearing a costume, say
11 N.Y.C. gallery
12 U-turn from WSW
17 Apply gently
18 Napkin's place
22 Greet the day
24 Battling
25 Daniel with a coonskin cap
26 "I don't want any part of it"
27 Cardinals' team letters
29 Dictatorship
31 Thumped fast, as the heart
32 Decorative jugs
34 Takes too much, briefly
36 Lennon's lady
39 Doofus
40 Kernel
45 Sheriff's sidekick
47 Cheap booze
50 Up to, informally
52 Fizzle out
53 Flu season protection
54 U.S.N. bigwigs
56 "Check this out!"
57 Norway's capital
58 "Exodus" author Uris
59 Fateful March day
60 ___ Lanka
61 Battery size

by Nancy Salomon and Harvey Estes

ACROSS

1 Was of the opinion
5 "Shake ___!"
9 Expensive wraps
13 Woodwind
14 Less welcoming
15 Straddling
16 Novelist Ambler
17 1970's–80's TV twosome
19 Recommended amount
20 Overseas Mrs.
21 Gerber offerings
22 Log holder
24 Syllables sung in place of unknown words
25 Winner
27 In the wrong
32 Pledge of Allegiance ender
33 Actor Bean
35 Androcles, e.g.
36 Fill the chambers, say
38 Arab League member
40 Put in storage
41 Company in 2002 headlines
43 Countrified
45 Barely maintain, with "out"
46 Mimics' work
48 Frequent ferry rider
50 "Kidnapped" author's inits.
51 Composer Boulanger
52 Black mark
56 Signal at Sotheby's
57 Steel mill by-product
60 1990's–2000's TV twosome
62 Coveted prize
63 Diva's delivery
64 Dust Bowl drifters
65 What Dubliners call home
66 Poverty
67 Jordan's Queen ___
68 Campus bigwig

DOWN

1 Worked in rows
2 Spain's second-longest river
3 1990's TV twosome
4 Iago's specialty
5 Hard nut to crack?
6 Money replaced by the euro
7 Rat alert?
8 Dads of dads
9 Evenhanded
10 Magazine of reprints
11 Took a cab
12 1974 Sutherland/Gould film
14 #1 hit for Brenda Lee
18 Imperatives
23 Outback hopper
24 ___ notes
25 Jacket holder
26 Massey of old movies
27 Personification of mockery
28 Oerter and Unser
29 1980's TV twosome
30 Elicit
31 Having a higher model number, say
34 Feudal laborers
37 John ___
39 Water nymphs
42 Silent film star Mabel
44 It was dropped in the 60's
47 Wine holder
49 Didn't speak clearly
51 More polite
52 E. B. White's "The Trumpet of the ___"
53 Goodyear product
54 Tennis great Nastase
55 Delighted
56 Scott of "Happy Days"
58 A celebrity may have one
59 Feds
61 "King Kong" studio

by D. J. DeChristopher

200

ACROSS

1 Broad comedy
6 H.S. math
9 Steinbeck family
14 Legend automaker
15 "Ben-___"
16 Dogpatch fellow
17 Wanted poster info
18 Drink in a mug
19 Botox targets
20 Chess endings that don't hold up?
23 Ad-___ committee
24 Rice Krispies sound
25 It makes pot potent: Abbr.
28 Ultimate degree
30 Look over, informally
35 Clarinet, for one
37 Brain-wave test: Abbr.
39 First name at the 1976 Olympics
40 Zombie calculation?
44 Resell illegally
45 Sign of summer
46 Numbskull
47 Sonora shawls
50 Granola morsel
52 European carrier
53 Yalies
55 ___ Cruces
57 Poisoned saltine?
63 Unclogged
64 Heston was its pres.
65 Imam's study
67 Waste maker, proverbially
68 Shrew
69 Singer Cleo or Frankie
70 Said "I'm in," in effect
71 Make like
72 Spanish hero

DOWN

1 Airways-regulating org.
2 Rights grp.
3 Undo
4 Wall Street debacle
5 Singer Sheena
6 Pequod skipper
7 Quiet times
8 Lorne or Graham
9 Pungent pepper
10 The last word
11 Green Gables girl
12 Stinky grades
13 Grads-to-be: Abbr.
21 Took steps
22 Kentucky Derby time
25 Bridge strengthener
26 "It follows that . . ."
27 Chest wood
29 H.R.H. part
31 Singer's backup
32 Baja "bye"
33 Supergirl's alias ___ Lee
34 Port east of Porto-Novo
36 Boxer Oscar ___ Hoya
38 Salon goo
41 Popped up
42 Corp. biggie
43 Australian "bear"
48 Polar helper
49 Reddish brown
51 Guard's neighbor
54 Deep-six
56 Swede's "Cheers!"
57 ___ Bator
58 Egg holder
59 More than fill
60 Frenzy
61 Idle in comedy
62 Indian princess
63 Chinese tea
66 Composer Rorem

by Jay Livingston

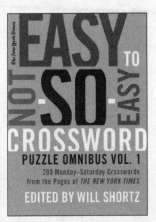

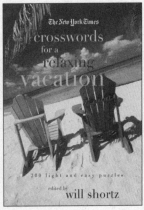
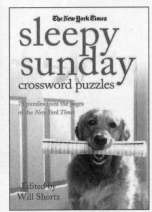

1

```
ROBS . TRASHY . ALF
OSLO . SUBLET . GEL
THUNDERROAD . IVE
SARGE . APR . ALEE
. SESAMESTREET
PTA . MER . TAR .
AARP . CUPS . PIETA
SUNSETBOULEVARD
STEAM . ALMA . ERIE
. LIP . UVA . LON
PRIMROSEPATH .
EONS . LAX . TIBET
AGO . TINPANALLEY
RUN . OCTOPI . LARK
LEE . WEASEL . SHOE
```

2

```
LARUE . TAMPA . QUM
ARENA . ALIAR . UNA
NEPLUSULTRA . ICH
ESSO . ITS . CRADLE
. CHE . SHARPER
BASKETS . PETER .
AMI . REWARD . SOWN
RINSE . ERA . TOQUE
TREK . LATINI . USA
. QUIET . NETCOST
TRUANTS . GOO .
ROASTS . OUR . SITE
USN . ADINFINITUM
CIO . CISCO . INERT
KEN . TETES . PERKS
```

3

```
AIOLI . LODE . FETA
SONIC . AMEX . ALAN
SWIPEADEBITCARD
NAT . BRUN . TEENSY
. SACK . TVAD .
LIFTTHEVEIL . SRA
ALEPH . ERS . AMAN
ZETA . MEDIA . NEJD
ANET . ARI . ONAIR
RED . PINCHANERVE
. CONE . ALEX .
ASTROS . MPAA . QED
STEALTHEPICTURE
SITZ . EMME . TRITE
TREY . MOON . SIZED
```

4

```
ATARI . SNIP . LUSH
ROBIN . TADA . AREA
KNUCKLESANDWICH
SITE . EPA . TRYSTS
. COMO . WHEE .
. SLAPONTHEWRIST
SPOKEN . HER . NCO
TIRED . JET . ASTRO
ACE . OAT . CLARET
BENDINGANELBOW .
. IDOS . ELSE .
PARLOR . ATL . RENT
SHOULDERHOLSTER
SOOT . ERIE . PAREE
TYKE . REAR . SWEDE
```

5

```
BETS . PAPAS . GRIP
MAUI . ATONE . RENE
TURNSLOOSE . ANTE
. ACOMPLETEFOOL
ANNEX . LOX . INS
ROD . FORM . HARE .
CROSSEYE . TAB .
. ATOTALFAILURE
. APT . ETCETERA
. PIKA . ARES . AIR
ROB . ULM . ISLET
AMILLIONBUCKS .
JESU . BRIANKEITH
ALEX . RANTO . EZRA
HOSE . ALOSS . TEAL
```

6

```
SODAS . TENAM . AHS
CNOTE . EXILE . HIT
ACORNFLAKES . ENE
REDEAL . MEX . DADE
. STAR . SIZEDUP
CRATERED . SEND .
OUT . SETIN . NERDS
STOW . DIVOT . BEET
ISLAM . PAROL . SMU
. LIED . STRAPSIN
BOBSLED . HOPE .
ALOT . ART . IDEALS
LEO . AROMADOWNEY
SOT . FINED . GETON
ASH . TEENS . SEINE
```

7

```
F I L C H   A R E S   T H I N
L O I R E   G U R U   W A C O
A T L A S   A T T N   O L E S
B A T S I N T H E B E L F R Y
    S T I E S   A M I
H U T   A B S   S T U T T E R
A L I S T   I C H   E R N O
S N A K E I N T H E G R A S S
N A R Y   S E E   I S S U E
T R A L A L A   S A N   H E S
    I R A   A M I G O
F R O G I N T H E T H R O A T
O A T H   D U E L   A N K L E
G R I T   E T A L   M O R O N
S A S S   R U D Y   S T A T S
```

8

```
L I L A C   P A L E   M E A T
O D O U R   R E A L   E L L A
C O C K A D O O D L E D O O M
I L K   T E N N   S N I P E S
  S P E N T   I C E S
M A M A   T O P D O G S
E R I C A   H A R M   F R O
L I T T L E K A N G A R O O M
D A H   L E I S   S A U T E
  B O L D E S T   I R O N
S H I V   T E L L S
A P O G E E   S E R A   C S A
C E N T R A L P A R K Z O O M
M A K O   R E A M   E E R I E
E R S E   N A R Y   R E E L S
```

9

```
I M P A L E   L A N G   S E R
T O O L E R   A P E R   H O I
S O L O N S   C L E O   A L B
  I H A T E T O R U S S I A
A T T A   R O M   N A T A L
L E I   V O W   B A D H A N D
E S C   O V I D   M C I
  H O W C A N I S E R B I A
  O A T   G I B E   C U D
H U R T L E D   S A W   E R A
E N I A C   E T A   S W A Y
I D O N O T B O L I V I A
N U T   R O A N   B I G T O P
I L E   D O S E   I N H E R E
E L D   S K E D   D E T R O P
```

10

```
A S I S   A T O Z   C R A B S
C O M P   R O P E   H A R E M
C H A I N M A I L   A C U T E
T O M E I   D U D   R E B E L
  G N P   M A I L C A L L
N I C E T R Y   S E A
C A L L H O M E   T Y R A N T
A G A   B A T C H   T E A
R O M A N O   H O M E L O A N
  M E N   M U T A N T S
L O A N W O R D   S H U
E R R E D   A R E   I G L O O
A B U S E   W O R D C H A I N
V I S T A   L O G O   I D L E
E T H Y L   S P O T   N E S S
```

11

```
A C N E   T E A S   O S C A R
D O E R   R A V I   S P O R E
I M P S   A R I Z   T A L K S
D E A T H I N V E N I C E
A T L   O P S   C A E S A R
S H I R R S   J A R   L T D
  I R E F U L   I P A N A
  D I V I D I N G I N T W O
W I N E D   S T A N C E
S E C   A H A   N U R S E S
J U L I U S   F O B   M I A
  I N T H E V I C I N I T Y
D O N U T   D A N E   E T H S
I S E R E   A L A N   W H E N
S E D E R   M E L T   T Y R O
```

12

```
A R M S   F O S S E   L P G A
L O O M   A V I A N   I R A N
T A R O T C A R D S   Z O R A
A R A R A T   A U K   T A L
R E S E W   A S T R O L O G Y
S D S   D E B T   E D U C E S
  C R I E R S   L O S T
  C R Y S T A L B A L L
O P I E   S N O O P S
U R G E O N   G E N L   D O R
T E A L E A V E S   O F E V E
A P R   N B A   E M O T E D
G A B S   O U I J A B O A R D
E R O O   B L O A T   L I D O
S E X Y   S T U B S   S L O G
```

13

```
HEARD ■ BUBBA ■ MBA
ALBEE ■ AREAS ■ RUN
MISSMANNERS ■ BET
■ ■ PUPAS ■ BATONS
ADMIRAL ■ BLUEJAY
SORTER ■ PAELLA ■
INKER ■ WORST ■ NIA
DUNS ■ PIPES ■ AGTS
ETO ■ PARIS ■ SPLAT
■ WARREN ■ TUPELO
SPIRITS ■ TELLSON
NOTIME ■ ABATE ■
OLA ■ MRSMALAPROP
OIL ■ ERROR ■ NIOBE
POL ■ REARS ■ SETIN
```

14

```
THIS ■ SLOGS ■ LAZE
REVIEWABLE ■ IRIS
ORANGEPEEL ■ BINS
DEN ■ RAISE ■ PEACE
■ PERSE ■ BAR ■
RECESS ■ CENTRAL
ALIAS ■ FOOD ■ YULE
NARC ■ BOWLS ■ BRIG
ITCH ■ AREA ■ LEAVE
SEABIRD ■ CALLER
■ RMN ■ GNARL ■
SCRAP ■ RAINY ■ ANA
OLIN ■ COTTONSWAB
LAND ■ OVEREXPOSE
EDDY ■ PESOS ■ ALAS
```

15

```
AESOP ■ PENAL ■ TET
BLISS ■ AMORE ■ AVE
NOTHINGISSO ■ KIN
EPEE ■ EERIE ■ BELT
RESALE ■ ■ ENROL
■ ■ ADMIRABLEIN
DEFENSED ■ LIGATE
ELUL ■ REA ■ EVES
PILLAR ■ ASPIRERS
POLITICSASA ■
■ TOOTH ■ ANGERS
BAIT ■ COBOL ■ AREA
OHM ■ SHORTMEMORY
USE ■ RISER ■ SUDAN
TOR ■ SEETO ■ STENO
```

16

```
OGLE ■ ANDS ■ MATES
PIER ■ DEEP ■ AROMA
ELSE ■ HULA ■ SLUMS
CATCHERINTHERYE
■ TARO ■ YIN ■
PET ■ VENTURE ■ LOT
ALONE ■ ORO ■ FETE
SOWONESWILDOATS
SPEW ■ RUE ■ RESET
EEL ■ PAPRIKA ■ TRY
■ IRS ■ TINS ■
JIMMIECRACKCORN
ADOBE ■ HULK ■ OBEY
VENUS ■ EDIE ■ RODE
ASSET ■ WEAR ■ NEST
```

17

```
ORCA ■ CCCP ■ OPALS
MEAD ■ REAL ■ ARIOT
ANIL ■ USNA ■ TODAY
RENAISSANCEMAN ■
■ INON ■ ORO ■
HOE ■ DEACONS ■ MPG
ENNUI ■ RIG ■ SOAR
LEONARDODAVINCI
GALE ■ ONA ■ OCTET
ALA ■ PLATEAU ■ ERS
■ CAL ■ DECA ■
■ DANTEALIGHIERI
RICOH ■ LUBE ■ SYST
ERATO ■ UCLA ■ LEVI
CEDES ■ MIEN ■ ESPN
```

18

```
ABCS ■ CAMUS ■ FLOP
KOLA ■ AMATI ■ LOVE
AMEN ■ SALAD ■ ASEA
■ BOCKINTHEUSSR ■
■ TINA ■ ASH ■
ELNINO ■ PERU ■ ESS
NEAT ■ KARMA ■ LET
DAVYJONESSLAGER
USA ■ ARISE ■ RATE
EEL ■ NATE ■ FURROW
■ JET ■ GAGA ■
■ ALETOTHECHIEF
QUIT ■ RIANT ■ GRAY
ETTE ■ INTRO ■ NILE
DOER ■ OTHER ■ SEAT
```

19

```
BASS  ⬛ UNDO ⬛ WALDO
OPAL  ⬛ PARS ⬛ AMOUR
USMARSHAL ⬛ RANEE
TEEPEE ⬛ BOOTHILL
⬛⬛ ATV ⬛ SIS ⬛⬛
SCALD ⬛ IBEAM ⬛ PST
ARRAY ⬛ DODGECITY
LOOM ⬛ SERGE ⬛ ATOP
TOMBSTONE ⬛ DRAKE
SKA ⬛ TASER ⬛ ESSES
⬛⬛ MAI ⬛ SOB ⬛⬛
OKCORRAL ⬛ TILDES
INAPT ⬛ WYATTEARP
LEVEL ⬛ ERTE ⬛ EZRA
SWEDE ⬛ SEER ⬛ REST
```

20

```
PUMP ⬛ CARAT ⬛ PARA
STAR ⬛ OVATE ⬛ EXIT
SARI ⬛ RECON ⬛ SLOE
THESTOCKMARKET
⬛ MON ⬛ NAY ⬛
OBI ⬛ FED ⬛ ACT ⬛ BAA
COMPUTERSYSTEMS
COMA ⬛ POI ⬛ WEBS
UNINVITEDPEOPLE
REX ⬛ ASH ⬛ EAR ⬛ SET
⬛ FRO ⬛ RIB ⬛
THEYMIGHTCRASH
SHOT ⬛ EDWIN ⬛ AUTO
IOWA ⬛ REEVE ⬛ GREG
NULL ⬛ SANER ⬛ SAWS
```

21

```
MOWS ⬛ AGAPE ⬛ MESH
ECHO ⬛ SHRED ⬛ AUTO
SHOOTHOOPS ⬛ CLEO
ASONE ⬛ SMU ⬛ AHEAD
⬛ PEN ⬛ TAPEWORMS
FAIRER ⬛ GEM ⬛
ITT ⬛ TUBING ⬛ ALAS
SMUT ⬛ FOCUS ⬛ NASH
HOPI ⬛ FLYBOY ⬛ NEA
⬛ PAL ⬛ NASDAQ
SNAPBEANS ⬛ CCS ⬛
LIBYA ⬛ FOE ⬛ HALOS
EXIT ⬛ FILMSTRIPS
DODO ⬛ ARTIE ⬛ ADIN
SNEE ⬛ REESE ⬛ BEES
```

22

```
CELLO ⬛ CBER ⬛ MALE
ORION ⬛ HONE ⬛ ALIT
COFFEEANDDANISH
ASET ⬛ TIE ⬛ ORIOLE
⬛ FUR ⬛ CLEANER
TAIPEI ⬛ ALES ⬛
ASSET ⬛ ASIN ⬛ SENT
MEATANDPOTATOES
PAYS ⬛ ADES ⬛ HENNA
⬛ AMEN ⬛ DOWSER
CRAMMER ⬛ HEY ⬛
AERIAL ⬛ DOE ⬛ FREE
PEACHESANDCREAM
ELBA ⬛ SIDE ⬛ HOIST
SSSS ⬛ STAY ⬛ AGNES
```

23

```
SCUFF ⬛ SCOT ⬛ SLOG
CAVIL ⬛ NANA ⬛ TALL
ARETE ⬛ ARMS ⬛ ERMA
GRAZEGRAYS ⬛ AVER
⬛ CALC ⬛ ENLACE
ROMPER ⬛ ARLES ⬛
AXEL ⬛ DESI ⬛ ATRIA
GETAWAY ⬛ SCREAMS
ANZIO ⬛ REEL ⬛ EVAS
⬛ NOMEN ⬛ ENLIST
HOOPLA ⬛ TARE ⬛
ELAL ⬛ CHECKCZECH
RITA ⬛ RIRE ⬛ TITHE
OVEN ⬛ OVER ⬛ ANNUM
DANE ⬛ SERB ⬛ REAMS
```

24

```
RABAT ⬛ NEST ⬛ DIME
IRANI ⬛ AXLE ⬛ ETAL
PIETA ⬛ RIOT ⬛ LARA
⬛ DIRECTORBILLY
TOECAP ⬛ PAR ⬛ ION
ELK ⬛ SORTS ⬛ INANE
AGED ⬛ COO ⬛ CEO
MARATHONERFRANK
⬛ DOS ⬛ TEA ⬛ ALEE
JABOT ⬛ SOLTI ⬛ LAG
AMO ⬛ ERA ⬛ ENTERS
NEWSMANMORLEY
GLEE ⬛ IDOL ⬛ ERODE
LIRA ⬛ SARA ⬛ TROOP
EAST ⬛ ELON ⬛ SEPTA
```

25

```
U S M A   E R R E D   T A L C
G O I N   L E A V E   O W E S
H U N D R E D Y A R D D A S H
    N I E C E S     A O R T A
J O E   S T E   R I M   D A R
A F L A C   M O U R N   S T P
W A L N U T   S T A Y S
  N I N E I N C H N A I L S
    A P N E A     I N T A K E
L A S   L E A R N   K E V I N
O A T   A S P   O D E   A P E
A C O R N     U N R E A L
T H R E E M I L E I S L A N D
H E E D   D O N E E   O M N I
E N D S   S C A D S   E P E E
```

26

```
E G B D F   F O A M   V A M P
L A N A I   E L L A   E T U I
B R A W N   L A M A   N A S A
A B I G A I L V A N B U R E N
      L O S     D O S I D O
A T M O S T   U M P S
C H I P   A N N L A N D E R S
C A D E T   O I L   S A M O A
T W I N S I S T E R   M I L L
      K N E E   O M E L E T
H O T T E A     B S A
I N E E D S O M E A D V I C E
P I P E   N O O N   C I D E R
P O E M   I Z O D   A L O N G
O N E S   T E N S   P E L T S
```

27

```
M A S S   F A T E   C O A S T
C R O C   A D I N   U N D E R
S M A R T B O M B   R E L A Y
  P A H   E L A L   A T O
  P O P U L A R O P I N I O N
G A P E D A T   C O C O
I C E S   L I P   U S H E R
G E R   H O T C A K E   A B E
I D A H O   S P A   T R O D
  A M I E   O N E I D A S
H I P R E P L A C E M E N T
A V A   F O A M   M I O
R A R E R   I N T R A N S I T
S N I D E   N O L A   T E R I
H A S T E . E T C H   O D E S
```

28

```
E L F   P O S T S   P E O N S
L I E   O N T O P   A L P H A
I N N   S C A L E   S M E L L
J A C K I E G L E A S O N
A G E N T   C U E   D O G
H E R O   P A T H S   D A M E
    W E I G H   F E T A L
T H E H O N E Y M O O N E R S
S O L O N   M A C R O
A N E W   E R E C T   T A N G
R E V   I R E   M E T O O
    A U D R E Y M E A D O W S
M E T R E   S W I R L   N I P
O M E G A   E C L A T   E S E
B U S E S   S A L S A   D E L
```

29

```
I N T E R   T I L   G U S T O
S A U D I   U N I   A S P E R
M I L I T A N T S   N O R S E
  F I T Z G E R A L D   I T S
  S P O I L S   A H I T
  R E O   H O W I T Z E R
H A D   S W O O N   T E T E
A T I L T   W O E   G O R E D
R A T A   E D S E L   S S S
I T Z W O R D S   M I R
  I N R E   B I T E R S
S U N   B A R M I T Z V A H
T R E V I   T E N S I O N A L
A S S E T   E R E   E K I N G
B A S E S   S E T   R E N E E
```

30

```
S C R I P   B A S H   L A D Y
H A I K U   A N T E   O L E O
I N D E P E N D E N C E D A Y
N E E   I Q S   P R O B O N O
    F L U   G O I N
T A P A   I R O N   J A F F E
O L E S   N I L   L O R E A L
S T A T U E O F L I B E R T Y
C E L E B S   P E P   T R E S
A R E N A   T R I S   H Y D E
    N E R O   Y M A
A T I N G L E   A N A   E E L
J U L Y I V M D C C L X X V I
A B L E   I O N E   T E P E E
R E S T   S R A S   A D O R N
```

31

```
SCAM ARAB CREAM
DARE DALE HALLE
SLAG RILE ABBES
 FLATONONESBACH
  WHIST  LEI
DEPART  PASTIME
ELATE  ERIN  BUN
MOSTWANTEDLISZT
OPT  LIED  ANEAR
SEESRED  SPUNKY
  AIR  COLIN
TOOHOTTOHANDEL
ECLAT OLAV ATOZ
SHARE MORE TALE
SONAR ERAS ELAN
```

32

```
DOIN EVITA EGAD
ARCO MACES  BEDE
HEARTBREAKHOTEL
LONGHAIR  ALONE
 TERSE  SERIF
ASH ESSENCE  FAT
DEEJAY XOO MONO
OGLED HUB ORFEO
RAPT PAR BUSMAN
ELM DELBERT YRS
 YMCAS  LILAC
ASSAI  DISALLOW
WHENIMSIXTYFOUR
EELS DEVIL RUSE
SAFE SCARY EDEN
```

33

```
JAIL METAL DAZE
UNTO ADORE EROS
STIR CIRCA LOOT
TENDERFOOT TAME
 LOY  HOARSE
BOWMAN FLEA
ALIEN COURTYARD
LALA TACKY ALAR
IVYLEAGUE BRAKE
 PIES CONNED
SQUEAL LAO
AUNT WATERMETER
BATH IRATE MAXI
OKIE NICHE IRIS
TELL DATER TATE
```

34

```
LOP FLASH ATLAS
ERA EERIE DUANE
ACU DARLA ELITE
HALT RALPHNADER
 RAINY ION
SMELTS VARIETY
WAVES FAXED HEF
ACES ERRED REAL
PAR AVAIL TERSE
 WELDING DONATE
 EAT TOMEI
JOHNMADDEN EDAM
ARENA IRANI EWE
BARON NOSED RAN
SLANT OPERA SYD
```

35

```
PAMPAS STEW PTA
ETERNE CODE EAR
NONONANETTE PRE
SMUT MONO VEEPS
 ELATE GILL
AMBIENT SALIENT
DUANE ATIT AMES
INB KIKIDEE OVA
NCAA DELE ASKER
SHARPEN SAVIORS
 UNIS ALIEN
STROP OBIS AIDA
AAH PUPUPLATTER
LIU IRES ERRANT
ELM NINE SCANTY
```

36

```
BLDGS SSW ATWAR
LEERS CHI RHINE
ATLAS REDGIANTS
SHUN OARED NEHI
TAXDODGERS BIZ
SLEEVE  SCALE
  ULCER EARLS
 HELLSANGELS
CLOVE ATARI
HIRES ONSITE
ASS STRAIGHTAS
USES TOEIN EARP
COMPADRES WILMA
EMAIL MDL ELIAN
RENTS EYE DACCA
```

37

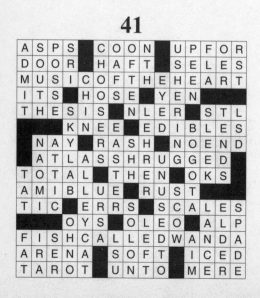

```
S T A N   A G O G   D A M E S
H I T E   D U N E   A L A M O
O N E A   M A T T   L Y S O L
W E A T H E R V A N E   E T O
M A S   I N D   L O Y   R I M
E R E C T   S N I T   T A C O
    H O B   O F A   I T O N
  I N A N O T H E R V E I N
D C O N   R H O   Y A T
R E S T   N E W S   S O L O S
A W E   R E B   P A C   E R E
C A R   Y O U R E S O V A I N
U T I C A   R E E K   I D E A
L E N I N   B I D E   V E N T
A R G O S   S N O W   A N T E
```

38

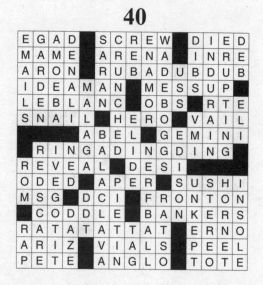

```
S O F A   S I T B Y   P A A R
A L U M   A D O R E   E C R U
A L T A   B E T E L   A C E S
R A Z Z Z O O O W L S   I N T
      E A T     S O M E D A Y
O S A   G A F F   W I R E
R O L E   G U R U   L E N D S
C A L L L E E E C L E C T I C
A R O M A   L O L A   T A D A
  C E L L   N A V E   L O T
P H A R A O H     I D O
L E T   W O O O S S S P I E S
A R I E   T R U T H   A G R A
Z O O T   E S T E E   R O L L
A N N A   R E S T S   T R E K
```

39

```
T O S C A   L E A S   A W L
I T H A D   P U M P S   T R A
P R I M E N U M B E R   S I T
S A P P   A T E E   C E N T
  B A R M I T Z V A H A G E
S H O R T E N   Z E T A
L O U I E   S L I M N E S S
A N N   O L D E N   L I T
M E D U L L A S   T R I P E
  L O A M   A B R E A S T
S I G N O F B A D L U C K
I D E A   S H O T   T A M E
G I T   B A K E R S D O Z E N
M O T   A V I A N   E R A T O
A M Y   T E N D   M Y N A S
```

40

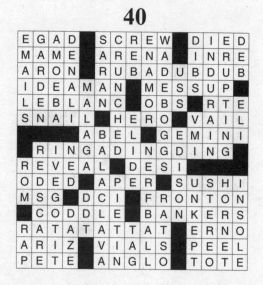

```
E G A D   S C R E W   D I E D
M A M E   A R E N A   I N R E
A R O N   R U B A D U B D U B
I D E A M A N   M E S S U P
L E B L A N C   O B S   R T E
S N A I L   H E R O   V A I L
      A B E L   G E M I N I
  R I N G A D I N G D I N G
R E V E A L   D E S I
O D E D   A P E R   S U S H I
M S G   D C I   F R O N T O N
  C O D D L E   B A N K E R S
R A T A T A T T A T   E R N O
A R I Z   V I A L S   P E E L
P E T E   A N G L O   T O T E
```

41

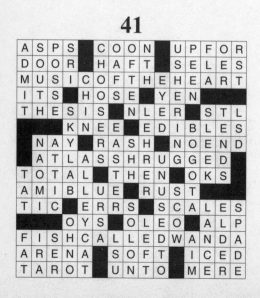

```
A S P S   C O O N   U P F O R
D O O R   H A F T   S E L E S
M U S I C O F T H E H E A R T
I T S   H O S E   Y E N
T H E S I S   N L E R   S T L
    K N E E   E D I B L E S
N A Y   R A S H   N O E N D
A T L A S S H R U G G E D
T O T A L   T H E N   O K S
A M I B L U E   R U S T
T I C   E R R S   S C A L E S
    O Y S   O L E O   A L P
F I S H C A L L E D W A N D A
A R E N A   S O F T   I C E D
T A R O T   U N T O   M E R E
```

42

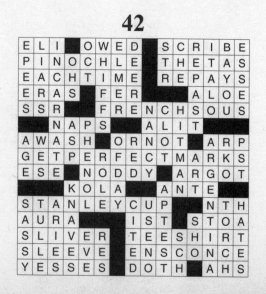

```
E L I   O W E D   S C R I B E
P I N O C H L E   T H E T A S
E A C H T I M E   R E P A Y S
E R A S   F E R   A L O E
S S R   F R E N C H S O U S
  N A P S   A L I T
A W A S H   O R N O T   A R P
G E T P E R F E C T M A R K S
E S E   N O D D Y   A R G O T
    K O L A   A N T E
S T A N L E Y C U P   N T H
A U R A   I S T   S T O A
S L I V E R   T E E S H I R T
S L E E V E   E N S C O N C E
Y E S S E S   D O T H   A H S
```

43

```
VISTA   DOIT   TRAY
OOHED   EDGE   HALE
TWEEDLEDUM    EMMA
EAST   IPSA   ATPAR
    HIES   NINO
  IDENTICALTWINS
ONE   TOGO   KEENON
EDITH   HOW   ALAMO
DISHES   THAT   LAW
SAMEOLDSAMEOLD
    BRRR   TART
JOLLY   OMNI   HALF
ARIA   TWEEDLEDEE
MESH   VSIX   ERASE
BOAS   SENT   ASYET
```

44

```
APNEA   INB   BLUM
DRAWL   ONEA   AURA
LABEL   HUGHGRANT
IDO   EPOS   AROUSE
BOBBYSHERMAN
   ASH   EAT   NSA
ADOS   ACTI   IDEAL
CIVILWARGENERAL
DRACO   LENT   ROBS
CEL   VOL   HOE
   JESSEJACKSON
PREAMP   PENT   ANY
HARPERLEE   ASKIN
ASIA   EYER   NIECE
THEN   YES   ESSEX
```

45

```
BEAST   OSCAR   TAG
ADLAI   CARPE   OIL
BUGSPRAYERS   ADO
ACE   TUT   POTSDAM
SERMON   CENSES
   TESLA   STITCH
CASS   TOTS   OSOLE
UGH   COWSLIP   OAR
PREGO   ECON   ELMO
SIERRA   AGAPE
   PASSON   WALKBY
POSSESS   LAB   NRA
IRK   TURKEYSHOOT
ELI   ERIKA   TOWNE
SYN   DECKS   SYNCS
```

46

```
SCABS   TABS   ISLE
ALLOT   ELAL   NEED
GOODY   NORA   ALOE
ATTY   STUDMUFFIN
   BLAH   BRO
STALAG   SHANGHAI
EUROS   CHIN   INN
DRAWSTRINGPANTS
EBB   HOLD   OLDIE
ROSEBOWL   DEPICT
   MOM   COMA
STRIPMALLS   CLAD
IRAN   CLEO   NIECE
PUZO   ASIS   INANE
SEER   NOSE   POKER
```

47

```
BLEAT   SPEC   AJAX
AUDIO   PIER   NORM
ETERNALTRIANGLE
ZEN   EMIT   MASON
   SLIT   SUE
  INCESSANTNOISE
SMERSH   DIE   PROG
LIVES   UMP   VIOLA
IDEA   ASI   SINNED
PERMANENTPRESS
   CAR   RATS
ORGAN   ZASU   HIS
PERPETUALMOTION
ELIE   ONCE   SANTA
LYNX   POKE   ONTAP
```

48

```
DORSA   FLORA   IDS
IRONS   LOCAL   TEL
ABOOKMUSTBE   SLA
   FRAME   EXPERT
MATT   ENCL   ILIE
ALOES   THEAXEFOR
IMPROV   ENTER
MSS   NEGATOR   HEM
   EATAT   MODENA
THEFROZEN   XRAYS
WELT   ADUE   ERAT
ERASER   ANGST
LET   SEAINSIDEUS
VIE   ADHOC   GENTS
END   ISSUE   INSET
```

49

```
UKES #ELBA #ACTED
NOAH REAP #LARVA
CARYGRANT #BREED
ALL #LASS #WIRERS
PAYMENT #MANY #
# ANT #SAYONARA
STERN #SHIN #AJAX
TAXI #AMAZE #TAKE
ARIA #DOME #TIRED
BATHMATS #RIO #
# COPE #SEANCES
AGHAST #FEAR #AVA
FLARE #JIMCARREY
RILEY #EDIT #CONS
OBEYS #BOSS #ALTO
```

50

```
MURAL #FLOWN #JAM
ACURA #AUDIO #AGO
SLIMPICKENS #NEO
HANA #RTE #DOOVER
# NIA #GUAVA #
# SKINNYDIPPING #
FIE #TIARAS #NERD
INTEL #CEN #KEYIN
RETD #SHANIA #CPA
# SLIGHTMISTAKE #
# ETHOS #AOL #
REDHOT #ADA #SKED
OAR #SPARECHANGE
DRU #TUXES #OCEAN
ELM #STEAK #NEEDY
```

51

```
TONGA #SOS #WEREA
USUAL #ANN #INALL
NOZZLE #YEA #DAZZLE
ALLEGRO #FEEBLER
SEEN #ENDUP #LENT
# ASTAR #IRE #
THESAURI #CYSTIC
AID #FRAZZLED #ODO
REDDEN #LINESMAN
# USE #ENTRE #
DOSE #RIDGE #SPAM
EVILEST #ERASURE
GUZZLE #ERR #FIZZLE
ALLEN #MOE #ALLES
SEEDY #SOD #REESE
```

52

```
BROW #PUMAS #HASP
LONE #ISIAH #YOKE
ONEEIGHTHUNDRED
BAH #NEET #TEETER
# ASTOR #PSI #ATO
CANTON #TOOLS #
ENDAT #SELF #COKE
ONETOUCHOFVENUS
SADE #NOES #INERT
# SIDLE #ASTUTE
MIA #CID #CRISP #
ANTHEM #CARO #PEA
ONEARMEDBANDITS
READ #EMILY #ONUS
IRMA #DOVES #AGIN
```

53

```
ADORN #SCAR #LOST
MELEE #HONE #ONTO
PEELS #HAYDNSEEK
SMOOTH #LODE #TEE
# ALAS #NEWBORN
GOODENPLENTY #
AIM #SERE #STRAW
GLIB #SYNOD #EACH
ASTER #TWIN #SHE
# NEESONNEPHEW
CANTINA #SAME #
ALI #GAME #HERDER
NIXONCUTS #SIEVE
AVEC #TENT #ISLES
LEST #SLAY #SHIRT
```

54

```
HAZES #SCAM #MAJA
EXERT #HUME #IRON
METER #URAL #SEWN
PLACEONTHESCALE
# TAD #LEER #
PEA #MIST #SPEEDS
ANTS #UNIT #TAROT
CUSTOMARYMANNER
TREAD #POKE #TIRE
SEATED #LEAD #ESP
# EURO #NEO #
MISSMUFFETSFARE
ADAM #MAID #AFTON
ZOLA #UGLI #LETBE
ELAN #PELT #TRUSS
```

55

```
L I N U S   G E N T   P F F T
A T O N E   A G R A   U L E E
B O R I N G B O A R   F E I N
      T O A S T   O F F E N D
S O M E R S   R I T A   I T S
A D E S   M A I N   T A N
L E W   T A M P A   L I G H T
V O L C A N O   P A I D F O R
O N I O N   U S E U P   L I E
    N O G   N E T S   M E S S
G I G   L A T E   T R E A T S
R O M P E R   S T E A M
E T U I   B A R I N G B E A R
T A L C   O M E N   E E R I E
A S E A   R I D E   D R A M S
```

56

```
R A M   H O P L I T E   C O W
A T E   A R O U S A L   A L E
T O N   C A S C A D E   L I B
    M U S I C I A N   V A L V E
      C E L T S   T E R S E R
E L A I N E   Z I N C
L I N E D   O P E N   H A M M
L E O N A R D O D A V I N C I
A U N T   A D D S   I T E M S
      I B I S   A C E T I C
S A S S E D   A Z T E C
P R A T T   S C U L P T O R
E E L   T I T U L A R   P A T
A N T   O V E R U S E   A K A
R A Y   R E P A S T S   L E G
```

57

```
H A G S   G O A D   E A S E S
T R A P   O N C E   N A P P Y
T I R E   B E D S   D R Y A D
P A P E R B A C K B O O
    D O L L   A R N E S S
S P O U S E   D I N S   S T E
P U M P E R N I C K E   T A T
O R E S   E G O   H A S T
O I L   T R A I N S T A T I O
N N E   H A R T   C A R E S S
S A T U R N   J A R S
    M E T A M O R P H O S I
M A M B A   M A U L   E R I N
A C T E D   I S L E   S E N T
P E A R S   S T E T   T O G O
```

58

```
B O C A   T S A R   J U T
A D A P T   A T T I C   O N O
W I L L A   T E M P O   N I N
L E M O N L A W   T R E A T Y
      M G T   I T C H Y
    L A B O R L E A D E R
A I L   I R R E G U L A R
M A P   M A L A I S E   O X O
P R O P A G A T E   N I T
    L I N C O L N L O G S
  T I E T O   A L B
S I T A R S   L A V A L A M P
P G A   E T H E L   M O N D E
E E L   D I A N A   A N K L E
D R Y   C M O N   G A I N
```

59

```
A B L A Z E   T H E C H A M P
S E E D E D   R E L E A S E R
W A S J U D G E A N D J U R Y
I N S   S A O   V I E
R I O T   S V E N   S L O E
L E N O   A S I   O P T I M A
    P A T I O S   A R E A S
T H E P E O P L E S C O U R T
H E L L O   S E R I A L
A L I E N S   T V S   L A S S
I D E S   E S S A   S T E W
    I N A   N I T   O R A
P O W E R O F A T T O R N E Y
C L A M O R E D   E T H E N E
S A Y O N A R A   M O O R E D
```

60

```
S A L S A   I R I S   S W A P
A V A I L   S I L K   L A C E
D O U B L E S O L I T A I R E
E N D   T A U T   P U T T E R
    L O S E   F O R E
S M A L L E R H A L F   P T A
N O M A D   O D E   W O E S
A T O M   G A P E S   H U R T
K O N A   R O E   R I N S E
E R G   R A N D O M O R D E R
    B O N E   T S A R
R O T U N D   N O R M   R C A
U N B I A S E D O P I N I O N
I C A L   O P A L   N I T R O
N E R D   N I K E   G L E N N
```

61

F	U	S	S		F	A	L	L		E	R	O	D	E
A	R	E	A		A	S	E	A		R	O	V	E	S
I	D	E	S		T	H	A	N		A	G	E	N	T
R	U	S	H	T	H	E	P	A	S	S	E	R		
		H	E	N		N	E	T						
C	A	E	S	A	R		C	L	A	D		G	O	P
O	R	L	O	N		L	E	A	F		S	U	L	U
S	T	E	A	K	M	E	D	I	U	M	W	E	L	L
T	I	C	K		A	G	E	D		O	A	S	I	S
S	E	T		P	R	O	D		E	L	Y	S	E	E
	B	A	G		B	R	A							
	F	I	R	E	W	H	E	N	R	E	A	D	Y	
S	T	I	N	T		H	A	Z	E		W	I	R	E
H	I	N	G	E		A	L	E	S		E	D	E	N
E	A	S	E	D		M	E	L	T		R	E	D	S

62

A	B	B	A		A	I	M		G	R	U	C	C	I
F	E	R	N	A	N	D	O		R	A	S	H	E	R
I	D	O	I	D	O	I	D	O	I	D	O	I	D	O
G	E	S	S	O		U	R	N		P	L	A	N	
				I	D	L	E		B	E	E	R	Y	
W	A	T	E	R	L	O	O		R	A	N			
A	B	A	S	H	E	D		M	E	D		D	R	S
D	A	N	C	I	N	G		S	W	E	D	I	S	H
E	S	S		N	E	E		D	I	G	I	N	T	O
			S	O	S		P	O	P	G	R	O	U	P
G	A	L	A	S		B	A	S	E					
O	M	A	N		I	A	N		T	R	I	A	L	
T	A	K	E	A	C	H	A	N	C	E	O	N	M	E
I	N	E	S	S	E		M	A	M	M	A	M	I	A
T	A	R	T	A	R		A	T	V		D	Y	E	D

63

A	L	E	C		R	O	M	P	S		H	E	L	P
D	I	V	A		I	N	T	R	O		A	P	E	S
E	V	E	N	S	T	E	V	E	N		N	E	T	S
P	E	R	D	U	E		S	A	D	D	E	S	T	
T	R	Y	O	N		A	S	T	R	A	Y			
			G	A	L	L	O		M	A	I	Z	E	
R	A	M	P		I	D	I		F	E	N	D	E	R
E	M	I	L		R	A	M	B	O		D	E	A	L
D	E	C	A	F	S		J	A	R		Y	A	L	E
S	N	A	I	L		M	I	K	E	S				
		N	O	N	A	M	E		T	O	D	A	Y	
V	A	L	J	E	A	N		L	A	R	E	D	O	
A	R	I	A		S	I	L	L	Y	B	I	L	L	Y
N	E	O	N		A	L	I	E	N		O	H	I	O
S	A	N	E		L	A	T	E	X		N	I	B	S

64

E	L	M	E	R		R	A	D	A	R		H	A	J
L	E	O	N	I		A	L	I	C	E		O	L	E
B	A	N	A	N	A	P	E	E	L	S		T	D	S
O	C	T		G	N	P		S	U	N	S	P	O	T
W	H	E	A	T	I	E	S		I	T	O			
			R	O	L	L	E	R	S	K	A	T	E	S
S	A	F	E	S		A	H	A		G	A	L	A	
E	R	A		S	L	I	P	O	N	S		T	A	G
R	E	N	A		I	D	O		I	L	O	N	A	
B	A	L	L	B	E	A	R	I	N	G	S			
	E	A	R		T	R	E	N	D	I	E	R		
C	A	T	S	E	Y	E		I	R	A		C	E	O
H	S	T		W	A	X	E	D	F	L	O	O	R	S
U	T	E		E	L	A	T	E		E	R	N	I	E
M	A	R		D	E	M	O	S		D	O	S	E	S

65

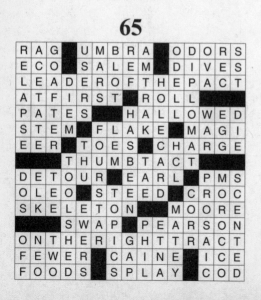

R	A	G		U	M	B	R	A		O	D	O	R	S
E	C	O		S	A	L	E	M		D	I	V	E	S
L	E	A	D	E	R	O	F	T	H	E	P	A	C	T
A	T	F	I	R	S	T		R	O	L	L			
P	A	T	E	S		H	A	L	L	O	W	E	D	
S	T	E	M		F	L	A	K	E		M	A	G	I
E	E	R		T	O	E	S		C	H	A	R	G	E
			T	H	U	M	B	T	A	C	T			
D	E	T	O	U	R		E	A	R	L		P	M	S
O	L	E	O		S	T	E	E	D		C	R	O	C
S	K	E	L	E	T	O	N		M	O	O	R	E	
	S	W	A	P		P	E	A	R	S	O	N		
O	N	T	H	E	R	I	G	H	T	T	R	A	C	T
F	E	W	E	R		C	A	I	N	E		I	C	E
F	O	O	D	S		S	P	L	A	Y		C	O	D

66

C	O	V	E		S	H	U	S	H		C	U	S	S
O	R	E	L		T	O	R	T	E		A	N	T	E
O	I	L	S		E	G	G	A	R		I	C	A	N
L	O	V	E	M	E	T	E	N	D	E	R	L	Y	
I	L	E		A	L	I		P	O	E	S	Y		
T	E	T	O	N		E	V	I	T	A		S	U	E
	O	N	O		E	C	O		R	A	P	S		
	I	H	A	V	E	R	H	Y	T	H	M			
I	N	N	S		E	R	S		S	E	E			
C	O	B		B	R	E	E	D		M	A	G	M	A
E	M	A	I	L		O	O	P		R	O	T		
	I	S	N	T	T	H	A	T	A	S	H	A	M	E
A	N	K	A		R	U	S	E	S		I	D	E	A
T	E	E	N		A	G	I	L	E		L	E	N	S
M	E	T	E		M	E	A	L	S		L	A	T	E

67

A	J	A	X		M	A	S	H		O	F	U	S	E
G	E	N	E		A	T	E	E		R	A	V	E	D
L	U	G	S		D	A	T	A		C	L	E	A	N
O	D	E		T	E	L		T	R	A	L	A	L	A
W	I	L	D	W	I	L	D	W	E	S	T			
			R	O	T		R	A	N		O	T	T	O
T	Y	P	E	B		P	A	V	E	D		I	O	N
W	E	E	W	I	L	L	I	E	W	I	N	K	I	E
A	T	E		T	O	O	N	S		V	O	I	L	A
S	I	P	S		I	T	E		Z	I	T			
			W	O	R	L	D	W	I	D	E	W	E	B
G	A	L	I	L	E	I		A	P	E		O	L	E
I	R	E	N	E		N	E	S	S		Q	U	I	T
M	A	N	G	O		E	T	T	U		U	N	D	O
P	L	A	Y	S		S	E	E	P		E	D	E	N

68

C	I	G	S		B	E	R	G		E	L	Y	S	E
H	A	R	T		O	V	E	N		L	O	O	T	S
E	M	I	L		L	A	L	O		A	G	U	E	S
F	A	M	O	U	S	N	A	M	E	S		N	N	E
			U	N	H		P	E	N	T	A	G	O	N
A	P	R	I	C	O	T		S	T	I	R			
G	U	E	S	S	I	N	G		O	C	T	O	P	I
O	L	D			T	U	B				R	O	D	
G	L	O	W	E	R		M	A	T	A	H	A	R	I
			A	X	E	D		S	I	L	E	N	T	E
C	H	I	R	P	I	E	R		N	A	N			
D	O	N		E	N	D	I	N	G	I	N	M	A	N
L	U	G	E	R		U	C	A	L		I	O	L	A
I	S	L	E	T		C	O	L	E		S	T	E	R
V	E	E	R	S		T	H	A	R		H	A	C	K

69

E	P	S	O	M		R	U	S	S	O		A	M	C
H	A	I	K	U		U	N	C	U	T		B	I	O
S	C	R	A	M		M	A	R	C	O	P	O	L	O
			P	B	S			I	C	E	R	I	N	K
M	A	R	I	O	C	U	O	M	O		O	L	E	S
A	D	A		J	E	S	U		R	P	M			
A	L	B		U	N	I	T	S		U	P	P	E	R
M	A	I	L	M	E	N		A	C	E	T	O	N	E
S	I	D	E	B		G	A	T	O	R		A	N	T
			T	O	A		L	I	N	T		C	U	R
A	P	O	S		T	O	L	E	D	O	O	H	I	O
C	A	R	G	O	E	S			O	R	R			
I	P	S	O	F	A	C	T	O		I	G	L	O	O
D	U	O		O	S	A	K	A		C	A	P	R	A
S	A	N		Z	E	R	O	S		O	N	S	E	T

70

T	A	C	K	Y		P	Y	G	M	Y		R	N	S
O	L	L	I	E		R	A	D	I	O		O	A	T
M	O	O	N	S		O	R	A	N	G		A	M	Y
B	U	G	S	B	U	N	N	Y		I	N	D	E	X
			M	U	T	E			I	B	A	R		
R	O	T	A	T	E		F	I	N	E	T	U	N	E
H	A	W	N		F	L	O	R	A		N	O	L	
I	K	E		P	L	A	I	N	E	R		N	B	C
N	E	E		O	U	T	R	E		D	E	L	I	
O	N	T	A	R	G	E	T		M	O	O	R	E	D
			Y	A	K	S		B	A	N	G			
A	T	B	A	Y		S	Y	L	V	E	S	T	E	R
C	H	I		P	E	W	E	E		T	H	O	L	E
T	A	R		I	D	E	A	S		W	O	O	E	D
S	T	D		G	U	E	S	S		O	W	N	E	D

71

B	E	E	F		A	M	O	S		A	H	E	A	D
A	I	D	A		L	I	V	E		Z	O	R	R	O
I	T	E	M		O	X	E	N		T	R	A	C	E
T	H	R	E	E	H	U	N	D	R	E	D			
E	E	L		L	A	P	S		I	C	E	S		
D	R	E	A	D			P	C	S		P	E	P	
			R	E	B	E	K	A	H		C	A	G	E
1	2	S	T	R	I	K	E	S	I	N	A	R	O	W
A	N	A	S		J	E	R	S	E	Y	S			
M	D	S		T	O	S			N	E	R	D	S	
		S	E	A	U		A	L	A	E		E	E	O
		X	X	X	X	X	X	X	X	X	X	X	X	X
Q	U	O	T	E		E	L	I	E		M	A	T	E
E	R	R	O	R		N	E	I	L		A	L	E	R
D	I	A	L	S		A	S	I	S		S	L	R	S

72

B	E	G	A	T		U	T	A	H		C	A	P	O
A	M	A	N	A		P	A	V	E		O	D	O	R
B	U	R	N	R	U	B	B	E	R		A	M	I	D
A	S	P	E	R	S	E		R	E	P	R	I	S	E
			Y	E	A	R			A	S	T	E	R	
C	O	M	A		S	T	E	P	O	N	E			
A	G	A	I	N		D	I	R	T		O	D	E	
S	L	A	M	O	N	T	H	E	B	R	A	K	E	S
H	E	M		B	O	N	E		Y	P	R	E	S	
			T	O	S	T	A	D	A		T	A	R	O
A	W	A	R	D		D	I	S	K					
D	E	L	A	Y	E	D		V	E	R	I	T	A	S
M	A	L	I		M	A	K	E	A	U	T	U	R	N
A	V	O	N		I	R	I	S		P	E	N	N	A
N	E	W	S		T	E	N	T		P	R	E	O	P

73

```
D E V I L ■ A C M E ■ P C B S
O V I N E ■ L O O T ■ H O R A
T E N D E R F O O T ■ O P I E
S N E E Z E ■ D U S T P A N
■ P A S S B Y ■ H O E R S
P O R T ■ T W A ■ F A I R
U H U H ■ C I R ■ A N D H O W
R I B ■ P U G N O S E ■ E G O
R O B B E R ■ O P T ■ B A R K
■ E R T E ■ N A B ■ I D E S
A G R E E ■ B E H A L F
G E N E R A L ■ L O O S E S
I N E Z ■ D O U B L E C H I N
L I C E ■ O C T O ■ S A U N A
E E K S ■ S K E W ■ S L E E P
```

74

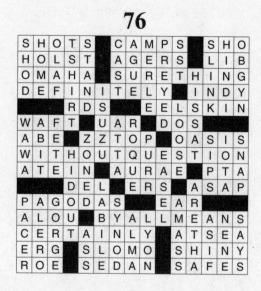

```
S A R A ■ A B B A ■ S T U P E
C H I C ■ M O L D ■ A R N A Z
H A F T ■ T R A M ■ N A D I R
■ B E F O R E H A N D ■ E R A
■ I R A ■ S N O R E R ■
P R O V O K E ■ W A R S A W
R A V E N ■ D E B I ■ E T N A
O D E ■ O M I G O S H ■ A D V
W I R Y ■ O T O S ■ A R N I E
L O W E S T ■ C C R I D E R
■ E N L I S T ■ A S P ■
E L I ■ A F T E R S H O C K
L E G I T ■ A M O I ■ S L I D
M A H R E ■ S P A N ■ T O N Y
O P T E D ■ H E R O ■ E D G E
```

75

```
O A F S ■ C O L D S ■ W H E T
S W A P ■ O N S E T ■ H Y D E
C A R E ■ S T A L E ■ E P I C
A R M E D T O T H E T E E T H
R E S C U E ■ I D O L ■
■ H E L L O ■ S N I F F S
E S C ■ L E V I ■ T E R R A
T H U M B O N E S N O S E A T
C O R E R ■ A N T E ■ D Y E
H O L D U P ■ S O U P S ■
■ I S L E ■ R A N C O R
L I V E H A N D T O M O U T H
O L A V ■ S T A R S ■ O T T O
A S I A ■ M E L E E ■ P I E D
F A L L ■ A R I E S ■ S E R A
```

76

```
S H O T S ■ C A M P S ■ S H O
H O L S T ■ A G E R S ■ L I B
O M A H A ■ S U R E T H I N G
D E F I N I T E L Y ■ I N D Y
■ R D S ■ E E L S K I N
W A F T ■ U A R ■ D O S ■
A B E ■ Z Z T O P ■ O A S I S
W I T H O U T Q U E S T I O N
A T E I N ■ A U R A E ■ P T A
■ D E L ■ E R S ■ A S A P
P A G O D A S ■ E A R ■
A L O U ■ B Y A L L M E A N S
C E R T A I N L Y ■ A T S E A
E R G ■ S L O M O ■ S H I N Y
R O E ■ S E D A N ■ S A F E S
```

77

```
L I B R A ■ A S E A ■ M A T E
I N L E T ■ B E A R ■ O X E N
S C U S E ■ I M R E ■ C L A D
T H E T I M E I T T A K E S
■ U N A ■ P H O B E ■
H A S P ■ F O R Y O U R N E W
A L A ■ C I A O ■ S Y L P H
R E L ■ A A R ■ A B E ■ E S E
D R E A R ■ O G O D ■ R O T
C O M P U T E R T O ■ I S M S
■ A S A M I ■ M A N ■
■ B E C O M E O B S O L E T E
Y E A H ■ A R L O ■ L O P E S
E A S E ■ L I E N ■ E V E N T
N U T S ■ E L S E ■ R E E S E
```

78

```
P I L O T ■ B A C K ■ I T C H
A R O S E ■ E L A L ■ C A R A
S A B L E ■ N I L E ■ E B A N
■ B O N D J A M E S B O N D
S O Y ■ A R I ■ K O O K Y
T W I G G Y ■ H E L I X ■
E L S I E ■ R E N E ■ P O D
M E T A R Z A N Y O U J A N E
S T S ■ E T N A ■ T A T A R
■ P A N S Y ■ B A R R I E
S A P I D ■ R A H ■ O R K
C A L L M E I S H M A E L ■
O R A L ■ A N T E ■ G A M A L
T O T O ■ S T A T ■ E V A D E
S N O W ■ T O R T ■ N E N E S
```

79

```
SHAQ  LALA  DALE
LULU  EPIC  EWERS
AMOI  HAGS  MOVIE
PEEL  ICH   AERATE
     TIGHTASADRUM
AFT  CHEATON
MORTE   SON  ALAS
PROUDASAPEACOCK
STYX  RAF   LEFTY
    SENESCE  TIE
SHARPASATACK
TATARS  TAR  ONTO
ALONE  PHIL  OAHU
GENOA  EERO  KNOT
 REND  ERST  YAMS
```

80

```
TRAC  BOAR  VALOR
HURL  ELSE  EMILE
ASIA  REST  NAMED
WHATSGOTINDIA
   TIES  CIEN
ASTERN  AUNT  AMT
BOHR  APLOT  FAA
AREYOUGHANADOIT
SRS  CHAIR  IONE
EYE  CATS  SISTER
   BLUE  SHOT
YOULLLAOSITUP
BLAND  IOWA  LORE
BARGE  NOEL  LISA
SYNOD  ENDS  SLAT
```

81

```
LIZA  SOME  TIBIA
ANON  ETAL  ONEND
STRAIGHTFORWARD
ERR  SUES  NOISES
ROOSTER  PSST
  PHD  PEP  HASH
SIXAM  LAPEL  CUE
COMMUNITYCENTER
ATE  SEATS  MAIZE
RANT  WRY  AMP
  HUBS  GRISHAM
ASSISI  MOAN  EGO
CATCHESOFFGUARD
EVOKE  AREA  FREE
SEWER  PERT  ODES
```

82

```
SOPS  PICA  BISON
TAIL  ADAM  ATONE
OTTO  RAVE  TUNED
WHATSTHESTORY
  MOO  ORB
POSTON  HON  IMAM
ACHOO  HOPIS  ADO
WHOSTHELUCKYMAN
ERR  HOMES  OMEGA
REEK  VID  SKATED
  APE  UPI
 WHERESTHEFIRE
ABOUT  TATE  ODOR
BORNE  CBER  LENO
SWEAR  HERE  DAIS
```

83

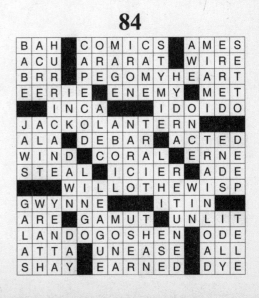

```
ABAB  KEN  DIARY
NAPA  BIDE  ONCUE
KNIT  UNEVENBARS
AGEISM  MALTED
ROCKYROADS  DEAL
ANE  NAB  AES  MMI
  HOPIN  IDIOM
AGAINSTTHEGRAIN
DEITY  HAUNT
ARR  MID  NCO  ITO
META  ROUGHRIDER
 INTERN  RAMONA
JAGGEDEDGE  PINT
ETHIC  MEAD  EDIE
BATES  IRS  LOSS
```

84

```
BAH  COMICS  AMES
ACU  ARARAT  WIRE
BRR  PEGOMYHEART
EERIE  ENEMY  MET
 INCA  IDOIDO
JACKOLANTERN
ALA  DEBAR  ACTED
WIND  CORAL  ERNE
STEAL  ICIER  ADE
 WILLOTHEWISP
GWYNNE  ITIN
ARE  GAMUT  UNLIT
LANDOGOSHEN  ODE
ATTA  UNEASE  ALL
SHAY  EARNED  DYE
```

85

```
F A L L   B A K E D   L A Z E
A L E E   E M E R Y   A X O N
H A N D E L B A R S   P E N D
D I S U N I O N   L A D L E S
      C O Z Y   D E F O G
M A N T L E   H E X A G R A M
A L O H A   T O S I R   E M I
N E B O   S I T K A   H A U T
O R E   M E T E S   H E S S E
R O L L C A L L   C A R E E R
      G U I S E   S A R A
T R A G I C   W A R P L A N E
H O S E   A B E L B O D I E D
E W E R   P A A V O   E D E N
M E S S   E L L E N   D A D A
```

86

```
S L U G   F O S S E   L I M A
P E S O   A L I E N   I S A S
R O N A   L I N E S   D A Z S
A N A P O L O G Y I S   B E E
W I V E S       A L A   E L S
L A Y   T A B S   E X A L T S
      D I M M E D   A L O E
A G R E A T W A Y T O H A V E
D E A L   S T E E P S
A T R I S K   O D E A   S M A
M T A   O A S     R O T O R
S H A   T H E L A S T W O R D
R E V S   U V U L A   E P E E
I R I S   N E R D S   N U N N
B E S T   A R E A S   S P O T
```

87

```
A B A C I   A M A H L   B E T
S E D A N   O L D I E   O R E
S E A S C A L L O P S   T I X
A P P E A L   E S P   S T E T
M S T   S E T   O N T O
      S H R I M P S C A M P I
D A H L   O P E R   A R S O N
A L I A S   I D O   A M U C K
B U T C H   N E W S   A P O S
S M O K E D S A L M O N
      R E D O   S A N   A W S
H Y M N   C H I   Z E A L O T
A M I   S T U F F E D S O L E
M C S   H O R S E   G A F F E
M A S   O R L O N   E N T E R
```

88

```
J A V A   C H O S E N   O A S
E L E M   O U T C R Y   B R O
E A R P I E R C I N G   E L F
P R Y   C R O   I S L E T
      B A C K B R E A K I N G
S T O L L E   L O R N E
C A V I L   I L L T I M E D
A D E S   I S T L E   N O D E
M A R T I N E Z   T I N G E
      E N T R E   D U N K E D
H E A R T R E N D I N G
O X E Y E   O V A   P I E
M I G   A R M T W I S T I N G
E L I   R U I N E D   A L F A
Y E S   S E T T L E   P L O D
```

89

```
A D J   A B U T   W R E A T H
M E A   G O N O   H A N K E R
A R C   R O D O M O N T A D E
Z I T I   S I T U A T E
E D I T   T E S T   O R F E O
D E T E R   S H A W   S A I L
      A M O R   I N R E   N R A
T U T   B O A S T E R   F E Y
U P I   E B R O   N A P A
B O O B   B M W S   S E R I F
A N N U L   A N T S   R O D S
      R A I N H A T   K N I T
B R A G G A D O C I O   A D O
A I R L O G   R E E L   D I P
M O R E S O   N Y S E   E T S
```

90

```
W A D S   E R I C A   B A T S
A R E A   V A L E T   U T A H
R U M B L E F I S H   M A K E
S T O L E N   E T E   B L E D
      C E N T S   A N T L E R S
A R R   D U E T   S E E
N O A H   A T O M   A B A S H
T U T U   L A P I S   E D N A
I T S M E   T A L C   E M I T
      B L T   Z E R O   I T E
A P P L I E S   S A V O R
M I R E   N U B   B A N A N A
B L I P   S T U M B L E B U M
L O N I   E R R O L   A L T O
E T T E   D A N T E   L E S S
```

91

```
BARN ■ SWISS ■ GOUP
EREI ■ CARAT ■ RUDE
BONNVOYAGE ■ ATAT
ENDEARS ■ RIPPLE
■ ILE ■ PENNPALS
AWARE ■ AUS ■ EAT
RENO ■ ULSTER ■ IDS
MANNINTHESTREET
SRI ■ LIMPET ■ ENCE
■ HEE ■ AIM ■ ACTOR
TAILFINN ■ ATA ■
ALLOTS ■ OUTPOST
SLAP ■ SWEPTUPINN
TATE ■ EAGER ■ ESAU
EYED ■ IRONY ■ DEPT
```

92

```
SODOM ■ ASS ■ APACE
OPERA ■ CPO ■ MELEE
STAIN ■ HOUSECALL
■ DOES ■ UTENSILS
FILLSINTHE ■
ICEE ■ ZEE ■ ITASCA
VAT ■ HEAD ■ NORMAL
ENTRY ■ ■ STARE
PSEUDO ■ WOOS ■ LOX
MORSES ■ INK ■ ALLI
■ CARTRIDGES
TEAMMATE ■ ANDA ■
UNDERRATE ■ USURP
GRIME ■ LAT ■ SUGAR
SYNOD ■ EPA ■ EPEES
```

93

```
DALI ■ SLUG ■ ACHES
ALAN ■ TORO ■ THESE
NUMEROUNO ■ TEASE
AMAZON ■ FREEDOM
■ DESK ■ ANKH ■
ASHEN ■ LIPID ■ OBS
SPIRE ■ ENID ■ GNAW
SAGGY ■ EGG ■ BUCKO
ECHO ■ EPPS ■ USHER
SEP ■ VISIT ■ THORN
■ REAR ■ NYSE ■
NAILSET ■ ONFIRE
AREAS ■ MISTERBIG
VISTA ■ EDIT ■ AIDA
EATER ■ NONO ■ USED
```

94

```
BUCK ■ HALL ■ STOOL
ACHE ■ OLEO ■ ARUBA
ALEE ■ OMIT ■ FETID
LAMPCHOPS ■ EMOTE
■ FRANZ ■ IRON ■
AGGIE ■ DIAS ■ RAPS
VERTEX ■ GNAW ■ LUC
ONE ■ PRO ■ NAH ■ IRE
WOE ■ SARI ■ CARMEN
SANG ■ YENS ■ TEPEE
■ TOES ■ QUAIL ■
PSHAW ■ DUMPFOUND
ROUTE ■ AIMS ■ AREA
ELMER ■ BRIE ■ DART
POPES ■ SETS ■ SLOE
```

95

```
ITS ■ CLAP ■ ASIANS
TIE ■ HIVE ■ TUCKED
EVE ■ OMEN ■ OREADS
MOSTMORNINGS ■
SLAVS ■ NEE ■ ASP
■ IWAKEUPGROUCHY
■ YETI ■ NATAL
ACRE ■ LENTO ■ WIDE
BRINE ■ OREO ■
BUTONSATURDAYS
AXE ■ SIR ■ DIVES
■ ILETHIMSLEEP
STALAG ■ IDEA ■ TOA
ARRIVE ■ DEAR ■ TUT
TEPEES ■ ESTE ■ ETE
```

96

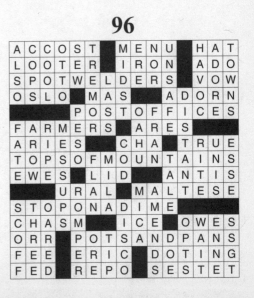

```
ACCOST ■ MENU ■ HAT
LOOTER ■ IRON ■ ADO
SPOTWELDERS ■ VOW
OSLO ■ MAS ■ ADORN
■ POSTOFFICES
FARMERS ■ ARES ■
ARIES ■ CHA ■ TRUE
TOPSOFMOUNTAINS
EWES ■ LID ■ ANTIS
■ URAL ■ MALTESE
STOPONADIME ■
CHASM ■ ICE ■ OWES
ORR ■ POTSANDPANS
FEE ■ ERIC ■ DOTING
FED ■ REPO ■ SESTET
```

97

```
F O A M S   P A R D   A C E S
I N L E T   A T E E   P O G O
S T A T E   J E F F E R S O N
H O S A N N A   S I M I A N S
      L O O M S   N I L
E V I L   H A T P I N   O V A
C O N I C   S A T E   N O B
L I N C O L N   K E N N E D Y
A L E   N O E S   T E A K S
T A R   S N E E R S   X M A S
      D O G   Q U I L T
A L F A L F A   B R I D G E T
B A L D E A G L E   T O R C H
B R A D   C O I N   H O O H A
E D G Y   E N D S   E R G O T
```

98

```
S H U T   M A N E D   O R B S
T O R I   I M A G E   N E A P
O R I G   N A T A L   E T T E
W A S H I G H O N   B A R O N
      T A L L   A L M O N D
S H O W M E   S A G E
L E D A   D R Y D E N W O R K
I R I D O   A R I   D O B I E
P R E S S U R I N G   N I T E
      A R E A   O R D E A L
R E S I G N   O T O E
A M O R E   F O L D E R O L S
L I S A   F R O D O   F R E T
P L A T   R E N E W   U L N A
H Y D E   Y E A R N   L Y O N
```

99

```
L A S   A N G L E R   S T U B
I S P   T I R A D E   P E R U
E L L   O N E I D A   H A N G
S E I S M O G R A P H E R
T E N P I N   S E R I A L
O P T I C   R A M   P E N T A
      C A V E M E N   T O W
S I Z E L I M I T A T I O N S
E S O   M I S R E A D
E L O P E   T H O   N E S T S
R E T O R T   A G A T H A
    S I G H S O F R E L I E F
N O U N   A T T A I N   L Y E
E X I T   N U T L E T   T V S
B Y T E   K N O L L S   S E T
```

100

```
F A C T S   A L B U M   V I P
A D O R E   B E A N O   E N E
D O N O R   C O N C O U R S E
    Q U A D   J U S T N O W
S T U B   A S C O T   T A L E
K E E L   W O O S   M E L E E
I N S E A S O N   E A R
T N T   C O N T E X T   C A B
    S E N   O N C E M O R E
P E S T S   J U D E   O N E L
A N T I   H O R S E   O V A L
S C A L P E R   D I R E
C O N T E N D E R   D I R T Y
A D Z   G N A S H   E N S U E
L E A   S A N T O   A G E N T
```

101

```
A W E S   A G A   I R W I N
D I A L   E R L E   S C H M O
A N G E L F A C E   T A I N T
M E L E E   M O R P H   T O E
  D E V I L M A Y C A R E
    E S E   S T O N E D
E K G   N O A H   S T I P E
S W O R D O F D A M O C L E S
M A L A Y   T O J O   E E K
E N D I N G   A L S
    F L A T A S A B O A R D
A P E   S O N A R   A L A R M
C O V E T   K I N G M A K E R
E L E M I   A L I S   D E C I
D O R I C   S E A   A S K S
```

102

```
S A L K   L E T M E   B L A H
A G U N   A V I A N   O A H U
J A M E S B E A R D   D I M E
A P P E A R   C O D E R E D
K E Y   H A S P   R A G
    L I T T L E S H A V E R
N A B O B   R A V E L   A G E
O W E S   C O T E S   C R O P
V O L   A L L E N   S A Y S O
A L L I N A L A T H E R
    S T P   U S E R   T A B
Q U A L I T Y   A B J U R E
U R S A   R A Z O R S E D G E
A D E N   A L E U T   S O U R
D U A D   P E E R S   T R E Y
```

103

```
W H I M S . A P S E . T G I F
I O N I C . R E E L . O R S O
S U N D A E O N A B A N A N A
E R S . M M M . W A R . S T L
. . O P I A T E . I D S .
B O W L E R S H E A D A C H E
O C H E R . E D S . G O A L
I C Y . S E A L S U P . U Z I
L A P S . D C I . H I R E D
S M A L L W I N E B O T T L E
. Y O U . D E V A N E .
P A M . C A R . O R E . L O U
S T O C K M A R K E T N E W S
S O R E . M I T E . A R N I E
T M E N . O N E S . G A T E S
```

104

```
C O P . C H I M N E Y . H A G
C I A . R E W A R D S . I N E
S L Y . I R O N A G E . J O E
. R O S E B U D . E R S A T Z
S I L O S . L R G . A C H E
E G A N . A D E N . J O K E R
A S S I S I . S A G E . S R S
. C H R I S T M A S .
A P E . E S T E . E N C A M P
N I N J A . E D E N . A M E S
T E R I . M I L . B R E S T
A B O M B S . N A I L E R S .
C A L . L A T R I N E . I I I
I L L . O R I E N T S . C A R
D D S . C I N D E R S . A H A
```

105

```
S W A T . B E T S . R A G O N
E A V E . O M I T . C L O W N
E R A S . H I D E . C A B L E
Y E S S I R R E E B O B .
A S T E R . P A L A C E S
. R O G U E . T A M A L E
W H O A N E L L Y . A R I D
H O P . S E A M A P S . G A G
I V E S . N O W A Y J O S E
T E R E S A . S N O R E .
E L A S T I C . I R I S H
. S O R R Y C H A R L I E
A N T I C . O O Z E . I O T A
I B O O K . A D A M . E V I L
D A N N Y . T A R P . S E N S
```

106

```
A P R I L . B E E T . O L A F
S A U C E . A L P O . T I L L
H U G H O B R I A N . T A P E
E L S . N U B . R A N E E
. J A M E S S T E W A R T
C A P O . T E L E C A S T .
A N G L E R . C O M A .
W Y A T T E A R P P L A Y E R
. E L S E . E L P A S O
. R E P R I N T S . E K E D
K E V I N C O S T N E R .
A L I C E . E E L . A O L
R I C K . H E N R Y F O N D A
M E T E . A G E E . I N N E R
A S S T . M O T O . N E A R S
```

107

```
B E S I E G E R . E M M E T T
O V E R R A T E . T O O T H Y
W E W O N D E R . O U C H E S
I R E N E . O B I S . I T O
E T R E . H O W E L S E C A N
. D E A L . D E E R .
A L A . S L A P . A S T A
B I R D S O F A F E A T H E R
S E M I . L I M P . Y E T
. S U R E . D I E M .
F L O C K I F N O T . O N E S
A O K . A S T O . S T O V E
U P R O S E . T O G E T H E R
N E A R E R . S H E L L I N G
A S S E S S . O M E L E T T E
```

108

```
A D A M . T H E R E . S U N G
G E N E . R E L A Y . K N E E
H E A R T I N T H E . I V A N
A R T . A E R O . B R E T T
. H A N D I N T H E T I L L
A V E R S . O U R . L Y E
S E M I . A S S A Y .
H E A D I N T H E C L O U D S
. N O I S E . L S A T
A P T . D O L . R E E D Y
F O O T I N T H E D O O R .
F L O R A . A T O M . B E D
E L L A . R I G H T P L A C E
C O E D . A T E A T . A S O F
T I D E . P E N N Y . B E N T
```

109

```
C B S . R E V I L E . S H O P
A N A . O L I V E R . P U Z O
P A N A M A C A N A L A R A B
P I G L A T I N . . A S T R O
. . I N E . T O Y . S K Y
G L O B . . S L A M
R A M A D A C A T A M A R A N
A L A B A M A M A H A R A J A
B A N A N A R A M A S A G A S
. . T E R I . . L A R A
R P M . D I D . A D S
E L O P E . C U T I E P I E
B A B A W A W A S A V A T A R
U Z I S . C A M E R A . A G O
S A L T . T H E S I S . S O S
```

110

```
S A I L . P S H A W . C H A R
K I T E . R A I S E . H I R E
I R O N O U T T H E K I N K S
. . . S A N I T Y . O L D I E
R I M . T E R I . . C L I N T
U S A G E . E N O C H
M A Y O R S . G O O . T H A I
B A B E S I N T H E W O O D S
A C E S . R A H . D I S M A L
. . . J E T E R . T H E M E
A T S E A . L E C H . S S T
P R A N K . P I G L E T
P U T T E R I N G A R O U N D
L E E R . M C K A Y . A V O N
E D D Y . N O S E S . D A D A
```

111

```
S P A S . M A S H . B A Y E R
C O R P . O R E O . E L I Z A
A S I A . D R A W I N G P I N
M I S C U E . M E M O . S O T
S T E E P L E . S P I T
. . N O S I R . A T H O M E
L I N E N . D E L I . I H O P
O N C E . S E W E R . M I R E
M E A D . T R E E . T B O N E
A Z A L E A . D R O O L
. . E N Y A . S T R E E T S
U S E . D E M S . H O W L I N
T H R E A D B A R E . E I N E
E A S E L . L I A R . E T T A
S H E L L . E L M S . D E S K
```

112

```
E R A T . B E L I E . A M E N
L A S H . A R E N T . N O N E
B I T E . T I N K E R T O Y S
A N I M A T E D . D E T A T
. . . A R E . H A N
T A I L O R M A D E . N A S A
A T O L L . A F A R . A C T I
S A T . L E C A R R E . E E L
S L A M . S A L E . L O R N E
E L S A . S O L D I E R B O Y
. . . L A O . R C A
A U D I T . E M I T T I N G
S P Y G L A S S E S . O V A L
S T E N . P A S T E . R A T E
N O D S . B L E S S . S N E E
```

113

```
M U M . D E C A F . P A G E R
O L E . E R A T O . A C O R N
U N A . C E L T I C C R O S S
R A N D R . S A T E D
N E T R E S U L T S . T A P
. . J E U N E . T A H I T I
P E A . R I G S . D E M O N
S P U R O F T H E M O M E N T
A C T O R . S O L D . S E A
T O O T O O . R I C C I
S T P . K I N G C O T T O N
. I C E I N . I S E R E
B U L L S E S S I O N . N B A
A L O E S . E L I D E . S I T
M E T O O . T O N E D . E T O
```

114

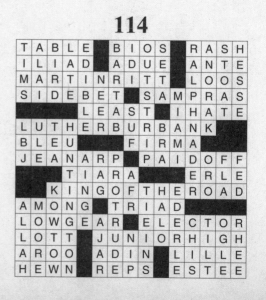

```
T A B L E . B I O S . R A S H
I L I A D . A D U E . A N T E
M A R T I N R I T T . L O O S
S I D E B E T . S A M P R A S
. . . L E A S T . I H A T E
L U T H E R B U R B A N K
B L E U . . F I R M A
J E A N A R P . P A I D O F F
. . T I A R A . E R L E
. K I N G O F T H E R O A D
A M O N G . T R I A D
L O W G E A R . E L E C T O R
L O T T . J U N I O R H I G H
A R O O . A D I N . L I L L E
H E W N . R E P S . E S T E E
```

115

E	L	A	L		S	P	A	S		A	D	O	B	E
M	A	M	E		P	R	I	M		L	A	N	E	D
T	W	O	F	O	R	O	N	E	O	F	F	E	R	S
	C	U	T	T	Y		T	A	P		T	I	N	E
H	O	N		T	E	N		R	E	C		L	I	L
M	U	T	T		R	E	P		N	O	B	L	E	S
O	R	T	H	O		H	E	A	T	E	R			
	T	O	O	F	O	R	E	B	O	D	I	N	G	
		S	U	B	U	R	B		S	N	E	R	D	
T	A	L	E	S	E		S	O	C		E	X	I	T
A	L	E		E	Y	E		T	A	B		T	D	S
S	C	A	T		E	L	M		M	E	R	C	I	
T	O	F	O	U	R	M	O	R	E	Y	E	A	R	S
E	V	E	N	T		E	V	I	L		A	S	O	F
R	E	D	Y	E		R	E	D	S		L	E	N	O

116

W	H	I	G	S		N	U	B		A	L	S	O	
R	E	T	R	O		C	A	S	A		L	I	E	U
A	R	E	A	S		Z	I	N	G		A	S	P	S
P	E	R	S	O	N	A	L	A	D	Z		Z	I	T
			S	O	A	R	S		A	O	R	T	A	S
D	E	C		N	O	S	E		D	R	O	P		
E	R	O	S		M	E	T	Z		B	A	R	G	E
S	O	M	A	L	I	A		O	N	A	D	I	E	T
C	O	M	B	O		T	O	N	E		S	C	A	N
		O	R	G	S		R	E	S	T		E	R	A
D	O	N	E	I	N		A	S	T	R	A			
O	N	E		C	A	T	C	H	S	O	M	E	Z	S
S	I	Z	E		P	O	L	O		J	I	V	E	S
E	C	R	U		A	B	E	T		A	N	E	N	T
D	E	A	R		T	E	S			N	O	N	O	S

117

D	E	L	E		U	S	M	C		J	U	M	B	O
A	P	E	X		P	H	I	L		A	C	U	R	A
S	E	N	T		T	I	L	E		C	O	L	O	R
H	E	A	R	T	O	F	D	A	R	K	N	E	S	S
			A	B	I	T		R	A	I	N			
B	A	R	D	O	T		F	I	R	E		O	P	T
A	G	A	I	N		T	I	N	E		O	P	E	R
C	E	N	T	E	R	O	F	G	R	A	V	I	T	Y
O	N	C	E		E	Y	E	S		G	E	N	E	S
N	T	H		C	U	S	S		A	R	R	E	S	T
			C	E	S	T		A	G	E	D			
M	I	D	D	L	E	O	F	T	H	E	R	O	A	D
A	M	O	R	E		R	I	T	A		A	S	T	O
R	A	Z	O	R		E	L	I	S		F	L	O	P
E	N	E	M	Y		S	E	C	T		T	O	M	E

118

A	D	L	I	B		H	O	U	S	E		G	S	A
L	E	O	N	A		E	P	S	O	M		A	W	L
L	E	G	A	L	B	R	I	E	F	S		Z	A	P
O	R	I		B	E	R	E	F	T		D	E	M	O
R	E	C	O	O	L		U	T	N	E				
		L	A	T	E	B	L	O	O	M	E	R	S	
B	R	A	E		S	R	A		P	H	O	B	I	A
A	U	R	A	S		A	N	T		O	L	O	G	Y
S	T	I	N	T	S		J	A	W		I	N	A	S
S	H	A	D	O	W	B	O	X	E	R	S			
			E	P	E	E			B	E	H	A	V	E
B	A	R	R		E	T	U	D	E	S		V	I	A
O	V	A		O	P	E	N	D	R	A	W	E	R	S
Z	I	T		C	E	L	I	A		L	A	R	G	E
O	D	E		T	A	S	T	Y		E	X	T	O	L

119

S	T	A	T	S		C	O	A	T		A	B	E	L
M	U	R	A	L		H	I	L	O		P	E	T	E
A	D	E	N	I	N	A	D	E	N		I	N	T	O
R	O	N		T	O	W		R	E	B	A	T	E	S
T	R	A	I	T	S		M	O	U	E	S			
			R	E	E	V	E		P	L	A	T	T	E
S	T	R	A	D		E	E	R		A	W	A	R	D
A	M	E	N		T	R	A			A	R	I	E	
B	E	E	F	S		S	K	I		S	P	O	O	N
U	N	D	O	E	R		A	D	L	A	I			
			R	E	A	C	T		E	N	A	B	L	E
C	O	R	I	N	T	H		O	F	F		O	A	R
O	V	E	R		T	O	G	O	T	O	T	O	G	O
S	E	L	A		A	S	A	P		R	A	Z	E	D
A	N	O	N		N	E	T	S		D	E	E	R	E

120

E	L	S	E		N	E	T	S		P	R	O	W	L
L	E	O	N		O	L	I	O		R	E	M	I	T
E	A	S	T		V	A	N	S		E	L	A	N	D
C	H	A	R	I	O	T	S	O	F	F	I	R	E	
			A	N	T	E			R	E	V			
A	V	E	N	G	E		L	O	R	E	L	E	I	
C	I	R	C	E		S	H	O	W			O	R	R
T	O	W	E	R	I	N	G	I	N	F	E	R	N	O
E	L	I		N	U	T	S			O	N	E	I	N
D	A	N	C	I	N	G			S	Y	D	N	E	Y
			A	N	E			I	K	E	A			
	I	S	P	A	R	I	S	B	U	R	N	I	N	G
A	L	L	O	W		S	O	O	N		G	L	E	N
D	I	A	N	A		A	M	O	K		E	S	A	U
D	E	W	E	Y		Y	A	K	S		R	A	T	S

121

```
N O T V   S W A G     D W A R F
I D E A   T I T O     I O N I A
N I T S   I N T O     A R D O R
O N E S E C O N D P L E A S E
      A S K S   G E M
P H E L P S   A R T   A V I D
A O L   R O S S I   P R I D E
T W O M I N U T E D R I L L S
C S P O T   N O F E E   L E K
H O E D   S S R   S M E A R S
      D O H   A C I D
T H R E E D A Y W E E K E N D
B E I N G   D E A N   O D A Y
A M A N A   E N I D   C I N E
R I L E S   S S T S   H E A D
```

122

```
BOX K I T E   A P U   S H O E BOX
C O C O A   P E P   A M P L E
A L E U T   E A R E D S E A L
R A S P  BOX S C O R E   R I D
    E E L   O A R   W A N E
I R R E G U L A R   H A T E R
N E E   O N I T   M A L I
BOX O F F I C E   B A L L O T BOX
  L U S H   B I T S   N A E
B R E S T   P R O C E S S O R
R A C E   B O O   H Y P
E M T   M U S I C BOX   A L O T
A S I R E C A L L   P R I M O
D E V I L   D E E   E S S A Y
BOX S E A T   A R F   G E A R BOX
```

123

```
A T L A S   S I S I     A N T E
C H A L K   E D E N     T A R A
R A B B I T E A R S   I S I S
E T S   I O N   G Y M S H O E
      E N D   H I N E S
  K A N G A R O O C O U R T
I N N S   T A P   W E A R Y
T O V   K E E P E R S   Z E D
S P I R O   E E E   J O Y S
  F L E A M A R K E T E R S
      S L A T S   S U B
W A R P A T H   E E R   T A I
A L O E   T O A D S T O O L S
D I S C   E M M A   L E G A L
S T E T   R E A M   E R A S E
```

124

```
T O M E   O R E M     S P A D E
O N E S   N A D A     A L I E N
A R E S   E Y E D     M A D T V
M A K E I T S N A P P Y
A M E N D E   M I A S A R A
N P R   I N I S   A N K L E T
      S O T T E D   O O N A
  G E T T H E L E A D O U T
F E A R   M E S C A L
C A V I E S   S I C K   A B A
C R E P T U P   R A N G E R
    M O V E Y O U R T A I L
K A U A I   R U D I   E T R E
O N A L L   I M I N   S H U N
P E R L E   L A N G   T A T E
```

125

```
S I L A S   A L F A     R I L E
K N E L T   R I A L   E D E N
I F Y O U W A N T L I F E T O
R U D E   A C E   C R A S S
T S E   G R A M E R C Y
S E N O R   R A R E   A S A
    B E G I N A T F O R T Y
A W E I G H     C A N C A N
D O N T G O E I G H T Y
D O E   S A G A   E X A M S
    P E T U N I A S   T A P
E T H E L   O T T   D O R A
W H E N Y O U R E T W E N T Y
E R I C   U S E R   H E C H E
S U R E   R O D S   O R E A D
```

126

```
A T L A S   L O L L     I D L E
Q U A R T   E D I E   N O U N
U L C E R   N O N O   B O L D
A S E A   F O R D T A U R U S
S A Y S N O   Y A R N
      E C O L   R E C O A T
G R A N T I N A I D   H A S H
A U T O   O R R   E T T A
P L O T   T R U M A N S H O W
S E N A T E   E A S Y
    T E R M   H E Y D A Y
B U S H L E A G U E   A E R O
O N T O   N U L L   T H A N K
A D A M   C L U E   N O L I E
Z O N E   E S T E   T O T E D
```

127

S	H	A	R	P		T	R	U	R	O		B	M	W
S	A	B	E	R		R	A	Z	E	D		O	A	R
T	H	E	P	O	S	I	T	I	V	E		A	G	E
S	A	T	I	R	E	S				S	A	T	I	N
			N	A	T	T	I	N	E	S	S			
A	M	S		T	H	E	N	E	G	A	T	I	V	E
C	O	T	T	A			S	R	A		U	R	A	L
U	T	A	H		E	L	T	O	N		T	O	L	L
R	I	F	E		L	E	A			S	E	N	S	E
A	F	F	I	R	M	A	T	I	V	E		Y	E	N
			R	H	O	D	E	S	I	A	N			
A	N	T	S	Y			A	N	T	E	N	N	A
B	O	O		M	R	I	N	B	E	T	W	E	E	N
U	S	E		E	E	R	I	E		L	E	M	A	N
T	E	D		S	T	A	L	L		E	L	O	P	E

128

A	S	T	A		T	A	M	E	R		G	O	G	O
G	L	I	B		A	M	I	L	E		A	R	I	D
R	O	T	S		C	A	C	H	E		L	E	N	D
I	T	H	I	N	K	H	A	I	L	T	O			
P	H	E	N	O	L				A	S	T	I	R
		T	H	E	C	H	I	E	F	H	A	S	A
T	A	C	H		H	A	S	N	T		P	A	N
O	P	I	E		C	A	R	L	O		M	E	A	T
O	R	R		E	L	I	D	E		A	R	C	S
N	I	C	E	R	I	N	G	T	O	I	T			
S	L	A	N	G			P	O	I	S	E	D
		J	O	H	N	F	K	E	N	N	E	D	Y
E	C	H	O		A	A	R	O	N		E	L	A	N
B	U	O	Y		S	T	A	K	E		E	M	M	E
B	E	E	S		H	O	N	O	R		S	A	S	S

129

D	E	S	K		A	S	H	E		S	H	O	U	T
E	T	O	N		S	W	A	T		H	O	R	S	E
E	C	H	O		H	A	L	T		E	M	C	E	E
	H	O	W	D	O	Y	O	U	P	L	E	A	D
		S	I	R	E			I	V	Y			
K	A	T		R	E	D	T	A	P	E		B	A	H
I	C	I	N	G		I	M	P		A	L	T	O
W	H	E	R	E	D	O	E	S	I	T	H	U	R	T
I	O	T	A		R	I	G		O	A	S	I	S
S	O	O		P	I	L	S	N	E	R		H	A	Y
		P	A	L		O	L	A	Y			
	W	H	A	T	L	L	Y	O	U	H	A	V	E
B	R	U	T	E		S	A	N	D		N	A	V	Y
B	E	G	I	N		A	L	A	E		K	N	E	E
S	N	O	O	T		T	E	N	D		S	E	N	T

130

I	S	L	A	M		C	H	A	W		V	E	E	P
T	H	U	D	S		H	A	L	O		L	I	V	E
C	O	L	D	S	H	O	W	E	R		A	S	I	S
H	O	L	E		A	S	K	E	D		S	E	C	T
			D	A	L	E			G	O	I	N	T	O
B	O	W	O	U	T		B	R	A	N	C	H
B	L	A	N	D		S	L	O	M	O		O	P	A
L	I	L		I	N	P	O	W	E	R		W	E	B
S	N	L		B	E	A	T	S		D	W	E	E	B
		F	E	L	O	N	S		P	E	A	R	L	Y
P	O	L	L	E	N			P	U	R	R
A	H	O	Y		S	I	R	E	N		Z	E	R	O
T	A	W	S		I	V	O	R	Y	T	O	W	E	R
C	R	E	E		G	E	T	S		O	N	E	A	L
H	A	R	E		N	Y	S	E		M	E	R	R	Y

131

E	L	G	A	R		M	A	G	N	A		T	B	A
L	E	A	S	E		A	P	R	I	L		I	O	N
F	I	R	S	T	S	T	R	I	K	E		G	L	O
			I	R	E		T	E	E	T	H	E	R
C	O	N	S	O	N	A	N	T	S		A	T	R	A
U	N	I	T		I	S	A	Y		I	T	S	O	K
B	I	G	S	H	O	T	S		L	A	I	C
E	T	H		O	R	A	C	L	E	S		R	O	D
		T	A	P	S		E	S	T	I	M	A	T	E
P	A	S	S	E		A	N	A	S		E	P	I	C
A	R	C	H		B	O	T	T	L	E	N	E	C	K
S	C	H	E	M	E	R			I	T	O
T	A	O		C	A	T	C	H	P	H	R	A	S	E
O	N	O		I	D	A	H	O		O	A	S	I	S
R	E	L		I	S	L	E	T		S	H	A	R	P

132

B	L	O	C		M	O	D	E		U	S	H	E	R
L	E	N	A		A	P	A	L		S	W	E	D	E
O	A	T	S		T	E	R	I		E	E	R	I	E
W	H	O	I	S	A	L	E	X	T	R	E	B	E	K
			N	A	H			I	E	S	T
L	A	B	O	R	A	T	O	R	Y		P	A	R	K
A	S	E		G	R	A	B		S	E	G	U	E
W	H	E	R	E	I	S	J	E	O	P	A	R	D	Y
N	O	N	O	S		E	N	D	O		E	E	E
S	T	E	T		C	U	T	C	O	R	N	E	R	S
			A	V	O	N		M	E	A
W	H	A	T	I	S	A	Q	U	E	S	T	I	O	N
E	U	B	I	E		B	U	R	T		U	S	M	A
E	L	B	O	W		L	O	G	E		R	E	A	R
B	A	R	N	S		E	D	E	R		E	E	N	Y

133

```
C A W S   B O N O   P S H A W
A M A T   A V O N   A W A K E
S U R E   B A L L E R I N A S
A L B A N Y   A I R I N G
B E L L A D O N N A   E S P O
A T E   G O P   E S P   O E R
    D O G L E G     I X N A Y
      B I L L Y J A C K
Z U B I N   M A R K E R
I K E   G A G   I R A   I F S
P E N S   B O L L I X E D U P
    T A K E T O   V E N D E E
B U L L E T H O L E   E L L E
A N E A R   A P I A   R E E D
H A Y D N   M Y S T   O R D O
```

134

```
A N N O   A S S T   U S H E R
N E E D   I N C A   T H E M E
T A X I   R O O K   T O X I N
E T T U B R U T E   E R A T O
      M O A T   T O R T
H O T   X I S T H E   T A B S
E L A T E D   E A R   E L L A
M I X E R   E X T   B R O I L
E V E S   E R A   M O M E N T
N E S T   W I N N E R   S K Y
      S P E C   A T N O
D E C C A   I N T H E W A S H
D R O O P   D O T O   E X P O
A G O R A   L I E D   N L E R
Y O K E L   E R R S   S E W N
```

135

```
E A R T H   U R A L   H A R I
A L O H A   N A N A   A G E D
S T A Y W I T H I T   N O E L
T O M   K R I S   H A G G L E
    N E I L   D E L I
  O B E Y S   M E R I N G U E
C L O V E   T E L E   T I N E
L I R E   W I E L D   H A I L
A V E R   A N T S   R E N T S
D E S S E R T S   P A R T Y
    A L M S   T I L E
A R G Y L E   A O N E   H B O
L E A D   D O N T G I V E U P
A N T I   U L N A   G I M M E
N O S E   P E A L   H A S P S
```

136

```
R O I L   O P T I C   A P S E
O M N I   F A R G O   S E A L
M A G N I F Y I N G C L A S S
P R E E N I N G   H E S S E
        N N E   S H U E
G E H R I G   S T A M P E D E
O C E A N   G O A T   M E N
G O I N G F O R T H E C O L D
O L D   A R T E   L A T T E
L E I S U R E S   S P R E A D
      E T O N   M T A
A M A N A   G O E S I N T O
F O R T H E L O V E O F C O D
R O A R   T I B E R   F A R E
O N L Y   H E I R S   Y A K S
```

137

```
S A L E M   L I E F   Y A P S
I N E R T   A T R A   O G L E
T I M E F L I E S L I K E A N
      S U E T   E S S E N C E
O T B   J A Y S   T O L T E C
T U R N I P   C R A B   S R A
O N E A   T O O F A R
  A R R O W B U T F R U I T
    C U R A R E   B N A I
N B C   S E R E   A T E S T S
O R A T E S   R A R A   O I L
N O V E L T Y   L I S P
F L I E S L I K E A M E L O N
A L A N   E P I C   A R E N A
T Y R A   S E N S   N U T T Y
```

138

```
S A D A   C A R D   O N K E Y
E L A L   A L O U   H A I L E
E L M E R F U D D   G O T I T
R E S C U E M E   L O M
E G E S T   N O S E D I V E D
D E L   F A U S T   J O V I
      R O I   T R I B U T E S
Y E S O R N O   S T U D E N T
E M I G R A N T   B C D
P I N E   G E E S E   C O T
S T O R Y L I N E   D R A N O
      M A E   S L O E E Y E D
A W F U L   B I L L Y B U D D
V E R D I   R O T E   A G A L
A B O D E   A N O S   G A Y E
```

139

```
X F I L E S   ■ T S H I R T
R E C I P E S ■ T H E O R E M
A R A B I A N ■ D E P L A N E
Y A M ■ C L A W S ■ T E N O N
S L E D ■ E R A ■ T I S ■
■ ■ E N D E R M I C ■ R E V
D I S C O ■ D E A N ■ V O L S
D O W A G E R ■ R A V I O L I
A W A Y ■ M U S S ■ I N D E X
Y A P ■ H U M P H R E Y ■
■ ■ G U S ■ A L E ■ L E S T
T S A R S ■ P S A L M ■ R I B
R E G A T T A ■ N I A G A R A
E A R F L A P ■ D E C A T U R
X R A T E D ■ ■ F S T O P S
```

140

```
H O A R ■ S M A S H ■ E Z R A
O N L Y ■ H E L L O ■ C O A X
R E I D ■ A T P A R ■ Z O N E
S A V E E V A S V A S E ■ ■
E M E R G E ■ ■ ■ E M A I L
■ ■ C A S T C A T S A C T S
C H A U D ■ R O S E S ■ M I A
R A S P ■ S A L S A ■ C E S T
U R L ■ U N I T E ■ O A S I S
S P O T P O T S T O P S ■ ■
T O W I T ■ ■ ■ W I T C H Y
■ ■ L O S E S O L E S L O E
J O W L ■ E X U D E ■ O A K S
A L O E ■ V A P O R ■ F R E E
B E E R ■ E M E R Y ■ F O Y S
```

141

```
P E R U ■ C L A D ■ E Q U A L
A X E S ■ R A S H ■ L U R I E
R E P S ■ E S T O ■ G I L D S
S M A R T A S A W H I P ■ ■
E P I ■ H M O ■ I N S T E P
S T R E E P ■ P A T ■ A L A
■ ■ R A I N E D ■ B A L M Y
■ W I S E A S A N O W L ■
N A A C P ■ M O R O S E ■
A D D ■ Y E S ■ A N D R E A
T S E T S E ■ P H I ■ E N S
■ S H A R P A S A T A C K ■
S I N A I ■ E L L A ■ A S I N
S C O R N ■ S E E R ■ N O N O
T E N S E ■ T A S K ■ K N O T
```

142

```
F L A R E ■ B A R B ■ S T O P
A I M E D ■ O L E O ■ I R M A
C R O C I ■ T I T O ■ B E A T
T A K E T O H A R T E ■ A H S
■ ■ D I G ■ S O L A R D A Y
A R L E N E S ■ E C O ■ ■
H I E ■ G E T H I G H M A R X
A R A B ■ A I R ■ E X A M
B E F R O N T M A N N ■ L I A
■ ■ A L A ■ N E A T E N S
R E M N A N T S ■ M P H ■ ■
O L E ■ F E E L N O P A I N E
L I A R ■ T R I O ■ E L L I S
E T N A ■ T R E E ■ R I L L S
S E T H ■ E A R L ■ S A Y S O
```

143

```
BACK B A Y ■ A L T O ■ C A L L BACK
O L G A ■ B E A N ■ A R I E L
F U E L ■ J O L T ■ Y A Z O O
F R E E L U N C H ■ C L A N G
■ ■ A R E ■ E N E ■ ■
C A N I N E ■ S R A ■ S H E S
A G A N A ■ S H O R ■ H E L P
B A C K I N T O A C O R N E R
E T R E ■ E Y E D ■ D U N C E
R E E D ■ I R S ■ R E B A T E
■ ■ U N O ■ C O T ■ ■
O A T H S ■ F O O D S T A M P
U R I A H ■ O G R E ■ A L I A
T I T L E ■ A L A N ■ N O S Y
BACK D O O R ■ M E L T ■ G E T BACK
```

144

```
S A S H ■ A S S A D ■ B L A H
T E A S ■ S H I R E ■ E A V E
A I N T ■ H A N D B U Z Z E R
R O D ■ F O R G E ■ S E E R S
R U B B E R P E N C I L ■ ■
■ L A D E ■ ■ L A S T L Y
O T A R U ■ A G R I ■ R I O
D I S A P P E A R I N G I N K
I N T ■ E R G S ■ O R A T E
N A S C A R ■ ■ N O O N ■
■ E X P L O D I N G G U M
P A D R E ■ A S O N E ■ U N I
S Q U I R T R O S E ■ O L D S
S U M S ■ A G L E T ■ T A U T
T A P E ■ N E E D Y ■ T R E Y
```

145

```
WEST  PARIS  DATA
AREA  ELEGY  ISON
RICKNELSON  STAT
METEOR  TREATISE
      SEW    DONTS
SAMMYDAVISJR
ARIA   KENT  THOR
MINI   BIRDS IAGO
EDEN   UNDO  ORLY
    SERGIOMENDES
SCOTS    RAE
HATRACKS  TRADER
ACHE  LESLEYGORE
RHEA  INTER  ODIN
PERM  POSTS  GONE
```

146

```
PLAN  TAMPER  ZIT
BALE  OBOIST  IDS
SWASHBUCKLE  PEE
     TEETHE  STPAT
ASSES   ARS   ALLS
LONGAGO   PERUSE
BRAG  ARMYANTS
STP  CLOSURE  FOG
    OUTOFGAS  SOHO
SPURNS   NEPTUNE
PITA  HAH  EUROS
ENOLA   REEARN
DEF  PANICBUTTON
URI  TRANCE  EIRE
PST  SIZZLE  DEED
```

147

```
SMOG  HEFTS  ABCS
CONE  EXERT  RULE
OVEN  MATEO  IMON
FEDERALEXPRESS
FIG  ANT  LUSTER
STERN  SATIE  EON
    CAL  LUG  ZEUS
 STATEOFTHEART
WHOS  MCI  TEN
DOE  VOTER  RESIN
SETSIN  HAI  PLY
 LOCALPHONECALL
RATE  ALONG  ORSO
ECON  WEEDS  DEAN
BEET  SADAT  EDYS
```

148

```
MARC  BEFIT  AMES
OLEO  ATONE  NERO
TERR  BARBARGAIN
INUNDATE  PULLEY
FENCE    STONE
     OBIS  STERILE
BATBATTLE  SLUR
OVA  ROASTED  ELL
PERU  BUSBUSTLE
SCANDAL  EBAN
     RELET  NUMBS
OCLOCK  BASEBALL
BOYBOYCOTT  BRAE
IDLE  LANKA  EIRE
TEED  SMEAR  DEEP
```

149

```
AMPS  SCREW  BALE
RIAL  ALONE  ISAY
EXTRALODGE  RISE
WET  PETE  STATS
ERICA  HOORAH
    ERLE  PUNDITS
PRONTO  KANGAROO
RAPT  ITALO  YARD
OVERSTAY  FACETS
MENACES  AFRO
 LURKER  MDCCI
SIXPM  ROSE  UAR
ELMO  TWOUNDERPA
ASEC  ANDSO  DIET
TANK  DWEEB  SERE
```

150

```
SAVOR  CABIN  JEW
TRIPE  AMANA  EPA
OGLES  PANTYRAID
PUERTORICO  ONCE
SERA  PAN  NAT
      SET  DEVILLE
SHA  LIBYA  ANAIS
PUBLICRELATIONS
AGLET  ARENA  SOO
TEETERS   GRR
    TSE  TOE  ELAN
ODIE  PAULREVERE
POTROASTS  MINCE
AGE  DITTO  IVIED
LEM  DRAIN  RENDS
```

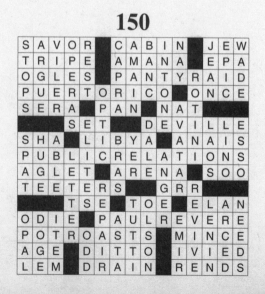

151

S	N	O	W		S	N	I	P	S		A	C	E	D
R	E	D	O		H	O	M	E	O		N	A	M	E
S	E	E	M		R	E	E	L	S		A	N	I	L
		B	U	I	L	T	T	O	S	C	A	L	E	
A	B	A		R	V	S			R	A	I	L	E	D
S	U	N	D	A	E		A	A	R	O	N			
H	O	T	E	L	L	O	B	B	Y			C	U	B
E	Y	E	S			J	O	E			V	O	T	E
S	S	S		P	A	I	D	A	V	I	S	I	T	
		B	A	S	I	L		D	I	A	B	L	O	
S	H	E	I	L	A		R	O	D		Y	E	N	
H	I	D	D	E	N	O	P	E	R	A	S			
I	N	G	E		D	R	A	P	E		L	A	D	Y
N	E	A	R		Q	A	T	A	R		A	R	I	A
S	S	R	S		S	L	E	D	S		T	E	E	M

152

C	A	P	R	I		T	B	A	R		C	A	R	Y
A	S	I	A	N		H	O	L	E		U	L	E	E
S	H	U	F	F	L	E	O	F	F		T	I	N	A
H	E	S		R	A	B	B	I		T	A	F	T	S
		D	O	U	R		E	A	R	N	E	S	T	
C	A	L	E	N	D	A	R		M	I	D			
U	B	O	A	T		D	I	I	I		D	R	O	P
B	U	L	L		S	Y	N	C	S		R	E	P	O
S	T	A	B		E	S	S	E		A	I	D	E	S
		R	I	P		E	L	A	T	E	D	L	Y	
I	Q	T	E	S	T	S		A	C	E	D			
M	U	R	A	L		C	A	N	T	I		P	O	I
B	E	A	K		F	O	L	D	I	N	H	A	L	F
E	R	D	E		A	U	D	I		T	O	T	E	S
D	Y	E	R		T	R	A	C		O	W	E	G	O

153

B	A	S	E	R		H	I	P	S		S	L	A	W
A	H	O	R	A		E	R	S	E		Y	A	L	E
J	E	N	N	Y	C	R	A	I	G		S	N	A	P
A	M	S		G	O	E	S		M	U	T	A	N	T
			O	U	T	S		S	E	R	E			
	H	E	N	N	Y	Y	O	U	N	G	M	A	N	
F	I	S	T	S		C	I	T	E		V	O	W	
O	T	T	O		K	E	A	T	S		B	A	B	E
R	U	E		S	E	L	L			T	R	I	E	D
	P	E	N	N	Y	M	A	R	S	H	A	L	L	
		A	A	H	S		O	T	I	S				
I	N	D	I	G	O		G	U	A	M		F	I	B
V	I	A	L		L	E	N	N	Y	B	R	U	C	E
A	N	T	E		E	G	A	D		L	E	M	O	N
N	E	E	D		S	O	W	S		E	V	E	N	T

154

B	R	U	T		B	U	D	S		S	A	L	E	M
L	U	T	E		I	T	I	N		E	R	O	D	E
U	P	I	N		G	A	G	A		E	E	R	I	E
R	E	C	O	R	D	H	I	G	H	S		A	N	T
B	E	A	N	I	E		T	S	A	R	I	N	A	S
			S	P	A	M			Z	E	N			
G	Y	M		S	L	I	P	P	E	D	D	I	S	K
N	O	A	H			L	E	I			Y	O	R	E
P	U	P	U	P	L	A	T	T	E	R		N	O	G
			G	E	O		A	D	A	M				
R	E	C	H	E	C	K	S		A	N	E	M	I	A
E	T	A		V	I	N	Y	L	S	I	D	I	N	G
M	U	L	T	I		O	R	A	N		U	L	N	A
I	D	L	E	S		T	U	N	E		S	K	I	M
T	E	A	C	H		S	P	A	R		A	S	E	A

155

M	G	R	S		A	C	T	I	I		R	E	F	
A	R	E	A	L		L	U	A	N	N		O	L	E
C	U	C	K	O	O	C	L	O	C	K		X	Y	Z
	B	E	E	R	T	A	P	S		I	W	A	S	
O	B	I		E	I	N			H	E	R	N	I	A
R	E	V	E	L	S		T	S	A	R	I	N	A	S
C	R	E	M	E		O	O	H	S		T	E	N	K
		B	I	R	D	W	A	T	C	H				
P	A	A	R		T	E	E	M		H	E	L	P	S
A	R	B	O	R	E	A	L		G	I	D	E	O	N
D	A	R	I	U	S			O	E	D		F	R	O
	P	E	L	F		R	E	T	R	E	A	T	S	
B	A	A		F	E	A	T	H	E	R	T	I	C	K
A	H	S		E	L	I	T	E			S	A	S	H	A
D	O	T		D	I	N	E	R			T	H	E	Y

156

A	D	E	P	T		A	M	I	S		P	S	S	T
P	A	Y	E	E		T	O	R	I		A	H	O⃝	Y
O	N	E	A	M		B	O⃝	A	R	D	W	A	L	K
P	A	R	K	P	L	A	C	E		A	N	G	I	E
			L	A	T	H		E	N	E				
F	A	B	L	E	S		S	N	I	D	E	S	T	
E	R	L	E		T	O	P	P⃝	L	E		P	H	I
R	E	A	D	I	N	G	R	A	I	L	R	O⃝	A	D
M	A	N⃝		S	A	L	O	N	S		A	C	M	E
I	R	K	S	O	M	E			T	I	T	H	E	S
			A	B	E		S	T	E	N				
S	C	A⃝	L	A		S	H	O	R	T	L	I	N	E
L	U	X	U	R	Y	T	A	X		R	A	C	E	R
O	B	I	T		A	L	L	I		A⃝	M	O	C	O
E	A	S	E		K	O	L	N		Y	A	N	K	S

The eight circled letters can be rearranged to spell MONOPOLY.

157

ASTA ALSO KATIE
BAAS DIEM IMAGE
ANKA DORA NYLON
STEPHENFROSTER
HAT ODE AKA
HAROLDPRINTER
PIEPAN IRS ERA
TARTS ANY TRAIT
AGA PRE SAUTES
SOPHIETRUCKER
ESE POE ORB
PHYLLISDRILLER
SUEDE NEAP ALEE
TREAT TATI NEVE
PEPYS OREO DYED

158

HOST EFLAT SPAM
ASTA LEERY EIRE
THIRTYDAYS NELL
CEL ASU ASCOT
HATHSEPTEMBER
ASE HAAS UNA
GUIDE LIST ASEC
APRILJUNEANDTHE
LOOT IRKS OASIS
ANN RBIS ABM
SPEEDOFFENDER
TRIAD ELL IRE
OEDS BURMASHAVE
BEET OPIUM URIS
ELSA SCORE TYNE

159

SAWN SLASH CUBA
INRE KOREA OVER
KNITPICKER VENT
HAT ONUS SLEAZY
BESS CHER
ALARM DONATION
SAFE GRIMES RNA
KNOWGREATSHAKES
EAU AISLES BENT
DILEMMAS BUDDY
IMAY MEET
FRUGAL KATE BEE
EACH KNIGHTCLUB
SILT IRENE AURA
SLAY NAVAL TROY

160

SPARTA SURGE
LINEAR CHOICEST
ATTICS OUTFOXES
THINKOFTHAT CEO
SONES EWERS
OFF NSW YODEL
REACT HUB ALDA
CANYOUBELIEVEIT
ATTN FAX GENOA
ADIOS ATO TNT
RESIN FLAME
OAT JUSTIMAGINE
TRIBUNAL ENAMOR
ENCIRCLE SIDING
TEHEE TASTES

161

SPCA MCGEE AQUA
PAAR ALERT BURP
LIVERWURST CAGE
ONENESS AAR REX
STATE TNT OTT
HST FREEZEDRIED
ASORT REALLY
AMEX ASTER CELS
DENIAL IBOOK
ORGANDONORS ISH
ILK IGN MOTTO
JON AIL IRISHER
ACED DIETICIANS
WHEY LEVEL ECCE
SORE ERASE RAHS

162

TWA CHAOS ABASE
WAD HELLO ROPER
ALI ISLEOFCAPRI
IDES TONI AVE
NOURISH ENSURES
IDLE REATA
BAA EARN GETUP
ILLHAVETHEUSUAL
DEPOT HOLA SRO
ITEMS CARE
DINEDIN KNOWHOW
IDI LAOS EACH
AISLELIGHTS NEE
NOTER LEONA OAT
ATSEA SEPTS INS

163

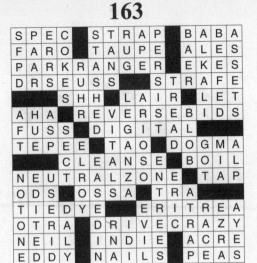

```
S P E C ■ S T R A P ■ B A B A
F A R O ■ T A U P E ■ A L E S
P A R K R A N G E R ■ E K E S
D R S E U S S ■ ■ S T R A F E
■ ■ S H H ■ L A I R ■ L E T
A H A ■ R E V E R S E B I D S
F U S S ■ D I G I T A L ■ ■
T E P E E ■ T A O ■ D O G M A
■ ■ C L E A N S E ■ B O I L
N E U T R A L Z O N E ■ T A P
O D S ■ O S S A ■ T R A ■
T I E D Y E ■ ■ E R I T R E A
O T R A ■ D R I V E C R A Z Y
N E I L ■ I N D I E ■ A C R E
E D D Y ■ N A I L S ■ P E A S
```

164

```
H A R P O ■ T O I T ■ F U S S
O C E A N ■ A H S O ■ A S T A
M I S T E R I N B E T W E E N
E D T ■ U P O N ■ E N D E D
■ C A C H E ■ E A S T L A
Y O U R B R I D G E S ■ O Y L
M A R E S ■ I R K E D ■ ■
A S E A ■ W A V E S ■ R A F T
■ S L O M O ■ S A D I E
A C H ■ A N O T H E R W O R D
T H E I S T ■ E N O L A ■
M A L T S ■ O M N I ■ N A P
O L D S O N G A N D D A N C E
S K I M ■ T R U E ■ A S I D E
T Y N E ■ H E I R ■ S P E C K
```

165

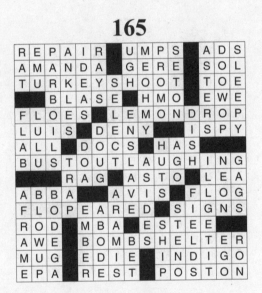

```
R E P A I R ■ U M P S ■ A D S
A M A N D A ■ G E R E ■ S O L
T U R K E Y S H O O T ■ T O E
■ B L A S E ■ H M O ■ E W E
F L O E S ■ L E M O N D R O P
L U I S ■ D E N Y ■ I S P Y
A L L ■ D O C S ■ H A S ■
B U S T O U T L A U G H I N G
■ R A G ■ A S T O ■ L E A
A B B A ■ A V I S ■ F L O G
F L O P E A R E D ■ S I G N S
R O D ■ M B A ■ E S T E E ■
A W E ■ B O M B S H E L T E R
M U G ■ E D I E ■ I N D I G O
E P A ■ R E S T ■ P O S T O N
```

166

```
D E A T H ■ J A W S ■ B O O K
A R T O O ■ A L A N ■ L O D E
M A T Z O M I A T A ■ I Z O D
P T A ■ P A L ■ E P O N Y M S
S O R E L Y ■ G R U N T ■ ■
■ ■ T A T A R ■ P U Z Z L E
T A C O ■ A S I P ■ S K O A L
A R O N ■ G O D O T ■ R O M E
R E A C H ■ F L O E ■ I T E M
P A T H O S ■ O H A R E ■ ■
■ ■ A N N E X ■ P E G L E G
N E W L E A F ■ O O P ■ O S U
O P E L ■ T R E N T L A T K E
R E B A ■ C E D E ■ A P S E S
M E S H ■ H M O S ■ Y E A R S
```

167

```
V C R ■ P A T T I ■ K E F I R
I R A ■ O L E A N ■ O X I D E
S A C ■ N O R T H ■ V A L E T
A M E D I U M S O C A L L E D
S P R E E ■ ■ T A C T ■ ■
■ ■ L S A T S ■ T S E T S E
B E C A U S E I T ■ D E A N
U S A ■ P E R S O N A ■ C S T
N A R C ■ ■ I S N E I T H E R
K I B O S H ■ Y O U R E ■ ■
■ ■ R U M P ■ ■ P E R C H
R A R E N O R W E L L D O N E
A B O L T ■ M A N I A ■ M O W
T E S L A ■ A C T O N ■ A T E
S T A I N ■ N O O N E ■ N E D
```

168

```
S A N G ■ R A V E ■ H E M E N
C L I O ■ E D E N ■ A L I C E
R O C K ■ F O R T H R I G H T
A H E A D ■ N E E D ■ S O S
M A R R I A G E R I T E ■ ■
■ ■ T E A R ■ R O A M E D
A I R S T R I P S ■ P R O X Y
I R E ■ P E L T S ■ P I E
L A N D S ■ G O A L P O S T S
S N O O T S ■ R E A R ■ ■
■ ■ W I L B U R W R I G H T
O A R ■ L O O N ■ E E R I E
G H O S T W R I T E ■ N E L L
R E V U E ■ E T A L ■ T A L E
E M E N D ■ S E R F ■ S T Y X
```

169

MAPS	TADA	FIFTY
ALOP	ATOM	INUSE
GAPE	NEWYORKSPA
IMPLY	ISSUE	SSR
COALMINE	NTH
SAD	ACREAGE
ARC	STATEABBRS
ROREM	ADO	PEROT
TWOLETTERS	AWE
SECEDES	ARA
CAP	LANDDEAL
ESC	LILAC	SAMOA
FLORIDAKIN	GORY
FOCUS	MEDE	ETTE
START	ERSE	SEAR

170

| JADE | SODAS | LAVA |
| ALUM | IPANA | OTIS |
| COTTAGEINDUSTRY |
| KEY | INNS | BEIGE |
| AMAT | AGO | COT |
| BUNGALOWBILL |
ASEAT	AIRTIGHT
LEAR	TAXED	QUAI
ESTIMATE	AUTRE
CABINCRUISER
FAA	RUT	LORD
ALBEN	LAMA	COS
LODGEACOMPLAINT
SNUG	CANOE	DATE
EELY	TBIRD	ZOOM

171

BORES	DELI	BANG
ABUSE	OVEN	ORCA
BOSSA	DENT	DIAL
YET	BRONZEMEDAL
BEETS	RAG
COULEE	PENTACLE
RACKS	TRIES	OAR
ASKS	SAINT	SPCA
TIE	ETUDE	ROPES
ESTIMATE	TALESE
GIG	OUTER
AUBURNTIGER	HIS
WHOA	AWOL	AGENT
NUNN	NOTE	CEASE
SHEA	TSAR	ENDOW

172

ELMS	ACME	BALES
BEET	GAIT	ACELA
ANNA	ALLTERRAIN
YOUBETYOURLIFE
LEX	RED
GRILLS	TROY	MAB
EERIE	SEER	BADE
THEPRICEISRIGHT
TANS	DAMN	ORNOT
OBE	PENS	SOLACE
ERA	STS
TOTELLTHETRUTH
LIGHTSABER	EPEE
EGRET	VAIN	BOND
BEERY	ARKS	ANDY

173

IRAN	SISQO	SAW
ROPED	CROUP	CRI
ISTHEREABEE	HEN
SILICONE	NAIAD
HEY	ILE	SHELL
IDLIKEANELLE
GESTE	REND	ION
RUNE	STAND	CNBC
ORO	OLAF	NAGEL
HOWABOUTAJAY
TILTS	RES	ELS
HEIDI	PATSAJAK
OAR	GIVEMEANEYE
PRE	ECOLI	UNCLE
ESS	DELTS	STAT

174

GRAPE	LASTS	WAN
ATLAS	ESTEE	ABE
BEATTHEHEAT	LBS
TAU	EAST	KIT
LETITBE	DELETES
ANA	ERAS	SETH
INK	SIGHS	STEMS
RUED	SLATE	UTAH
SITUP	ELAND	ARA
HORS	LIME	LID
PRESOAK	DEBAKEY
LIC	FLIP	SET
ONA	FILLTHEBILL
TSK	ENLAI	RADIO
ZOE	RESTS	STOUT

175

```
F I R   I T S M E   K I C K
A M A T   G O T O N   E T O N
U P T O N O G O O D   L A M E
N A T T E R S O N   I L L B E
A L L O W     P E N N Y
S E E   A F T   D O T   C O P
    I D I O M   T H R O N E
C O U L D N T B E B E T T E R
C A M E R A   A N A M E
S R S   E L M   O D O   S H E
    A S S A M     N A T A L
B L O T S   N O I S E L E S S
R O U E   S U N D A Y B E S T
E C R U   O A T E N   A R L O
W I S P   B L E A K   S E N
```

176

```
B A B E S   S C U D S   R I D
A Q U A S   T O M E I   I S R
J U S T W H A T W A S   P L Y
A I D E   A R T   D I P P E R
    E R S T   A A H   A L T O
E A P   T H E G R E A T E S T
L D O P A   R E C A N T
M A T I L D A   A T T I M E S
    C A E S A R   H E E L S
T H I N G B E F O R E   N I T
H E M I   A R R   U M P S
I P E C A C   I R E   A W L S
R C A   S L I C E D B R E A D
D A S   T E N A M   O S A K A
S T Y   A S S N S   D E R E K
```

177

```
H E D D A   T R E E D   C S T
A L A I N   H E N C E   R E B
J O I N T H E C L U B   U R I
    S T O O L   R I S E R
E L Y   N E I L D I A M O N D
S O M E   S P O O N   P E A S
C L A S S   O S C A R
    L E T S M A K E A D E A L
    R E A R S   A S I A N
S P C A   S C E N T   S R T A
W I L D A T H E A R T   H E P
O N E A L     M O O S E
R N A   G A R D E N S P A D E
D E N   E M A I L   C A D E T
S D S   R A N G Y   A T S E A
```

178

```
  A H A B   V A S T   I B I D
A G O G O   A M O R   N O S E
G O O E Y   P T U I   B L E W
A R E   O U I S   P H O O E Y
L A Y A B E D   B L U R
    T O Y   G R E E N T E A
D E W E Y   B L A T S   A N T
O B O E   L O U I S   S P O T
E A R   W O O E D   C H E W Y
S Y M P H O N Y   S H E
    R E N E   D U E L L E D
S C R E W Y   B O I L   O V A
U L E E   B U O Y   S O O E Y
E V A N   I D O L   E R I N S
Y I P S   N O P E   A B E T
```

Sixteen answers rhyme: GOOEY, PTUI, LOUIS, DEWEY, CHEWY, SUEY, BUOY, PHOOEY, SCREWY, SOOEY, HOOEY, DEWY, UEY, GLUEY, SUI, LOOIE.

179

```
D E L T A   M I F F   R A M P
E Q U U S   O R E O   E G A L
B U G L E   I M A X   G O T O
T I E S   F L A S H L I G H T
S P R A W L   T O S S
    R O O T   L U T H E R
P E R R Y W H I T E   R I D E
A L O E   I T E   A L G A
G A T E   C O L E P O R T E R
E L I X I R   E M I L
    A D A R   L A B E L S
F A R M A N I M A L   A L A W
E L O I   K N I T   A N I S E
U P O N   U S E R   A C H E D
D O M E   P E N A   H O U S E
```

180

```
J I H A D   C S P A N   S S T
A T A R I   A L E U T   T W O
W A T E R T R O U G H   A I R
    S T O R M   E T N A
S N L   G O O D E N O U G H
L A U G H A T   R A I S E S
I S L E Y   P A C T
T H U M B I N G T H R O U G H
    R H E A   I S S U E
C A V I A R   E S C H E R S
B R E A D D O U G H   R U S
R E N T   D R U I D
A C E   G O L D E N B O U G H
C H I   A R I E S   I N T R A
T E D   P E E R S   S E E R S
```

181

```
CASH  CRASS  MAZE
ANTE  YECCH  OPEN
ROAM  ADORE  NENE
HITEANDWAITE
ONEND    PLAYPEN
PTS  DASH  ALBUMS
   GENIES    ASIA
 REEDANDWRIGHT
CART   ODIUMS
HIATUS  AGEE  EGG
ALSORAN    ACURA
 KNIGHTANDDEY
ELAN  LAIRD  ROTE
LOCO  EIEIO  ORES
FLEW  DODOS  MALT
```

182

```
ARS  ADD   ESCROW
SHA  BORG  ACHEBE
SOFTSHOE  TEETER
ADAR  ANN  INESSE
MARIA  EDENIC
  ICU  REV  CHALK
STPETE  REQD  LIE
KIA  OCONNOR  LEM
IRR  ROVE  MISTUP
PEKOE  AUG  VMI
  SVELTE  EAMES
FLAWED  RYE  LEGO
RADARS  ASWELLAS
ORELSE  LEOX  OLA
MANDEL  RKO  WED
```

183

```
CHIC  CAVE  YIELD
HIDE  ARID  ERROR
EVEN  MANE  SALSA
FEATHERONESNEST
  SARA   III
AAH  RATTLER  PTA
TRESS  ASI  SOON
LEATHERSTOCKING
ANDY  VAT  LINER
SAY  CAYENNE  TRY
  SOD   EARS
HEATHERLOCKLEAR
AGREE  EACH  URSA
HALER  AROO  MIEN
ADORE  PANS  PEAK
```

184

```
EXPAT  JOVE  PTAS
MEESE  AHEM  LAME
INAWE  LARA  EXEC
LAKESHORECABIN
   SHAPE  IRE
CAMPILY  BAT  BMT
ICIER  EAT  FAIR
VACATIONGETAWAY
ISAK  MTV  HILTS
LES  GAB  JEERSAT
  DUG  FORAY
 SEASIDECOTTAGE
PAWN  NERO  RADON
BRAT  EVAS  ILIAD
SANE  SOLE  CENTS
```

185

```
RAH  EMCEE  AGORA
INA  LIRAS  VIPER
STRAYDOGSHELTER
KIDS  CLEON  ISA
 SIXTEENOUNCES
MOHAIR    TEA
ELI  VISTA  SCHMO
ALPS  POUND  LIEN
LASIK  ONTAP  TAU
  RAF   ROMANS
MONEYINLONDON
ETO  ALOOF  NDAK
STRIKEWITHFORCE
TEASE  AREAL  UTE
ARDOR  YENTA  NIL
```

186

```
CHOP  LENS  SIFTS
AONE  ALOU  IDIOT
PAIR  NEAL  LARGE
GROUNDCHUCK  EST
USN  EMT  AHAB
NESTEA  INARUSH
  STRAPS  TIGER
DAME  KNEAD  SSTS
ROOTS  DANUBE
SLOSHES  CESSNA
 NEAR  AKA  AIR
BAR  TRUSTBUSTER
ALOFT  SARI  NICE
EMCEE  EVIL  ORES
RAKER  DEAL  WEST
```

187

```
N A A C P ■ E M M A ■ D O O R
O C C U R ■ M O A T ■ A N N E
T H R E E R I N G C I R C U S
E Y E ■ P O G O ■ H O N E S T
■ ■ F A I R ■ F I N ■ ■ ■
J E R R Y L E W I S ■ L A M A
A L I A S ■ I D O ■ A V I D
N O D S ■ F E L O N ■ B E A M
E P E E ■ A D M ■ N O R M A
T E R R ■ D E A N M A R T I N
■ ■ P E N ■ E A T S ■ ■ ■
A N G O R A ■ M E N U ■ J A I
H O L L Y W O O D O R B U S T
O P E D ■ A L O E ■ A O R T A
Y E N S ■ Y A R D ■ L O Y A L
```

188

```
V A T ■ B A L M S ■ J E R K Y
I S R ■ A T E U P ■ U N T I E
C H A I N M A I L ■ I N E P T
T O U R D E F R A N C E ■ ■
I R M A S ■ S O Y ■ I D S
M E A N ■ O U G H T ■ A C R E
■ ■ N A N A ■ I N A B I T
F I V E T I M E C H A M P ■
G O T H A M ■ E V E L ■ ■
T G I F ■ E A S E D ■ G I T S
E S C ■ P A T ■ M E N S A
■ Y E L L O W J E R S E Y
Q U E E N ■ A E R O S M I T H
B R O W N ■ S N A G S ■ S S E
S I S S Y ■ T O P S Y ■ T E Y
```

189

```
R A P T ■ I L I A D ■ D A D A
I S L A ■ N A C R E ■ U S E D
C L A N ■ O N E O F A K I N D
H A N G I N G L O O S E ■ ■
I N T O W ■ M R T ■ I D S
E T A ■ O C T O ■ M I L T I E
■ ■ T E N D E R S ■ A S A N
F I T T I N G E N D I N G ■
A L O T ■ S A L E R N O ■ ■
M O N E T S ■ N A D A ■ B I O
Y E S ■ R E S ■ F L I T S
■ S I T T I N G T I G H T
B A B Y B O O M E R ■ E G A L
O M E N ■ F L A R E ■ N I C E
Z I N C ■ F E N D S ■ S E A R
```

190

```
B I B B ■ P I A F ■ O F O L D
O N E A ■ U G L I ■ R E N E E
M E L O N B A L L ■ Z E S T A
B R I B E S ■ T I T O ■ L I D
■ T E A M ■ S O A K ■ E A T S
■ B O U I L L O N C U B E
A D D S ■ M A D ■ R O G E T
C R O ■ S A M ■ P T A ■ H M O
T Y P O S ■ A A A ■ S T E N
I C E C R E A M C O N E ■
V E N T ■ S C A T ■ E E L S
I R A ■ G E T Z ■ R E S O L E
S E N S E ■ S O L I D F O O D
T A C I T ■ U N T O ■ I S P Y
S L E D S ■ P S S T ■ T E E S
```

191

```
A C R E S ■ P S S T ■ A M A N
S O U T H ■ A W A Y ■ L E N A
I N T H E B L I N K O F A N I
A S H O R E ■ N E E D ■ N I L
■ S P A D E ■ D A T E S ■
B I D ■ A T E ■ S K I D ■
O D I E ■ P O L I T I C A L
H E R E S M U D I N Y O U R I
R E T R E A T E D ■ S E G O
■ I N D Y ■ E R A ■ S O N
P A R E D ■ G R E C O ■ ■
A D E ■ U S S R ■ E R U P T S
T H E A P P L E O F O N E S I
T O S S ■ R O T E ■ S C O O T
I C E S ■ Y E A R ■ S E N S E
```

192

```
S M A C K ■ S H E D ■ S H O P
P U R E E ■ P E T E ■ M O M A
A S T O R ■ A L U M ■ O P E N
T H E S C O R P I O N K I N G
■ ■ H E E ■ T O Y ■ ■ ■
O R C H I D ■ C A I N ■ J F K
R E L E E ■ H A L O ■ T E L E
T H E A F R I C A N Q U E E N
H A F T ■ E L H I ■ U N P E N
O B S ■ D A L E ■ Y E A S T Y
■ ■ S E C ■ H I E ■ ■ ■
T H E L I T T L E P R I N C E
H U L A ■ I R A S ■ E V I A N
I S I S ■ N E W S ■ S O C K O
S H A H ■ G E N E ■ T R E Y S
```

193

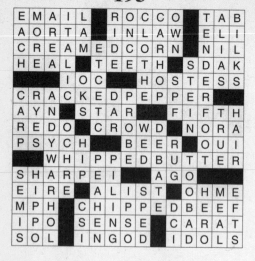

```
EMAIL ROCCO TAB
AORTA INLAW ELI
CREAMEDCORN NIL
HEAL TEETH SDAK
IOC HOSTESS
CRACKEDPEPPER
AYN STAR FIFTH
REDO CROWD NORA
PSYCH BEER OUI
WHIPPEDBUTTER
SHARPEI AGO
EIRE ALIST OHME
MPH CHIPPEDBEEF
IPO SENSE CARAT
SOL INGOD IDOLS
```

194

```
ETAL SCAB SETTO
TUTU TOME KNEAD
URIS IRIS YIELD
INTHEFASTPLANE
ILLS LAC
ALLAGES MOB SAG
POOCH HAY AURA
SAINTLOUISPRAMS
ETRE ERE LEVEE
SHE JOB AMUSERS
SUN BRIM
UNCLEBENSPRICE
SNORE ENOS ASHE
ADDAP TILE COAL
POEMS ANDS ENDS
```

195

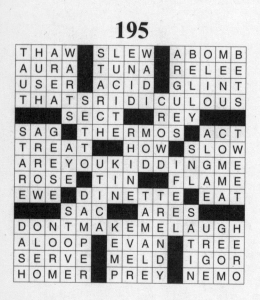

```
THAW SLEW ABOMB
AURA TUNA RELEE
USER ACID GLINT
THATSRIDICULOUS
SECT REY
SAG THERMOS ACT
TREAT HOW SLOW
AREYOUKIDDINGME
ROSE TIN FLAME
EWE DINETTE EAT
SAC ARES
DONTMAKEMELAUGH
ALOOP EVAN TREE
SERVE MELD IGOR
HOMER PREY NEMO
```

196

```
SILL DECI HANDY
ARIA ELAN EIEIO
FEARLESSFOSDICK
ENNEAD HRH ALEE
READS CLAIM
OHARE OATERS
SEW VISA INDIA
PAINLESSDENTIST
ATSEA PSAT TEE
TSETSE ORDER
SPACE RASTA
ACTS ELI INSTEP
SLEEVELESSSHIRT
TORME ETAL ELSE
ADMIT NYSE SEER
```

197

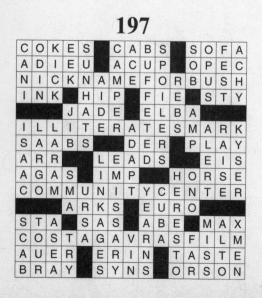

```
COKES CABS SOFA
ADIEU ACUP OPEC
NICKNAMEFORBUSH
INK HIP FIE STY
JADE ELBA
ILLITERATESMARK
SAABS DER PLAY
ARR LEADS EIS
AGAS IMP HORSE
COMMUNITYCENTER
ARKS EURO
STA SAS ABE MAX
COSTAGAVRASFILM
AUER ERIN TASTE
BRAY SYNS ORSON
```

198

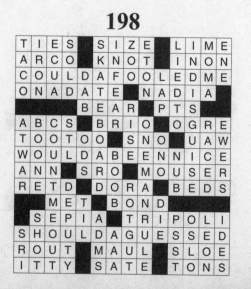

```
TIES SIZE LIME
ARCO KNOT INON
COULDAFOOLEDME
ONADATE NADIA
BEAR PTS
ABCS BRIO OGRE
TOOTOO SNO UAW
WOULDABEENNICE
ANN SRO MOUSER
RETD DORA BEDS
MET BOND
SEPIA TRIPOLI
SHOULDAGUESSED
ROUT MAUL SLOE
ITTY SATE TONS
```

199

```
HELD  ALEG  FURS
OBOE  ICIER ATOP
ERIC  MORK&MINDY
DOSE  SRA  PUREES
  &IRON  LAS
VICTOR  MISTAKEN
ALL ORSON  SLAVE
LOAD YEMEN  STOW
ENRON  RURAL  EKE
TAKEOFFS  ISL&ER
  RLS  NADIA
STIGMA  BID  SLAG
WILL&GRACE  PLUM
ARIA  OKIES  EIRE
NEED  NOOR  DEAN
```

200

```
FARCE  ALG  JOADS
ACURA  HUR  ABNER
ALIAS  ALE  LINES
 UNSTABLEMATES
  HOC  SNAP
THC  NTH  EYEBALL
REED  EEG  NADIA
UNDEADRECKONING
SCALP  LEO  DODO
SERAPES  OAT  SAS
  ELIS  LAS
 UNSAFECRACKER
CLEAR  NRA  KORAN
HASTE  NAG  LAINE
ANTED  APE  ELCID
```